C000069891

MARGARET

CHRISTMAS

Paris

Mrs Beeton's
Original Recipes

Mrs

Jeni Wright

CONSULTANT EDITOR
Jenni Fleetwood

Beeton's
Original Recipes

CASSELL

First published in the United Kingdom in 1999
by Cassell

Text, Design and Layout copyright © Cassell 1999

Mrs Beeton's is a registered trademark of Cassell ltd

All rights reserved. No part of this publication
may be reproduced in any material form (including
photocopying or storing it in any medium by
electronic means and whether or not transiently
or incidentally to some other use of this publication)
without the written permission of the copyright
owner, except in accordance with the provisions
of the Copyright, Designs and Patents Act 1988
or under the terms of a licence issued by the
Copyright Licensing Agency,
90 Tottenham Court Road, London W1P 9HE.
Applications for the copyright owner's written
permission to reproduce any part of this publication
should be addressed to the publisher.

A CIP catalogue record for this book is available
from the British Library

ISBN 0 7063 7815 6

Designed by Harry Green
Typeset in Bembo/Helvetica/Snell Roundhand
Printed and bound in Great Britain by
Hillman Printers (Frome ltd), Somerset

Cassell
Illustrated Division
The Orion Publishing Group
Wellington House
125 Strand
London WC2R 0BB

NOTE

As is explained in the Introduction,
Mrs Beeton's original (Imperial) measure
are given, with their metric equivalent.
Follow one set of measures only, not a mixture.

Where it is not vital to use precise quantities,
measure like 'a wineglassful' or 'a teacupful'
have been retained.

Equivalents are given where necessary in notes,
but as a guide, a Victorian teacup held about
7 fl oz (200 ml); a Victorian breakfast cup held
about ¼ pint (150 ml). In this book, a glass of
sherry is equivalent to 2 fl oz (60 ml); a glass
of port is about 4 fl oz (120 ml) and a glass
of wine is about 6 fl oz (175 ml).

ABOUT THE AUTHOR

Jeni Wright has been writing about food,
ingredients and cooking for 30 years. She
started her career in cookery on the Cordon
Bleu Cookery Course in the late sixties, then
worked as a cookery writer for *Woman*
magazine before writing her first book,
The St Michael All-Colour Cookery Book, which
was published in 1976. It was the first cookery
book to be sold in a supermarket and it became
a classic over the years – it ran to more than 20
reprints. Since then she has written well over
30 cookery books, at the same time as bringing
up a family. Like many of her generation, Jeni
was first inspired by Mrs Beeton and feels she
owes her a considerable debt. She would like to
dedicate this book to the memory of Isabella
Beeton and the contribution she made to
British cooking.

CONSULTANT EDITOR

Jenni Fleetwood has a long and devoted
association with the work of Mrs. Beeton.
A member of both the Guild of Food Writers
and the Society of Authors, Jenni lives and
works in Suffolk

Contents

~ Introduction

T HE 'MRS BEETON' PHENOMENON has been – and continues to be – unique in the history of cookery book publishing. Mrs Beeton has been a household name in Britain for almost 150 years. Her book *Beeton's Book of Household Management*, in all its various forms and editions, has stood the test of time like no other cookery book before or since.

As we approach the end of the twentieth century, there will inevitably be those – especially in the younger generation – who may never have seen an original or early 'Mrs Beeton'. This new book is a celebration of her work, returning to the first edition of 1861 and taking from it a selection of material will appeal to today's new cooks. The days when the mistress ruled the house and the servants are long gone; snippets of the original household management sections are occasionally included for historical interest, but this is essentially a practical cookery book, as was Mrs Beeton's original work.

Mrs Beeton's recipes were beautifully written, clear and concise. This new book endeavours to keep the spirit of the original alive by using Mrs Beeton's own words wherever possible. The charm and idiosyncratic nature of the recipes have been retained, and you will find them a joy to read. Her informative and often amusing hints, tips and anecdotes are also included and many of them are as relevant today as they were when Mrs Beeton penned them. They appear as direct quotations under the heading "Mrs Beeton writes". Under this heading, too, you will find some of the paragraphs Mrs Beeton wrote describing the ingredients used in the recipes.

Mrs Beeton intended her book for the new housewife, so the recipes are generally easy to follow and understand. When this is not the case, particularly as regards unfamiliar ingredients and terminology, recipes have been sensitively edited and extra information has been added. On the few occasions when substantial changes were needed, this is mentioned in the recipe introduction. Variations with alternative ingredients are also sometimes included to help the novice, and a small number of new recipes has been added to make the collection comprehensive for today's new cooks. Care has been taken not to introduce foreign ingredients that would not have been known in Mrs Beeton's day.

The Recipes

For authenticity the titles of the recipes have been retained as close to the original as possible, but some old-fashioned words have been changed so that ingredients can be identified easily. For example, fowl is now chicken and mutton has been updated to lamb. Words like dredge (meaning 'to sprinkle') and pare (peel) have been left, as their meanings are clear when read in context.

The writing style of the original recipes was not as consistent nor as rigid as that of most modern cookery books. Inconsistencies give the book extra charm and they have been retained unless they might lead to confusion, in which case they have been changed. Errors of grammar and punctuation in the original have been corrected.

Mrs Beeton's original ingredients and method form the backbone of the recipes in this edition, but for each recipe a new introduction and a series of notes have been added. Before starting to shop and cook, it is important to read each recipe right through from start to finish. The introduction and notes provide indispensable information for cooks today. They clarify any points which are unclear in the original recipe; they also contain additional information which a new cook will find invaluable.

Alongside each recipe there are three headings – 'time', 'sufficient for' and 'seasonable'. In the original book these were listed at the end of the recipe, together with the approximate cost of the ingredients. The headings have been moved a more prominent – and practical – position; the cost has been omitted because it is of no practical value to today's cooks.

Time The original timings were rather vague. It was not clear whether they referred to cooking alone, or cooking plus preparation. Cooking times were not often given in the recipe methods. If they were listed, they tended to be longer than is usual today, and this is especially the case in the fish and vegetable chapters. More efficient cookers are partly responsible. For today's cooks, timings have been added to the methods and the total preparation and cooking time has been recalculated and included in the statistical information for each recipe. Timings are necessarily approximate, because much depends on the experience and dexterity of the cook.

Sufficient for Sometimes the quantities given in the original book were for large numbers of people. If this was the case, either the recipe has been scaled down and the number of servings proportionately reduced or the original quantities have been retained and suggestions given on or what to do with leftovers. If quantities have been scaled down, this is mentioned in the introduction to the recipe. In other cases the original number of servings did not reflect today's appetites, so these have been brought up to date.

Seasonable Although most ingredients are now available all year round, Mrs Beeton's information on this subject has been retained. Her 'seasons' were for home-grown produce and these are still worth noting: British vegetables and fruit in season are often the best quality and flavour – and less expensive than alternatives; meats like pork are often preferred in colder weather; and specialities like marmalade, pancakes, mincemeat and plum pudding are associated with specific seasons or festivities.

Imperial measurements were used in Mrs Beeton's day and these have been retained with their equivalent metric measures.

Ingredients have been put in order of use, as is the custom in modern cookery books, but they were not originally listed in this way. Measuring was often by volume rather than weight. In cases where it is quicker and easier to do this, the volume measures have been left in the list of ingredients, but for those who prefer the scale to the measuring jug, equivalent weights are given in the notes that follow the recipe. Measures like 'glass of sherry' and 'teacupful of stock' have been retained when an accurate amount is not crucial to the success of a recipe. Where quantities were vague or missing altogether, they have been supplied if it is necessary to know them, but expressions like 'a little butter' have been retained when it is not essential to have an exact amount.

Modern oven temperatures are given at the end of methods where applicable. Coal-fired kitchen ranges were used in Mrs Beeton's day, and these made accurate temperatures and timings impossible.

Seasoning was not always mentioned by Mrs Beeton. It has been included in this edition, either in the ingredients or the notes, but in many cases it is left to the reader to decide on the amount to use.

The First Edition

A lot of people have heard of Mrs Beeton, but many may be surprised to learn that her reputation was largely due to a single (though undeniably extraordinary) book, *Beeton's Book of Household Management*. The publisher was her husband, Samuel Orchart Beeton, and the book was a bound edition of material that had been published in instalments in the *Englishwoman's Domestic Magazine*, one of Sam Beeton's many publications. The first instalment came out towards the end of 1859, then subsequent parts appeared at monthly intervals to make up twenty four in all. The book ran to well over a thousand pages and was published in 1861. It contained over 4000 recipes and a wealth of practical advice about every aspect of running a home. By all accounts, the first edition sold 60,000 copies.

Isabella Beeton was twenty one and in the first year of her marriage when she embarked on the task of compiling the material. It took her four years, during which time she gave birth to two sons, both of whom died while still babies. Another son was born in 1863, in the same year that the book was reprinted. In 1865 she gave birth to a fourth son. Both of these boys survived, but Isabella tragically died following the birth of her last son. She was only twenty nine.

In the short time between publication of the book and Isabella's death, Isabella and Sam did not rest on their laurels. An ambitious and hard-working young couple, they continued to update 'Household Management' while working on numerous other publications. Isabella was checking the proofs for another book – the *Dictionary of Everyday Cookery*, only days before her death. In 1868, Samuel Beeton published a new edition of 'Household Management'. He said in a note at the beginning of the book, 'In this New Edition I have striven, with feminine aid of the most valuable kind, to make a few improvements upon the original model of this work, and I have infused some new and modern information which, seven years ago, did not exist'.

Since then there have been numerous reworkings of Mrs Beeton's material in new editions of the book. In the latter part of the nineteenth century these were fairly faithful to the original – admirable attempts to keep the material up to date and take into account new ingredients, culinary innovations and changes in domestic tastes and habits. None of these took anything away from the original. On the contrary, the book was constantly being enlarged and the number and size of the pages increased. An 1888 edition claimed it was 'nearly half as large again as the former edition', while an editor in the 1920s boasted his volume was 'nearly twice the number of pages and four times the size of its modest ancestor'.

Throughout the twentieth century, editors have kept Mrs Beeton's spirit alive in a succession of books that have kept pace with the rapidly changing world. By 1960 the book had changed almost beyond recognition. In an edition published 'to mark the book's entry into its second century', liberal use was made of the latest colour photography – the original 1861 edition had only black and white engravings and twelve colour plates – and the editors even saw fit to change its name. In the book's preface we read: 'Many newcomers to

Household Management thought the book covered only the running of a home, so to guard against any further misapprehension the title has been expanded to include the word "Cookery".' From then until the present day the book has been known as *Mrs Beeton's Book of Cookery and Household Management*.

Mrs Beeton – A Short Biography

Isabella Beeton combined a demanding career with running a home and having children. This was in mid-nineteenth century Britain, long before the days of the suffragettes and their fight for the vote. In her own way she was a liberated woman, years ahead of her time. To understand Isabella, it is helpful to know a little about her early life. Her childhood was as remarkable as her achievements, and without doubt had an influence on her work.

Born in 1836, Isabella Mayson was the eldest of four children. Her family was well-to-do and middle class, and they lived in Milk Street in the City of London. Her father died when Isabella was five and her mother subsequently married Henry Dorling, a rich widower who was in the printing business. He too had four children, and the couple went on to have thirteen more – making twenty one children in all. As the eldest daughter in a large Victorian family, Isabella was expected to help to look after the little ones. With twenty siblings, her childhood could never have had a dull moment.

Henry Dorling became the clerk of the race course at Epsom, and in 1845 took over the lease of the grandstand. From then on, that was where the children lived – for the simple reason that there were too many of them to fit comfortably into Henry's house in town. The 'little Dorlings' slept in the committee rooms, ate in the salon, played in the paddocks and even on the racecourse itself. Isabella and her maternal grandmother lived with the children in the grandstand and the two of them looked after the children together there. Their mother stayed with her husband in the house in town.

Despite her domestic and nursery duties, Isabella had a good education at school in Islington and later on at finishing school in Heidelberg, where she learnt both French and German – and developed a passion for pastry making. She was a striking-looking young woman, intelligent, well educated and energetic. She was also a gifted pianist, and went for lessons to Sir Julius Benedict, the most fashionable piano teacher in London at that time.

At the age of nineteen Isabella fell in love with the lively and fun-loving Samuel Beeton, whose successful publishing company was just off Fleet Street. At the time of their meeting he had just launched the first women's magazine in this country, the *Englishwoman's Domestic Magazine*. He himself wrote most of its contents, and it was a runaway success.

The couple bought a house in Pinner, a leafy suburb on the outskirts of London, and Isabella set about learning how to run a home of her own. Having looked after the little Dorlings for so many years, she had more practical experience of domestic life than many young women of her age. It seems that she relished the prospect of managing her own home, but was disappointed in what she saw around her, contending that wherever she looked she saw 'mismanagement', which in her view brought about domestic unhappiness. Isabella believed that only when a home was properly managed could a family ever be happy.

'Why has no-one written a book – a good book for brides,' she said at this time, 'to help them learn these things?'

Only a handful of practical cookery books had been published in Victorian England, and there were even fewer on running a home. Young middle class newly-weds were plunged in at the deep end and often left at the mercy of their staff. Just like young people today, they did not always have their mothers and grandmothers nearby to give advice when needed.

After their marriage in 1856, Isabella began to help Sam on the magazine, editing the cookery and household columns. Within a year the couple decided to publish a cookery book, and Isabella started to collect and edit material for it. Most of this came from friends, family and acquaintances. Sam also placed an advertisement in the *Englishwoman's Domestic Magazine* asking readers to send in their favourite recipes, and Isabella set about testing these in her kitchen, just as a cookery writer would do today. One of Sam's rules for the book was that 'nothing was to go untried'.

The recipes needed sorting, classifying and re-writing as well as testing. Many were rejected and substitutions made. Reams of informative text were written on the subect of food, ingredients and cooking, and household tips and words of advice were gathered, researched and written. The book embraced all aspects of running a home, from the duties of the mistress and the art of dining to the managing of household servants, cleaning, the rearing of children, and medical and legal advice. The project was completed in just four years, and Isabella masterminded it all.

CHAPTER 1

Soups

In her introduction to 'Soups', Mrs Beeton began with an apology for the poor reputation of English cooking. 'It has been asserted that English cookery is, nationally speaking, far from being the best in the world. More than this we have been frequently told by brilliant foreign writers, half philosophers, half chefs, that we are the worst cooks on the face of the earth, and that the proverb which alludes to the divine origin of food and the precisely opposite origin of its preparers, is peculiarly applicable to us islanders.'

Soups, however, she saw as our salvation...

'We are glad to note that soups of vegetables, fish, meat and game are now very frequently found in the homes of the English middle classes as well as in the mansions of the wealthier and more aristocratic, and we take this to be one evidence that we are on the right road to an improvement in our system of cookery.'

There was a huge choice of soups in the original book. Puréed fruit and vegetable soups came first, then meat, poultry and game recipes, some of which were more like stews or meals in themselves than soups to be served as a first course. Finally, there was a handful of soups based on fish and shellfish.

According to the Bills of Fare in a chapter towards the end of the book, soup was sometimes, but not always, served at family dinners. For formal dinner parties, it was compulsory. It was placed on the table at the same time as the fish, and served as a first course. The serving instructions were most explicit.

'The guests being seated at the dinner table, the lady begins to help the soup, which is handed round, commencing with the gentleman on her right and on her left, and continuing in the same order till all are served. It is generally established as a rule not to ask for soup or fish twice, as, in so doing, part of the company may be kept waiting too long for the second course, when, perhaps, a little revenge is taken by looking at the awkward consumer of a second portion. This rule, however, may, under various circumstances, not be considered as binding.'

Mrs Beeton attached great importance to stock-making and recipes for 'stocks for all kinds of soups' appeared at the beginning of the original chapter. In this edition they can be found in Basic Recipes on pages 334-336.

ᑌᓂ *Apple Soup*

Time 1¼ to 1½ hours
Sufficient for 10 persons
Seasonable from
    September to December

INGREDIENTS
2 lb (1 kg) good boiling
    apples
6 pints (3.6 litres) Medium
    Stock (page 334)
6 cloves
¾ teaspoon white pepper
ground cayenne pepper or
    ginger to taste

FRUIT SOUPS ARE NOT sweet as you might imagine, and this one is a good example. Made with tart cooking apples, it has a tangy flavour from the spices and is quite refreshing to the palate. It is ideal for late summer or early autumn when you may have a surplus of windfall apples. It makes a large amount, so you can halve the quantities if you like, but it freezes well and is equally good hot in winter or chilled in summer for entertaining.

METHOD

Peel and quarter the apples, taking out their cores. Put them into a large saucepan with the stock and the cloves and cook them gently until tender – about ¾ hour. Rub through a sieve, add the seasonings and heat through until boiling.

NOTES

Good boiling apples Bramley cooking apples are the best variety for boiling. Their flesh softens during cooking and quickly reduces down to a pulpy consistency.

Medium Stock is meaty, made with beef or veal and poultry trimmings, but you can use a vegetable or chicken stock if you prefer. Chicken stock will give the soup a deep savoury flavour, especially if you use homemade or the fresh stock that is sold in cartons at supermarkets. Vegetable stock will give a lighter flavour.

Sieve You can purée the soup in a food processor or blender instead of sieving it. For an ultra-smooth texture, work the soup through a sieve after puréeing.

Mrs Beeton writes

"THE APPLE – As a food the apple cannot be considered to rank high, as more than the half of it consists of water, and the rest of its properties are not the most nourishing. It is, however, a useful adjunct to other kinds of food, and, when cooked, is esteemed as slightly laxative."

AN OVEN-BAKED SOUP like this one needs no attention for several hours, allowing you time to get on with other things. Years ago, cooks were frugal with their use of oven heat: if the oven was used at all, it would be used to full capacity, so dishes like this that were usually cooked on top of the stove were often adapted for oven cooking. The quantity of this soup is enough for a large gathering or to last for more than one meal, but it can easily be halved.

METHOD

Cut the meat and vegetables in slices, add them to the rice and peas and season with pepper and salt. Put everything in a jar, fill up with the water, cover very closely and bake for 4 hours.

The oven should be preheated to 300°F (150°C) Gas 2.

NOTES

Meat In her original recipe Mrs Beeton said to use '… any kind of meat, any trimmings or odd pieces'. Boneless stewing or braising beef would be appropriate here, so too would a cut of lamb like neck or shoulder. Trim off as much fat as possible or the soup will be greasy. A ham knuckle could also be used (ham and split pea soup is a traditional favourite), in which case the ham should be removed from the bone and cut into bite-sized pieces at the end of cooking. Return the pieces to the soup and reheat them before serving.

Jar A flameproof casserole with a tight fitting lid would be the modern-day equivalent. To get the soup cooking at the start, bring it to the boil on top of the stove, then transfer it to the oven.

Mrs Beeton writes

"This will be found a very cheap and wholesome soup,
and will be convenient in those cases where baking
is more easily performed than boiling."

Time 4¼ hours
Sufficient for 10 or 12
   persons
Seasonable at any time

INGREDIENTS
1 lb (500 g) meat
2 onions
2 carrots
2 oz (60 g) rice
1 pint (600 ml) split peas
pepper and salt to taste
8 pints (4.8 litres) water

✆ Cabbage Soup

Time 1 hour
Sufficient for 8 persons
Seasonable in winter

INGREDIENTS
1 large cabbage
3 carrots
2 onions
4 or 5 slices of lean bacon
4 pints (2.4 litres) Medium
   Stock (page 334)
salt and pepper to taste

THIS IS A WONDERFUL WINTER SOUP. It is warming and nourishing, yet inexpensive and very easy to make. For vegetarians, simply omit the bacon and use vegetable stock. You can halve the quantities if you like, although it is the ideal soup for a main meal served with hot crusty bread and cheese. If you have any left over, keep it in the covered pan in the refrigerator and reheat it within a day or two.

METHOD

Separate the cabbage leaves, scald them, then cut them up. Slice the carrots and onions. Line a saucepan with the bacon, put in the cabbage, carrots and onions and moisten with a few skimmings from the stock. Simmer very gently until the cabbage is tender – about 5 minutes. Add the remaining stock, simmer for half an hour, and carefully skim off every particle of fat. Season and serve.

NOTES

Cabbage Any cabbage is suitable. Savoy cabbage has a good strong colour and flavour and attractive crinkly leaves. Spring greens are sweeter and more delicate than Savoy. Hard Dutch white cabbage will make a milder, paler soup, and may need longer cooking.

Scald means to plunge the cabbage into a large saucepan of boiling water, bring the water quickly back to the boil, then drain immediately. It helps cleanse the cabbage and remove any bitterness.

Mrs Beeton writes

"THE CABBAGE – The Egyptians adored and raised altars
to the cabbage tribe, and the Greeks and Romans ascribed
many of the most exalted virtues to them. Cato affirmed
that the cabbage cured all diseases, and declared that it
was to its use that the Romans were enabled to live in health
and without the assistance of physicians for 600 years."

YOU NEED REALLY GOOD CARROTS for this simple soup, so buy organically grown ones. You may spend more time scraping them than you would ordinary carrots, but the difference in flavour will make the extra work worthwhile.

METHOD

Scrape and cut out all specks from the carrots, wash and wipe them dry, then cut them into quarter-inch (5 mm) slices. Put the butter into a large saucepan. When it is melted, add the sliced carrots and let them cook gently without browning. Add the stock and allow to simmer until the carrots are tender – say for nearly an hour. Press them through a sieve with the stock, and add salt and cayenne if required. Boil gently for 5 minutes, skim well, and serve.

NOTES

Stock Use vegetable stock for a vegetarian soup, otherwise use chicken stock.

Stewing In Mrs Beeton's original recipe she recommended stewing the carrots in the butter for an hour, but this length of time is not necessary – about 10 minutes is sufficient. This culinary technique is called 'sweating', and is used at the beginning of cooking hard vegetables to soften them and release their flavour. The pan should be covered and the heat kept very low so that the vegetables and butter do not brown. Some cooks press a piece of buttered greaseproof paper over the vegetables to help keep them moist.

Sieve You can purée the soup in a food processor or blender instead of sieving it. For an ultra-smooth texture, work the soup through a sieve after puréeing.

Mrs Beeton writes

"THE CARROT – The garden carrot in general use was introduced in the reign of Queen Elizabeth and was, at first, so highly esteemed that the ladies wore leaves of it in their head-dresses. A pretty winter ornament can be obtained by placing a cut from the top of the carrot-root in a shallow vessel of water, when the young leaves spring forth with a charming freshness and fullness."

Time 1¼ hours
Sufficient for 10 persons
Seasonable from October to March

INGREDIENTS
2 lb (1 kg) carrots
3 oz (90 g) butter
4 pints (2.4 litres) stock
seasoning to taste of salt and cayenne pepper

✥ Chantilly Soup

Time ½ hour

Sufficient for 8 persons

Seasonable from June to the
   end of August

INGREDIENTS

2 pints (1.2 litres) young
   green peas

a small bunch of parsley

2 young onions, chopped

4 pints (2.4 litres) Medium
   Stock (page 334)

Mrs Beeton writes

"Cold peas pounded in a
mortar, with a little stock
   added to them, make a
very good soup in haste."

NAMED AFTER CHANTILLY in northern France, an area renowned for its vegetables, this soup is simply delicious when made with freshly picked young peas. If you can't get homegrown peas, buy them from a reputable greengrocer as early in the season as possible.

METHOD

Boil the peas in plenty of water with the parsley and onions until quite tender – about 20 minutes. Drain the peas, then rub them through a sieve into a saucepan and pour the stock into them. Heat until very hot, but do not boil after the peas are added or you will spoil the colour.

NOTES

Young green peas The quantity given here is for shelled peas measured by volume in a measuring jug. You will need about 2½ lb (1.2 kg) peas in the pod to yield 2 pints (1.2 litres) shelled peas.

Medium stock is recommended in the original recipe, but its meaty flavour could easily mask the delicate sweetness of the peas. Vegetable stock would be a better choice.

Sieve You can purée the soup in a food processor or blender instead of sieving it. For an ultra-smooth texture, pour the soup through a sieve after puréeing.

Chestnut Soup ❧

This is the perfect soup at Christmas time, when you are most likely to have chestnuts in the house. Chestnuts and turkey are traditional partners, so it is also ideal for using turkey stock made from the leftover carcass.

METHOD

Take the outer rind from the chestnuts and put them into a large saucepan of warm water over a high heat. As soon as this becomes too hot for the fingers to remain in it, take out the chestnuts, peel them quickly and immerse them in cold water, then wipe and weigh them. Now cover the chestnuts with a third of the stock in a clean pan and cook them gently for rather more than three-quarters of an hour, or until they break when touched with a fork. Drain, pound and rub them through a fine sieve back into the saucepan, which has been rinsed. Add the remaining stock, mace, cayenne and salt to taste and stir until it boils, then put in the cream.

NOTES

Chestnuts are notoriously fiddly to peel and skin, yet Mrs Beeton's description seems to make light work of removing the 'rind' (shell). You will find the task easier if you first make a small slit in the outer shell of each chestnut, then immerse them in boiling water for 10 minutes. Drain and immerse in cold water, then put them in warm water and proceed as described above to remove the skins.

Sieve You can purée the soup in a food processor or blender instead of sieving it. For an ultra-smooth texture, pour the soup through a sieve after puréeing.

Cream If you take care not to let the soup boil after adding the cream, single cream can be used, otherwise use double or whipping cream, both of which can be boiled and will give a richer result than single cream. For a more tangy flavour, use crème fraîche.

Mrs Beeton writes

"The stock in which the chestnuts are boiled can be used for the soup, when its sweetness is not objected to, or it may, in part, be added to it. The rule is that ¾ lb chestnuts should be given to each quart of soup."

Time 1½ hours
Sufficient for 4 persons
Seasonable from October to February

INGREDIENTS

¾ lb (375 g) chestnuts
2½ pints (1.4 litres) Medium Stock (page 334)
seasoning to taste of ground mace, cayenne pepper and salt
¼ pint (150 ml) cream

✍ Cock-a-Leekie

Time 4 hours
Sufficient for 6 persons
Seasonable in winter

INGREDIENTS
about 2 lb (1 kg) fine leeks
1 boiling fowl, trussed
5 pints (3 litres) Medium
   Stock (page 334)
pepper and salt to taste

MRS BEETON'S ORIGINAL RECIPE used a capon or large fowl, 2 to 3 bunches of fine leeks and 10 pints (6 litres) stock. Today these would not be practical amounts, so the quantities have been scaled down. According to Scottish custom, cock-a-leekie should be served before the haggis on Burns night, and Mrs Beeton informed us that, 'Cock-a-leekie was largely consumed at the Burns Centenary festival at the Crystal Palace, Sydenham, in 1859'.

METHOD
Well wash the leeks, taking off the roots and part of the heads. Cut the leeks into lengths of about 1 inch (2.5 cm). Put the bird into the pan of stock with half of the leeks, and allow it to simmer gently. In half an hour, add the remaining leeks, and then it may simmer for 3 or 4 hours longer. It should be carefully skimmed and seasoned to taste. In serving, take out the bird and carve it neatly, placing the pieces in a tureen and pouring the soup over them. The soup should be very thick of leeks (a purée of leeks the French call it.)

NOTES
Boiling fowl It is still possible to buy boiling fowls at traditional butchers, although a roasting chicken can be used instead. Boiling fowls are older birds that benefit from long cooking, whereas a roasting chicken needs very gentle poaching or the flesh will toughen and become stringy.

Medium stock was recommended by Mrs Beeton, but most cock-a-leekie recipes use plain water. Given the length of the cooking time, it would seem hardly necessary to use stock.

Mrs Beeton writes

"Without the fowl, the above, which would then be merely called leek soup, is very good, and also economical."

Courgette Soup ∾

MRS BEETON CALLED THIS 'Vegetable Marrow Soup' and specified 'young vegetable marrows' in the ingredients. This was in the days before we borrowed the word courgette from France, and began to cultivate miniature vegetable marrows by their French name.

METHOD
Pare and slice the courgettes and put them in the boiling stock. When done almost to a mash – about 50 minutes – press the mixture through a sieve into a clean pan and reheat. At the moment of serving, add the boiling cream and seasoning.

NOTES
Pare means to peel or remove the skins of the courgettes, but this is hardly necessary when the soup is pressed through a sieve because most of the skins will be left behind. You can purée the soup in a food processor or blender rather than using a sieve, in which case you can leave the skins on or off as you prefer – most cooks prefer to leave the skins on, for extra colour and fibre.

White stock is made with veal, poultry and ham. A mild-flavoured chicken stock would be a good substitute, or a vegetable stock if you want to make a vegetarian soup.

Cream The cream is boiled before being added to the soup, so it is essential to use double cream (with a butterfat content of at least 40 percent) or it will curdle.

Mrs Beeton writes

"THE VEGETABLE MARROW – This is a variety of the gourd family, brought from Persia by an East-India ship, and only recently introduced to Britain. It is already cultivated to a considerable extent, and, by many, is highly esteemed when fried with butter.
It is, however, dressed in different ways, either by stewing or boiling, and besides, made into pies."

Time 1 hour
Sufficient for 8 persons
Seasonable in summer

INGREDIENTS
4 courgettes, or more, if very small
4 pints (2.4 litres) boiling White Stock (page 335)
½ pint (300 ml) boiling cream
salt and white pepper to taste

ISABELLA BEETON'S
NO-NONSENSE MANNER
AND STEELY ATTITUDE
TO THE RIGHTS AND
DUTIES OF THE MISTRESS
OF THE HOUSE ARE
NOWHERE MORE
APPARENT THAN IN THE
FOLLOWING
QUOTATIONS, WHICH
CAME UNDER THE
FOREBODING TITLE OF
'THE MISTRESS'.

AS WITH THE COMMANDER of an army, or the leader of any enterprise, so is it with the mistress of a house. Her spirit will be seen through the whole establishment. Of all those acquirements, which more particularly belong to the feminine character, there are none which take a higher rank, in our estimation, than such as enter into the happiness, comfort and well-being of a family.

EARLY RISING is one of the most essential qualities which enter into good Household Management, as it is not only the parent of health, but of innumerable other advantages. Indeed, when a mistress is an early riser, it is almost certain that her house will be orderly and well-managed. She who makes her husband and her children happy, who reclaims the one from vice and trains up the other to virtue, is a much greater character than ladies described in romances, whose whole occupation is to murder mankind with shafts from their quiver, or their eyes.

FRUGALITY AND ECONOMY are home virtues, without which no household can prosper. We must always remember that it is a great merit in housekeeping to manage a little well. Economy and frugality must never, however, be allowed to degenerate into parsimony and meanness.

HOSPITALITY is a most excellent virtue; but care must be taken that the love of company, for its own sake, does not become a prevailing passion; for then the habit is no longer hospitality, but dissipation.

IN MARKETING, that the best articles are the cheapest, may be laid down as a rule; and it is desirable, unless an experienced and confidential housekeeper be kept, that the mistress should herself purchase all provisions and stores needed for the house. If the mistress be a young wife, and not accustomed to order 'things for the house', a little practice and experience will soon teach her who are the best tradespeople to deal with, and what are the best provisions to buy.

A HOUSEKEEPING ACCOUNT-BOOK should invariably be kept, and kept punctually and precisely. The housekeeping accounts should be balanced not less than once a month; so that you may see the money you have in hand tallies with your account of it in your diary.

GOOD TEMPER should be cultivated by every mistress, as upon it the welfare of the household may be said to turn; indeed, its influence can hardly be over-estimated, as it has the effect of moulding the character of those around her, and of acting most beneficially on the happiness of the domestic circle. Every head of a household should strive to be cheerful, and should never fail to show a deep interest in all that appertains to the well-being of those who claim the protection of her roof.

CHARITY AND BENEVOLENCE are duties which a mistress owes to herself as well as to her fellow-creatures; and there is scarcely any income so small, but something may be spared from it, even if it be but 'the widow's mite'. It is to be always remembered, however, that it is the *spirit* of charity which imparts to the gift a value far beyond its actual amount, and is by far its better part.

THE TREATMENT OF SERVANTS is of the highest possible moment, as well to the mistress as to the domestics themselves. On the head of the house the latter will naturally fix their attention; and if they perceive that the mistress's conduct is regulated by high and correct principles, they will not fail to respect her.

✎ Soupe à la Crécy

Time 1¾ hours
Sufficient for 8 persons
Seasonable all the year

INGREDIENTS
4 carrots, sliced
2 onions, sliced
1 lettuce, cut small
a bunch of chervil
2 oz (60 g) butter
¼ pint (150 ml) lentils
4 pints (2.4 litres) Medium
   Stock (page 334)
crumbs of 2 French rolls
half a teacupful of rice,
   boiled

MANY CLASSIC FRENCH DISHES containing carrots are described as *à la Crécy* because the best French carrots are said to come from Crécy, a town in the *Ile de France*, the lush and fertile region that surrounds Paris. This is more than just a carrot soup, it is thick and substantial with the addition of lentils, rice and bread.

METHOD

Put the vegetables and chervil with the butter in a saucepan and let them simmer for 5 minutes. Add the lentils and half of the stock and cook gently for half an hour. Now fill it up with the remainder of the stock and let it boil another hour. Put in the crumb of the rolls. When well soaked, rub all through a sieve. Reheat the soup in a clean pan, add the boiled rice and serve.

NOTES

Lentils can be green, brown or red, although Le Puy lentils would be most appropriate for a French soup. Mrs Beeton measured them by volume; the weight of ¼ pint (150 ml) lentils is about ¼ lb (125 g).
French rolls Use about 2 oz (60 g) fresh crumbs from a baguette.
Half a teacupful of long-grain rice weighs about 2½ oz (75 g). Put it in a saucepan with ½ pint (300 ml) cold water and bring it to the boil. Cover and simmer for 15 minutes, by which time it will be tender and will have absorbed all of the water.
Sieve You can purée the soup in a food processor or blender instead of sieving it. For an ultra-smooth texture, work the soup through a sieve after puréeing.

Mrs Beeton writes

"THE LENTIL – is a variety of the bean tribe, but in England it is not used as human food, although considered the best of all kinds for pigeons. On the Continent it is cultivated for soups, as well as for other preparations for the table. Among the Romans it was not much esteemed and from them the English may have inherited a prejudice against it, on account of its rendering men indolent. It takes its name from lentus, 'slow' and, according to Pliny, produces mildness and moderation of temper."

MRS BEETON DESCRIBED THIS as a French recipe, no doubt because of the rich egg yolk and cream liaison used as a thickening at the end. It is a special recipe, which for our tastes would be better as a puréed soup, particularly if it is to be served for a dinner party first course. After cooking, work it in a food processor or blender until smooth, then reheat it gently before adding the egg yolks and cream.

METHOD

Pare the cucumber, quarter it and take out the seeds. Cut it in thin slices and put these on a plate with a little salt to draw out the water from them. Drain and put them in your saucepan with the butter. When they are warmed through without being browned, pour the stock on them. Add the chervil, sorrel and seasoning and boil for 40 minutes. Mix the well-beaten yolks of the eggs with the cream and add at the moment of serving.

NOTES

Pare means to peel the cucumber thinly.

Sorrel, a member of the leafy lettuce family, is sharp and acidic, with a flavour reminiscent of gooseberries. It was used frequently in soups and as a vegetable in Mrs Beeton's time, but it is not often seen for sale these days, although some shops are beginning to stock it as a herb item and it is easy to grow in the garden from seed. If you cannot get it, use more chervil or a few leaves of rocket.

Medium stock may be too meaty in this recipe for today's tastes. A light chicken or vegetable stock is better suited to the delicate flavour of cucumber.

Double cream is best for an egg-yolk liaison because it has a high fat content and is less likely to curdle. As a precaution, mix a little of the hot soup with the egg yolks and cream in a small bowl, then stir this slowly back into the soup. Do not let it boil.

Mrs Beeton writes

"THE CUCUMBER – is a cold food, and of difficult digestion when eaten raw."

Time 1 hour
Sufficient for 4 persons
Seasonable from June to
September

INGREDIENTS
1 large cucumber
salt and pepper to taste
a piece of butter the size of
a walnut
2 pints (1.2 litres) Medium
Stock (page 334)
a little chervil and sorrel cut
in large pieces
the yolks of 2 eggs
¼ pint (150 ml) cream

✌ Soupe à la Flamande

Time 1 hour
Sufficient for 6 persons
Seasonable from May to
   August

INGREDIENTS
2 onions
a head of celery
4 moderate-sized potatoes
2 oz (60 g) butter
½ pint (300 ml) water
2 pints (1.2 litres) Medium
   Stock (page 334)
½ pint (300 ml) cream

THE INGREDIENTS IN THIS Flemish puréed vegetable soup are inexpensive, and it makes an excellent meal in itself, served with bread. The smooth and creamy texture also makes it suitable for a first course, in which case it would look good swirled with a little extra cream and garnished with a sprinkling of chopped chervil or parsley or snipped chives. Mrs Beeton's original quantities make an enormous amount of soup, so this is a scaled-down version.

METHOD

Slice the onions, celery and potatoes and put them with the butter and water into a saucepan. Simmer for 10 minutes. Fill up the saucepan with stock and boil gently until the potatoes are done, which will be in about half an hour. Rub everything through a sieve, reheat in a clean saucepan and add the cream. Do not let it boil after the cream has been put in.

NOTES

Sieve You can purée the soup in a food processor or blender instead of sieving it. For an ultra-smooth texture, work the soup through a sieve after puréeing.

Seasoning was not mentioned by Mrs Beeton, but this was probably an oversight. Add salt and pepper to taste at the reheating stage.

Cream You can use single cream if you take Mrs Beeton's advice and do not let the soup boil.

Mrs Beeton writes

"This soup can be made with water instead of stock."

Soupe à la Julienne ∾

STRIPS OF VEGETABLES cut matchstick-thin are called *julienne* in French *haute cuisine*. Here they look very pretty floating in a clear broth, and they make this simple vegetable soup worthy of a professonal chef.

METHOD
Cut the carrots, turnips, onion, leeks and celery into strips of about 1¼ inches (3.5 cm) long, and be particular they are all the same size or some will be hard whilst the others will be done to a pulp. Cut the lettuce, sorrel and chervil into larger pieces. Fry the carrots in the butter, and pour the boiling stock on to them. When this is done, add all the other vegetables and the herbs and cook gently for at least half an hour. Skim off all the fat, pour the soup over thin slices of bread, cut round about the size of a shilling, and serve.

NOTES
Medium stock gives the soup a deep meaty flavour, but you may prefer to use vegetable stock in a vegetable soup. The flavour will be lighter, but equally delicious.

Seasoning was not mentioned in the original recipe, although it seems unlikely that it would not be needed. Taste the soup at the end of cooking and season with salt and pepper to your liking.

A shilling was a silver coin worth one-twentieth of a pound. It was about 1½ inches (4 cm) in diameter.

Mrs Beeton writes

"In summer, green peas, asparagus tops, French beans &c.
can be added. When the vegetables are very strong,
instead of frying them in butter at first, they should be blanched,
and afterwards simmered in the stock."

Time 1 hour
Sufficient for 8 persons
Seasonable all the year

INGREDIENTS
4 carrots
2 turnips
1 large onion
2 or 3 leeks
½ head of celery
1 lettuce
a little sorrel and chervil if
   liked
2 oz (60 g) butter
4 pints (2.4 litres) boiling
   Medium Stock (page 334)
thin slices of bread

✑ *Macaroni Soup*

Time ¼ hour or rather more
Sufficient for 8 persons
Seasonable all the year

INGREDIENTS
3 oz (90 g) macaroni
4 pints (2.4 litres) clear
  stock
salt to taste
grated Parmesan cheese, to
  serve

THIS IS MRS BEETON'S VERSION of *pasta in brodo*, a traditional Italian soup that is still very popular today. It is simple and quick, and very nourishing and satisfying. In Italian homes where lunch is the main meal of the day, *pasta in brodo* is often served in the evening.

METHOD
Throw the macaroni into boiling stock, with a pinch of salt, and simmer for ¼ hour. Serve grated Parmesan cheese with it.

NOTES
Macaroni is a hollow pasta that comes in long and short varieties. In Mrs Beeton's original recipe she used the long variety and pre-boiled it in water with a walnut-sized piece of butter before cutting it into short lengths. Today we use the short dried macaroni for convenience. In fact you can use any short pasta shape you like – the special tiny soup pasta called *pastina* would be a good choice.
Clear stock Homemade meat stock clarified with egg whites would have been used in Mrs Beeton's day. For a convenient and superb-tasting substitute, use canned beef or chicken consommé.
Parmesan cheese Buy a piece of genuine Parmesan (*Parmigiano-Reggiano*) and grate it yourself.

Mrs Beeton writes

"MACARONI – This is the favourite food of Italy, where, especially among the Neapolitans, it may be regarded as the staff of life. As it is both wholesome and nutritious, it ought to be much more used by all classes in England than it is. It generally accompanies Parmesan cheese to the tables of the rich, but is also used for thickening soups and making puddings."

THIS SOUP IS SIMILAR to French onion soup, although Mrs Beeton originally called it 'Cheap Onion Soup', to distinguish it from another of her onion soup recipes made with stock and cream.

METHOD

Cut the onions small, put them in a saucepan with the butter and fry them well until golden. Add the flour, water, seasoning and sugar and simmer until the onions are tender – about ¾ hour.

NOTES

Water If you like, you can use stock instead of the water suggested here. French chefs tend to use beef stock when they make onion soup, to give it body and a meaty flavour, but you could also use chicken or vegetable stock.

Thickening In the original recipe the soup was thickened at the end with a paste (*beurre manié*) made by mixing together butter and flour. The consistency of this soup is very good without thickening, but if you prefer it thicker, mix 1 oz (30 g) each of butter and flour to a paste and add it to the soup a little at a time. Stir constantly and simmer until the soup thickens.

Mrs Beeton writes

"THE ONION – Although all the species have highly nutritive properties, they impart such a disagreeable odour to the breath that they are often rejected even when they are liked. Chewing a little raw parsley is said to remove this odour."

Time 1 hour
Sufficient for 8 persons
Seasonable in winter

INGREDIENTS
8 middling-sized onions
3 oz (90 g) butter
1 tablespoon flour
4 pints (2.4 litres) water
salt and pepper to taste
1 teaspoon caster sugar

Parsnip Soup

Time 2 hours
Sufficient for 4 persons
Seasonable from October
   to April

INGREDIENTS
1 lb (500 g) sliced parsnips
2 oz (60 g) butter
2 pints (1.2 litres) stock
salt and cayenne pepper
   to taste

PARSNIPS MAKE EXCELLENT SOUP. The consistency is beautifully smooth and thick, and the flavour has a pleasant hint of sweetness. Serve sprinkled with chopped parsley or chervil for a warming winter meal, or swirled with cream for an elegant first course.

METHOD
Put the parsnips into a saucepan with the butter, which has been previously melted, and simmer them for about 10 minutes. Then add nearly 1 pint (600 ml) of the stock and boil together for half an hour. Pass all through a fine sieve, and add it to the remainder of the stock. Season, simmer for 10 minutes, and serve immediately.

NOTES
Stock The original recipe used an economical stock made from meat and poultry trimmings, vegetables, herbs and spices. If you don't want to make your own, buy a good-quality chicken or vegetable stock and add a fresh bouquet garni.
Sieve You can purée the soup in a food processor or blender instead of sieving it. For an ultra-smooth texture, work the soup through a sieve after puréeing.

VARIATION
To inject a little more flavour into the soup, sprinkle 1 to 2 teaspoons curry powder over the parsnips when cooking them in the butter at the beginning.

Mrs Beeton writes

"THE PARSNIP – This is a native of Britain and, in its wild state, may be found in many parts, growing by the road-sides. It is also to be found generally distributed over Europe, and in Catholic countries is mostly used with salt fish in Lent. In Scotland it forms an excellent dish, when beat up with butter and potatoes; it is also excellent when fried. In Ireland it is found to yield, in conjunction with the hop, a pleasant beverage."

MRS BEETON DESCRIBED THIS SOUP as inexpensive, which it certainly is. Split peas make a cheap and nourishing main meal soup, and the fresh mint at the end is an inspired addition. Served with chunks of wholemeal bread, butter and cheese, this is a good soup for cold winter days.

Time 2½ hours
Sufficient for 12 persons
Seasonable in winter

INGREDIENTS
¼ lb (125 g) onions
¼ lb (125 g) carrots
2 oz (60 g) celery
a little butter
8 pints (4.8 litres) water
¾ lb (375 g) split peas
1 tablespoon coarse brown
   sugar
salt and pepper to taste
a little mint, shred fine

METHOD

Fry the vegetables for 10 minutes in a little butter, previously cutting them up in small pieces. Pour the water on them and, when boiling, add the split peas. Let them simmer for nearly 2 hours, or until the peas are thoroughly done. Add the sugar and seasoning and simmer for ¼ hour. Add the mint and serve.

NOTES

Coarse brown sugar Use a light or dark soft brown sugar, or demerara sugar.

Seasoning It is important not to add salt until towards the end of cooking. If salt is added to split peas at the beginning of cooking it will toughen their skins and the peas will not soften.

VARIATION

Mrs Beeton suggested using 'the liquor in which a joint of meat has been boiled' as an alternative to water. You could use the water in which a ham has been boiled, checking first that it is not too salty (a possibility if a smoked ham was used). You could also use chicken or vegetable stock for added flavour, or you could even cook an unsmoked ham bone in the soup, then take the meat off the bone at the end, cut it into bite-sized pieces and reheat it in the soup.

Mrs Beeton writes

"MINT – The common mint cultivated in our gardens is known as the *Mentha viridis*, and is employed in different culinary processes, being sometimes boiled with certain dishes, and afterwards withdrawn. It has an agreeable aromatic flavour, and forms an ingredient in soups, and sometimes is used in spring salads. It is valuable as a stomachic and antispasmodic; on which account it is generally served at table with pea-soup."

∾ *Potage Printanier*

Time ¾ hour

Sufficient for 8 persons

Seasonable from May to
October

INGREDIENTS

½ pint (300 ml) green peas

a little chervil

2 lettuces, shredded

2 onions, chopped fine

a very small bunch of
parsley

2 oz (60 g) butter

1 pint (600 ml) water

seasoning to taste

4 pints (2.4 litres) Medium
Stock (page 334)

the yolks of 3 eggs

THIS RECIPE WAS ALSO GIVEN its English name of 'Spring Soup' by
Mrs Beeton, but the French sounds prettier, and both the ingredients
and the method are very French. It makes a good first course soup,
and is very versatile in that it can be made with frozen peas at other
times of the year.

METHOD

Put the peas, chervil, lettuces, onions, parsley, butter and water in a
saucepan. Season with salt and pepper and let them simmer until
tender – about 20 minutes. When done, strain off the vegetables and
put two-thirds of the cooking liquid into the stock in another pan.
Bring to simmering point. Beat the egg yolks with the remaining
third of the cooking liquid and heat through very gently in a separate
pan. At the moment of serving, add this to the simmering stock with
the strained vegetables.

NOTES

Peas The volume given here is for shelled fresh peas or frozen peas. If
you are buying peas in the pod, you will need about ¾ lb (375 g).

Medium stock is meaty, and may have too strong a flavour for the
delicate peas. Chicken or vegetable stock would be a better choice,
but make sure it has a good flavour. Use either homemade or the
fresh kind that is sold in cartons.

Egg yolks You can use just 1 or 2 egg yolks if you prefer a less rich
soup, or omit them altogether. Up to ¼ pint (150 ml) double cream
can be used instead.

Turkey Soup ๛

AS YOU MIGHT EXPECT, this soup is described by Mrs Beeton as 'a seasonable dish at Christmas'. It is the perfect way to use up the leftover turkey carcass when you have had the best part of the meat off it.

METHOD

Cut up the turkey in small pieces, and put it in the stock. Let it simmer slowly until the bones are quite clean – up to 4 hours. Take the bones out and work the soup through a sieve. When cool, skim well. Mix the arrowroot with a little of the soup, then add it with the seasoning and sauce or ketchup. Bring to the boil and serve.

NOTES

Medium stock is hardly necessary when you are going to make a very tasty stock from boiling the turkey for 4 hours. Years ago, cooks would have a pot of stock at the ready at all times, and would use it frequently. In this instance, water is perfectly adequate.

Arrowroot was a popular thickener in Mrs Beeton's day, favoured because of the translucent appearance it gave to soups and sauces.

Harvey's sauce and **mushroom ketchup** were two very popular condiments in Victorian times. You could buy them ready made in bottles – and you can still do so today – although Mrs Beeton did give recipes for them. Harvey's sauce is a thin liquid made from anchovies, soy sauce, walnuts, garlic, shallots, vinegar and cayenne pepper, while mushroom ketchup is made from fresh mushrooms, cayenne, allspice, ginger and mace. You can buy these sauces in some specialist delicatessens and gourmet food shops, but if you can't get them you can flavour this soup with a dash or two of Worcestershire sauce, soy sauce, anchovy essence or even chilli sauce.

Mrs Beeton writes

"Instead of thickening this soup, vermicelli or macaroni may be served in it."

"THE TURKEY – According to Tusser's *Five Hundred Points of Good Husbandry*, about the year 1585 turkey began to form a dish at our rural Christmas feasts.
'Beef, mutton, and pork, shred pies of the best,
Pig, veal, goose, and capon, and turkey well dress'd,
Cheese, apples, and nuts, jolly carols to hear,
As then in the country is counted good cheer'."

Time 4 hours
Sufficient for 8 persons
Seasonable at Christmas

INGREDIENTS
the remains of a cold roast turkey
4 pints (2.4 litres) Medium Stock (page 334)
2 oz (60 g) arrowroot
salt and pepper to taste
1 tablespoon Harvey's sauce or mushroom ketchup

✤ Hodge-Podge

Time 2½ hours or rather
more
Sufficient for 12 persons
Seasonable at any time

INGREDIENTS
2 lb (1 kg) shin of beef or
stewing steak
2 onions
2 carrots
2 turnips
a head of celery
1 pint (600 ml) table beer
6 pints (3.6 litres) water
pepper and salt to taste
thickening of 1 oz (30 g)
each butter and flour
mixed to a paste

As its name suggests, this hearty beef and vegetable soup is a kind of hot-pot. It makes a meal in itself, and would easily serve 6 people for a main course. Mrs Beeton suggested serving it with turnips and carrots, or spinach and celery, but bread makes a much easier accompaniment – and is good for mopping up the gravy.

METHOD
Cut the meat and vegetables into small pieces. Put the meat, beer and water in a saucepan. Simmer for a few minutes and skim carefully. Add the vegetables and seasoning and simmer gently until the meat is tender – about 2 hours. Thicken with the butter and flour paste.

NOTES
Table beer today would be pale ale or light ale, although you could also use bitter or stout, depending on the flavour you prefer.
Thickening The paste referred to is *beurre manié*, which is made by mixing together butter and flour until smooth. Add it to the hot soup in small quantities and stir constantly after each addition until the liquid boils and thickens.

Mrs Beeton writes

"TABLE BEER – This is nothing more than a weak ale, and is not made so much with a view to strength, as to transparency of colour and an agreeable bitterness of taste. It is, or ought to be, manufactured by the London professional brewers, from the best pale malt, or amber and malt. As a beverage it is agreeable when fresh; but it is not adapted to keep long."

Prawn Soup ೞ

THIS IS A DELICIOUS SMOOTH SOUP, which you can purée in a food processor or blender rather than working it through a sieve as cooks had to do in Mrs Beeton's day. She suggested it could be thickened with tomatoes, which would also deepen its colour, or that it could have vermicelli served in it, either or both of which would make it 'very tasteful'.

METHOD

Peel the prawns and put the heads and shells in a saucepan with the mace, vinegar and the same quantity of water. Cook for ¼ hour, then strain off the liquor. Put the fish stock or water into a saucepan and add the strained liquor. Reserve a few prawns for later and pound the remainder with the crumbs of the roll moistened with a little of the soup. Rub them through a sieve, and mix them by degrees with the soup. Add anchovy essence or ketchup to taste with a little lemon juice, then whisk in the thickening paste a little at a time and bring to the boil. Simmer until the soup is well cooked – about ¼ hour. Put in the reserved peeled prawns, let them get thoroughly hot and serve.

NOTES

Prawns used to be measured in a pint pot by the fishmonger, but today they are more likely to be weighed. You will need 1 lb (500 g) raw prawns in their shells.
French roll Use 2 oz (60 g) fresh crumbs from a baguette.
Anchovy essence and **mushroom ketchup** can be bought in bottles from good delicatessens. Anchovy essence will accentuate the fishy flavour of the soup; mushroom ketchup is quite spicy. Both are strong-tasting and should be used in very small quantities – stir in no more than ½ to 1 teaspoon.

Mrs Beeton writes

"THE PRAWN – This little fish bears a striking resemblance to the shrimp, but is neither so common nor so small. It is to be found on most of the sandy shores of Europe. The Isle of Wight is famous for shrimps, where they are potted, but both the prawns and shrimps vended in London are too much salted for the excellence of their natural flavour to be preserved."

Time ¾ hour
Sufficient for 8 persons
Seasonable at any time

INGREDIENTS
2 pints (1.2 litres) prawns
1 blade of mace
½ pint (300 ml) vinegar
4 pints (2.4 litres) Fish Stock
   (page 336) or water
the crumbs of a French roll
anchovy essence or
   mushroom ketchup
   to taste
a little lemon juice
thickening of 1 oz (30 g)
   each butter and flour,
   mixed to a paste

CHAPTER 2

Fish & Shellfish

M rs Beeton began her introduction to this chapter in the original book with a long lesson on 'the natural history of fishes', followed by a potted history of the popularity of fish 'as an article of human food among civilized nations'.

'We know that the British shores, particularly those of the North Sea, have always been well supplied with the best kinds of fish, which we may reasonably infer was not unknown to the inhabitants. By the time of Edward II fish had become a dainty, especially the sturgeon, which was permitted to appear on no table but that of the king. In the fourteenth century, a decree of King John informs us that the people ate both seals and porpoises, whilst in the days of the Troubadours whales were fished for and caught in the Mediterranean Sea for the purpose of being used as human food.'

Next came sound practical advice for cooking and serving fish.

'In cooking fish of any kind, the first point to be attended to is to see that it is perfectly clean. It is a common error to wash it too much, as by doing so the flavour is diminished.

'Fish should be put into cold water and set on the fire to do very gently or the outside will break before the inner part is done. Unless the fishes are small, they should never be put into warm water, nor should water, either hot or cold, be poured on to the fish as it is liable to break the skin. If it should be necessary to add a little water whilst the fish is cooking, it ought to be poured in gently at the side of the vessel.

'In garnishing fish, great attention is required, and plenty of parsley, horseradish and lemon should be used.

'In choosing fish, it is well to remember that it is possible it may be fresh, and yet not good. Nothing can be of greater consequence to a cook than to have the fish good; as if this important course in a dinner does not give satisfaction, it is rarely that the repast goes off well."

According to the 'Bills of Fare' at the end of the original book, fish was served at formal dinners as a first course at the same time as the soup. For family dinners, either fish or soup (not both) was served as a first course before the meat, poultry and game. Mrs Beeton's concluding remarks illustrate how popular fish had become.

'When well done, and with very good sauce, fish is more appreciated than almost any other dish.'

⨳ Cod Pie

Time 1 hour
Sufficient for 4 to 6 persons
Seasonable from November
    to March

INGREDIENTS

2 slices of cod fillet or other
    white fish such as haddock
    or halibut, total weight
    about 1 lb (500 g), skinned
pepper and salt to taste
½ teaspoon grated nutmeg
1 large blade of mace,
    pounded
2 oz (60 g) butter, diced
½ pint (300 ml) White Stock
    (page 334)
a pastry crust
FOR THE SAUCE
1 tablespoon White Stock
    (page 334)
¼ pint (150 ml) cream or
    milk
thickening of 1 oz (30 g)
    butter and ½ oz (15 g)
    flour, mixed to a paste
lemon peel, chopped very
    fine, to taste

THIS IS A VERY SIMPLE and quick fish pie if made with bought puff pastry – there is no need to make your own. In Mrs Beeton's original recipe, 12 shelled oysters were added to the sauce, which was poured into the pie at the end. This was a traditional custom for fish pies in the days when oysters used to be plentiful and cheap, but as this is no longer the case they have been omitted in this recipe. You can add them if you like, or use peeled cooked prawns instead.

METHOD

Wash the cod, cut it into chunks and place it in a dish. Season, and add the nutmeg, mace, butter and stock. Cover with the crust and bake until golden brown and crisp – about 25 to 30 minutes. Now make the sauce by mixing the ingredients named left in a saucepan. Bring to the boil, stirring constantly, and pour into the pie by a hole made in the top of the crust, which can easily be covered by a small piece of pastry cut and baked in any fanciful shape.

The oven should be preheated to 375°F (190°C) Gas 5.

NOTES

White stock is made with veal, poultry and ham, but you may prefer to use fish or chicken stock.

Pastry crust The type of pastry was not specified by Mrs Beeton, and her instructions were rather vague. Puff pastry is very good on top of fish pies, and sheets of frozen ready-rolled puff pastry are most convenient. You will need a 11 x 9 inch/280 x 229 mm sheet to fit a 2 pint (1.2 litre) pie dish, and it should be glazed with beaten egg before baking. The trimmings can be cut into fanciful shapes as suggested, and baked for a few minutes on a baking sheet. If you prefer to make Mrs Beeton's Puff Pastry, there is a recipe on page 337.

Cod à la Crème ❧

SIMPLE AND QUICK, this makes a good supper dish served with rice, and it can be made with other thick white fish such as haddock, halibut, brill or monkfish. If you like more sauce, simply add more stock at the same time as the milk or cream. For a special occasion, use cream and dry white wine instead of some or all of the stock and milk.

METHOD

Cook the cod, and while hot, break it into flakes. Put the butter, shallot, parsley and stock into a saucepan and let them boil for 5 minutes. Stir in sufficient flour to thicken and pour in the milk or cream. Simmer for 10 minutes, add the cayenne and sugar and, when liked, a little lemon juice. Put the fish in the sauce to warm gradually, but do not let it boil. Serve the fish in a shallow dish garnished with croûtons.

NOTES

Cook the cod Mrs Beeton originally said to boil the cod, but this seems rather plain. To give the cod flavour, season it well with salt and pepper, then either poach it in fish stock with a bay leaf, fresh herbs or a piece of lemon peel, or pan-fry it in butter or olive oil and butter. Cooking time should be 8 to 10 minutes depending on the thickness of the fish. It should flake easily when tested with a fork. When flaking the fish, remove and discard the skin.

White stock Use fish stock for preference. A Victorian teacup held about 7 fl oz (200 ml).

Cream Double cream or crème fraîche is the best choice. These have a high butterfat content and will therefore not separate when simmered or boiled.

Flour to thicken Sprinkle in about 2 teaspoons flour, stirring vigorously with a wooden spoon.

Time rather more than
½ hour
Sufficient for 3 persons
Seasonable from November
to March

INGREDIENTS
1 large slice of cod fillet
weighing ¾ lb (375 g)
1 oz (30 g) butter
1 shallot, chopped
a little chopped parsley
1 teacupful of White Stock
(page 334)
flour to thicken
¼ pint (150 ml) milk or
cream
cayenne pepper to taste
¼ teaspoon caster sugar
lemon juice to taste
croûtons to garnish

Mrs Beeton writes

"The remains of fish
from the preceding day
answer very well
for this dish."

Cod à la Maître d'Hôtel

Time ½ hour
Sufficient for 4 persons
Seasonable from November
  to March

INGREDIENTS
2 slices of cod fillet, total
  weight about 1 lb (500 g),
  skinned
¼ lb (125 g) butter
a little chopped shallot and
  parsley
pepper to taste
¼ teaspoon grated nutmeg
  or rather less when the
  flavour is not liked
the juice of ¼ lemon

FOR THIS RECIPE Mrs Beeton first boiled the cod, then said, 'either leave it whole or, what is still better, flake it from the bone and take off the skin'. In fact the very best method of all is to cook the fish as described here – in the butter with the *maître d'hôtel* flavourings.

METHOD
Wash the cod and cut it into chunks. Put the butter into a frying pan with the shallot, parsley, pepper and nutmeg. Melt the butter gradually and when all is well mixed and thoroughly hot, add the fish. Cook gently for 5 to 8 minutes or until the fish flakes easily. Sprinkle the lemon juice over and serve.

NOTES
Maître d'hôtel is French for 'head waiter'. Maître d'hôtel butter is butter with chopped fresh parsley and salt and pepper beaten into it. It is a classic garnish for fish in French cuisine, and often has additional flavourings of chopped shallot and grated lemon peel.

VARIATION
Any white fish can be cooked in this way, even flat white fish like plaice and skate.

Mrs Beeton writes

"THE SEASON FOR FISHING COD – The best season for catching cod is from the beginning of February to the end of April, and although each fisherman engaged in taking them catches no more than one at a time, an expert hand will sometimes take four hundred in a day. The employment is excessively fatiguing, from the weight of the fish as well as from the coldness of the climate."

FISH & SHELLFISH

Mrs Beeton's recipe was for live freshwater eels. Their flesh is meaty and rich, with a hint of sweetness, and her method of double cooking them suits it very well. Ask your fishmonger about getting live eels – in the parts of the country where they are caught, they are not difficult to obtain. If you can't get them, you could use a firm white fish such as monkfish instead.

METHOD

Skin, wash and fillet the eels, then cut them into 3 inch (7.5 cm) pieces. Cut up the carrot and onion. Rub the butter over the bottom of a saucepan, add the carrot and onion and stir them over a low heat for 5 minutes. Add the sherry and the same quantity of water. Season and bring to the boil, then add the pieces of eel. Cover and simmer until tender – 20 to 30 minutes. When they are done, take them out and let them get cold. Cover the pieces of eel with egg and bread crumbs and fry them in hot oil until a nice brown. Put them on a dish, pour the sauce over and serve them hot.

NOTES

Eels Freshwater eels (*Anguilla anguilla*) are always kept live, so ask your fishmonger or fisherman to prepare them for you. He will kill, skin and fillet the eels and cut them into serving pieces. The fish should be used on the same day. Don't make the mistake of buying conger eel, a seawater fish usually sold as cutlets.

Bread crumbs You will need about 2 oz (60 g) and you can use fresh or dried.

Sauce Piquante is made from herbs, spices and vinegar. If you don't want to go to the trouble of making it, serve the fried eels with lemon wedges and ready-made tartare sauce.

Mrs Beeton writes

"VORACITY OF THE EEL – We find in a note upon Isaac Walton, by Sir John Hawkins, that he knew of eels, when kept in ponds, frequently destroying ducks. From a canal near his house at Twickenham he himself missed many young ducks, and, on draining in order to clean it, great numbers of large eels were caught in the mud. When some of these were opened, there were found in their stomachs the undigested heads of the quacking tribe which had become their victims."

Time ¾ to 1 hour plus
  cooling
Sufficient for 6 persons
Seasonable from August to
  March

INGREDIENTS
2 lb (1 kg) eels
1 carrot
1 onion
a walnut-sized piece of
  butter
1 glass of sherry
salt, pepper and grated
  nutmeg to taste
1 egg, beaten
bread crumbs
oil for shallow frying
Sauce Piquante (page 228)
  to serve

✍ *Fish Cakes*

Time ½ hour
Sufficient for 4 persons
Seasonable at any time

INGREDIENTS

1 onion

1 pint (600 ml) water

a bunch of sweet herbs

salt and pepper to taste

1 lb (500 g) thick white fish
  fillets

2 oz (60 g) fresh white bread
  crumbs

1 lb (500 g) potatoes, boiled
  and mashed

½ teaspoon chopped
  parsley or more to taste

1 egg white

1 whole egg, beaten

about ¼ lb (125 g) dried
  bread crumbs

oil for shallow frying

lemon and parsley to
  garnish

FISH CAKES ARE HOMELY COMFORT FOOD that everyone loves, and if you make them yourself you know exactly what is in them. Mrs Beeton made hers with leftover cold fish, and used the bones, head and fins to make a sauce to serve with them. We are less likely to have enough leftover fish to make fish cakes, so these are made with fresh fish.

METHOD

Chop the onion and put it in a saucepan with the water, herbs and salt and pepper. Boil for 10 to 15 minutes, then add the fish, cover and poach for 5 minutes or until the flesh flakes easily. Leave the fish to cool in the liquid. Chop the fish fine, removing all skin and any bones. Mix it well with the fresh bread crumbs and cold potatoes, adding the parsley and seasoning. Make into 8 cakes with the white of an egg, brush them over with egg and cover with the dried bread crumbs. Fry in hot oil until a light brown – about 2 to 3 minutes on each side. Garnish with slices of lemon and parsley and serve hot.

NOTES

Sweet herbs These should be fresh herbs, such as parsley, chervil, dill, thyme or chives and a bay leaf or two. You can tie the sprigs together with string or just sprinkle them loose into the pan. If you tie them into a bouquet garni, you could include a stick of celery.

Baked Whole Fish ~

A WHOLE STUFFED FISH IS GOOD for a large gathering. You can
prepare it up to the baking stage several hours in advance and pop it
in the oven once your guests have arrived – it cooks very quickly.
Mrs Beeton used a small haddock for this recipe, but haddock are
rarely sold whole these days. This recipe works equally well for whole
bream, sea bass or salmon.

METHOD
Scale and clean the fish, without cutting it open much. Put in a nice
delicate forcemeat and sew up the slit. Put the fish in a baking dish
and dot with pieces of butter. Cover with buttered paper and bake
until the flesh flakes easily – 25 to 30 minutes. Garnish with parsley
and cut lemon.

The oven should be preheated to 350°F (180°C) Gas 4.

NOTES
Fish You can use bream, sea bass, salmon or salmon trout. Ask your
fishmonger what is best on the day, and if he hasn't got a large whole
fish, buy two smaller ones instead. You could also buy trout, each
weighing about 1 lb (500 g), and serve 1 fish for each person. The
fishmonger will scale and clean the fish for you, and there is no need
to sew up the slit as Mrs Beeton suggested, it will hold together just
as well with wooden cocktail sticks or a metal skewer. If you use small
trout, the baking time will be 15 to 20 minutes.
Forcemeat A suitable forcemeat can be found on page 340, but any
fresh herb stuffing can be used – there are plenty of these to choose
from in supermarkets. Alternatively, you can simply stuff the fish with
a handful of fresh herbs and some lemon peel.

Mrs Beeton writes
———————

"Haddocks may be filleted, rubbed over with egg and bread crumbs,
and fried a nice brown; garnish with crisped parsley."

———————

"THE HADDOCK – On each side of the body, just beyond the gills,
it has a dark spot, which superstition asserts to be the impression of
the finger and thumb of St. Peter, when taking the tribute money out
of a fish of this species."

Time ¾ hour
Sufficient for 3 to 4 persons
Seasonable from August
   to February

INGREDIENTS
a whole fish weighing 3–4 lb
   (1.4–1.8 kg)
a nice forcemeat
about 2 oz (60 g) butter or to
   taste
parsley and lemon to
   garnish

✑ Baked Herrings

Time ¾ hour plus cooling
Sufficient for 4 to 6 persons
Seasonable all the year

INGREDIENTS
12 herrings
4 bay leaves
12 cloves
12 allspice berries
2 small blades of mace
cayenne pepper and salt to
   taste
sufficient vinegar to fill the
   dish

ALTHOUGH MRS BEETON didn't say so, these are really soused herrings, a dish of cold spiced herrings that have been 'soused' or drenched in spiced vinegar. Herrings have oily flesh, and the vinegar cuts the richness and gives the herrings a most delicious flavour. They are good served chilled for a first course or lunch, with soured cream and snipped chives.

METHOD

Take the herrings, cut off the heads, and gut them. Put them in a pie dish, heads and tails alternately, and sprinkle the herbs and spices between each layer. Cover the fish with vinegar and bake for ½ hour, but do not use until cold. The herrings may be cut down the front, the backbone taken out, and closed again. Sprats done in this way are absolutely delicious.

The oven should be preheated to 350°F (180°C) Gas 4.

NOTES

Herrings are an inexpensive fish, but their flesh is very meaty and tasty. For this recipe, use small herrings, weighing about ½ lb (250 g) each. Ask your fishmonger to cut off their heads and gut them. He will also remove their backbones if you want to follow Mrs Beeton's advice at the end of the recipe. Sprats are small relations of the herring, which you may find at the fishmongers at certain times of year, especially in the winter when the weather is frosty. They are the ideal size for a first course, or you could use sardines.

Vinegar You may prefer to use equal quantities of vinegar and water for a milder flavour.

Mrs Beeton writes

"TO CHOOSE THE HERRING – The more scales this fish has, the surer the sign of its freshness. It should also have a bright and silvery look; but if red about the head, it is a sign that it has been dead for some time. The moment the herring is taken out of the water it dies. Hence the origin of the common saying 'dead as a herring'."

Mrs Beeton intended her recipe for kegeree (as she spelled it) to be for leftover cold fish and boiled rice. Her instructions were very vague, calling for 'any cold fish and 1 teacupful of boiled rice', then saying at the end, 'the quantities may be varied according to the amount of fish used'. This recipe uses fresh fish and rice and precise quantities, but otherwise the ingredients and method are the same as Mrs Beeton's.

METHOD

Put the rice in a saucepan and add the water and a pinch of salt. Bring to the boil, cover and simmer gently for 15 minutes. Remove the pan from the heat and leave undisturbed until the rice is cold. Poach the fish, then carefully remove any skin and bones. Shell the eggs and roughly chop them. Melt the butter in a large frying pan, add the mustard and stir until dissolved, then add the rice and fish and salt and cayenne to taste. Toss over a moderate to high heat until all the ingredients are very hot.

NOTES

Poaching fish Put the fish in a wide pan and just cover with fish stock or cold water. Bring just to the boil, cover the pan and simmer for 5 minutes or until the fish flakes easily when tested with a fork. Drain. If using smoked fish, you could use half milk and half water as an alternative poaching liquid to stock or plain water.

Soft boiled eggs Mrs Beeton gave explicit instructions for boiling eggs. For this recipe, the whites should be set nicely, so follow her advice on page 187 and boil them for 3¾ to 4 minutes.

Rice It helps if the rice is cold when you combine it with the mustard butter, because the grains will absorb the flavour and stay separate, but if you don't have time to wait for it to go cold, this is not absolutely necessary.

VARIATION

Use 1–2 teaspoons curry powder or garam masala and/or 1 teaspoon turmeric instead of the mustard powder.

Time ½ hour plus cooling
Sufficient for 2 persons
Seasonable at any time

INGREDIENTS
¼ lb (125 g) long grain rice
½ pint (300 ml) water
salt
½ lb (250 g) white or smoked fish fillet (cod or haddock)
2 soft-boiled eggs
1 oz (30 g) butter
1 teaspoon mustard powder
cayenne pepper

✑ Grilled Mackerel

Time ¼ hour or rather more

Sufficient for 4 persons

Seasonable all the year

INGREDIENTS

4 mackerel

pepper and salt to taste

a small quantity of oil

a little parsley

2 oz (60 g) butter

lemon juice

Maître d'hôtel Sauce (page
214) to serve

Mrs Beeton writes

"THE MACKEREL –
This is not only one
of the most elegantly
formed, but one of the
most beautifully coloured
fishes, when taken out
of the sea, that we have.
In choosing this fish,
purchasers should, to a
great extent, be regulated
by the brightness of its
appearance. If it have a
transparent, silvery hue,
the flesh is good;
but if it be red about
the head, it is stale."

MACKEREL IS AN INEXPENSIVE oily fish with meaty flesh. It has a distinctive flavour and is best cooked simply, without embellishment, so its natural flavour can be enjoyed to the full. Quick grilling is one of the best cooking methods for it, and the parsley and lemon flavourings complement it well.

METHOD

Mackerel should never be washed when intended to be grilled, but merely wiped very clean and dry, after taking out the gills and insides. Sprinkle the mackerel inside and out with a little pepper, salt and oil. Put the fish on the grill pan, place under high heat and grill for about 10 minutes, turning them over halfway. When sufficiently cooked, the flesh will start coming away from the bone. Chop a little parsley (about 2 to 3 tablespoonfuls) and work it into the butter with pepper and salt to taste and a squeeze of lemon juice. Serve the mackerel hot, topped with the butter before it is quite melted, with a maître d'hôtel sauce in a sauce boat.

NOTES

Mackerel are sold gutted and cleaned but left whole with their heads and tails intact. The ideal ungutted weight for each fish is ¾–1 lb (375–500 g). To facilitate grilling and to make the mackerel look more attractive, make 3 diagonal slashes on each side of each fish.

Maître d'hôtel sauce is made with butter, parsley and lemon. It was recommended as an accompaniment by Mrs Beeton, but you will probably find the parsley butter sufficient.

This simple recipe is Mediterranean in feel, with its flavouring of anchovies and sherry, and it makes a very pretty dish for a summer lunch or supper. Red mullet are imported from the Mediterranean in the summer months – look for them at the fishmonger or supermarket in June and July, when they are at their best.

Method

Clean the fish and take out the gills, but leave the inside. Fold in oiled paper and bake them gently for 15 minutes. When done, take the liquor that flows from the fish, put in a saucepan with the other ingredients and boil for 2 minutes. Serve the sauce in a sauce boat, and the fish with or without the paper cases.

The oven should be preheated to 375°F (190°C) Gas 5.

Notes

Red mullet weigh about ½ lb (250 g) each and 1 fish is usually sufficient for 1 person, but you may like to serve more than this because they are bony fish. The fishmonger will clean and scale the fish and remove the gills. By 'leave the inside', Mrs Beeton meant that the liver should be left inside the fish. This was, and still is, regarded as a great delicacy.

Oiled paper Greaseproof paper, baking parchment or foil are all suitable, and you should use a generous amount of olive oil to keep the fish moist. If you plan to serve the fish in the paper at the table, as Mrs Beeton suggests, greaseproof paper and baking parchment look better than foil. Rather than serving such a small amount of sauce in a sauce boat, open each parcel and drizzle sauce over each fish.

Mrs Beeton writes

"Red mullet may be broiled, folded in oiled paper the same as in the recipe above, and seasoned with pepper and salt. They may be served without sauce, but if any is required, use melted butter, Italian or anchovy sauce."

"THE STRIPED RED MULLET – This fish was very highly esteemed by the ancients, especially by the Romans, who gave the most extravagant prices for it. Those of 2lbs weight were valued at about £15 each; those of 4lbs at £60. In the reign of Tiberius, three of them were sold for £209."

Time ½ hour
Sufficient for 4 persons
Seasonable at any time, but more so in summer

INGREDIENTS
4 red mullet
½ teaspoon anchovy essence
1 glass of sherry
cayenne pepper and salt to taste

ᴓ *Fried Plaice*

Time ½ hour
Sufficient for 4 persons
Seasonable from May to
 November

INGREDIENTS
4 plaice fillets
1 large egg
about 2 oz (60 g) dried bread
 crumbs
1 tablespoon flour
hot lard or clarified dripping
fried parsley and cut lemon
 to garnish

THE TECHNIQUE DESCRIBED HERE for egging, crumbing and shallow-frying plaice can be used for any fish fillets – cod, haddock and sole are the usual fish besides plaice to be prepared and cooked in this way. Served with a parsley sprig garnish and wedge of lemon for squeezing, fried fish is a quintessentially English dish, simple but absolutely delicious. Mrs Beeton also suggested serving the fish with Shrimp Sauce (page 225).

METHOD
Wash, wipe and thoroughly dry the fish, then let them remain in a cloth until it is time to cook them. Brush them over with egg and cover with bread crumbs mixed with a little flour. Fry until a nice brown in hot lard or dripping, and garnish with fried parsley and cut lemon. Serve with shrimp sauce when liked.

NOTES
Plaice A whole plaice yields 4 fillets, 2 fillets from each side of the fish. The fillets from the top of the fish have black skin, those from underneath have white. For fish that is to be coated in egg and breadcrumbs, both the white and black skin are usually removed first, and you can ask your fishmonger to do this for you.
Lard and **dripping** were the traditional fats for frying fish. They can be heated to a very high temperature without burning, and so give the fish a good crisp coating. The best alternative is groundnut oil. You will need 3 to 4 tablespoons.

Mrs Beeton writes

"Plaice may be boiled plain and served with melted butter. Garnish with parsley and cut lemon."

"THE PLAICE – This fish is found both in the Baltic and the Mediterranean, and is also abundant on the coast of England. Its flesh is inferior to that of the sole and, as it is a low-priced fish, it is generally bought by the poor."

Poached Salmon ๛

Mrs Beeton gave instructions for boiling whole salmon in heavily salted water, but the taste and texture of this exquisite fish are better preserved if the fish is gently poached with subtle flavouring ingredients rather than salt alone. She also said, 'experience alone can teach the cook to fix the time for boiling fish, but it is especially to be remembered that it should never be undercooked, as then nothing is more unwholesome'. The time given here reflects today's preference for cooking salmon so that it is succulent and juicy when served.

METHOD

Scale and clean the fish, and be particular that no blood is left inside. Pour sufficient cold water into a fish kettle to half fill it and add the flavourings. Lay the salmon on the rack and lower it into the kettle, then bring the water quickly to the boil and take off all the scum. Cover and simmer gently until the fish is done, which will be when the flesh separates easily from the bone – about 20 minutes. Lift the fish out of the kettle on the rack and, if not wanted for a few minutes, keep it warm by means of warm cloths laid over it. Serve on a hot napkin, garnished with cut lemon and parsley.

NOTES

Salmon You can buy farmed or wild salmon, depending on your budget. Wild salmon is more expensive, but it has far more flavour than the farmed varieties. If the fish is too long to fit in the fish kettle, you can cut off the head and tail and poach them separately, then re-assemble the fish whole for serving. If you don't have a fish kettle, you can improvise by using a large roasting tin on top of the stove and covering the salmon with foil.

Flavourings Use 8 fl oz (250 ml) dry white wine, 4 tablespoons white wine vinegar, 1 carrot and 1 onion, sliced, 1 bouquet garni or a few bay leaves, 12 peppercorns and 2 tablespoons salt.

Serving Mrs Beeton recommended serving a Lobster or Shrimp Sauce (page 225) and plain melted butter with the salmon, plus a dish of Dressed Cucumber (page 153), but it is very good served perfectly plain, with side dishes of boiled new potatoes and seasonal vegetables. Poached salmon can also be served cold, in which case Mayonnaise (page 231) is the usual accompaniment, often flavoured with dill.

Time ½ hour
Sufficient for each person
½ lb (250 g) or rather less
Seasonable from April to
August

INGREDIENTS
1 whole salmon weighing
about 5 lb (2.25 kg)
flavourings
cut lemon and parsley to
garnish

∾ Salmon à la Genevese

Time ¾ hour or rather more

Sufficient for 4 persons

Seasonable from April to
August

INGREDIENTS

a knob of butter

2 shallots, chopped

a little parsley

a small bunch of herbs

2 bay leaves

2 carrots, chopped

pounded mace, pepper and
salt to taste

4 tablespoons Madeira or
sherry

1 pint (600 ml) White Stock
(page 335)

4 slices of salmon fillet,
each weighing 4–6 oz
(125–175 g)

1 teaspoon anchovy essence

the juice of 1 lemon

cayenne pepper

By '*A LA GENEVESE*', we can assume that Mrs Beeton was referring to *Sauce Genevoise*, also called *Sauce Génoise*, which was traditionally served with salmon or trout in classic French cuisine. Strictly speaking, this sauce should be made with fish stock and red wine, but Mrs Beeton had her own version, as with most things.

METHOD

Rub the butter over the bottom of a saucepan and put in the shallots, parsley, bunch of herbs, bay leaves, carrots, mace and seasoning to taste. Stir them for 10 minutes over a low heat, then add the Madeira or sherry and half of the stock and simmer gently for ½ hour. Put the fish in a sauté pan. Strain the liquid from the cooked vegetables and herbs over the fish. Cook the fish in this liquor for 6 to 8 minutes, turning it over halfway. As soon as the fish is sufficiently cooked, take away all the liquor, except a little to keep the salmon moist, and put the liquor into another saucepan. Add the remaining stock, the anchovy essence, lemon juice, cayenne and salt to taste. Boil rapidly for a few minutes until reduced. Lay the salmon on a hot dish, pour over it part of the sauce, and serve the remainder in a sauce boat.

NOTES

White stock is made with veal and poultry trimmings, but fish stock is more usual, and more practical.

VARIATION

For a special occasion, add a few tablespoons of double cream or crème fraîche to the sauce just before serving, and sprinkle the dish with chopped fresh herbs such as parsley or dill.

Mrs Beeton writes

"AN AVERSION IN THE SALMON – The salmon is said to have an aversion to anything red, hence fishermen engaged in catching it do not wear jackets or caps of that colour. As food, salmon, when in perfection, is one of the most delicious and nutritive of our fish."

Skate with Caper Sauce ❧

CAPERS ARE OFTEN COOKED or served with skate. Their sharp, vinegary flavour complements the richness of this delicious fish and its unusually soft, almost gelatinous, texture. In this French recipe a caper sauce is made and served separately from the poached skate, while in the variation below, butter, capers, parsley and vinegar combine to make another favourite – Skate with Black Butter.

METHOD

Cut the skate into serving-sized pieces and put into a fish kettle with all the other ingredients. Add sufficient water to just cover the fish, cover the kettle with the lid and simmer the skate until tender – about 15 to 20 minutes. When the skate is done, remove it from the pan and skin it neatly, then pour over it some of the liquor in which it has been cooking. Drain the skate and put it on a hot dish. Pour some of the caper sauce over it and serve the rest in a sauce boat.

NOTES

Fish kettle Fish has a strong smell, so it is a good idea to keep a pan especially for cooking it. A fish kettle is a stainless steel pan containing a perforated rack that makes the handling of a whole fish very easy, while the pan itself can be used for smaller fish and portions of fish as here. If you do not have a fish kettle for this recipe, you could use a sauté pan or a deep frying pan with a lid.

Caper Sauce is made from melted butter, capers and anchovy essence. Its piquant flavour is good with fish.

VARIATION

Skate with Black Butter Cook the fish in a deep sauté pan or frying pan, lift it out and place it on a platter. Pour away the liquid from the pan, add 2 oz (60 g) butter and stir it over a moderate to high heat until it is a dark golden brown. Drizzle the butter over the fish and sprinkle it with a few capers and a little chopped parsley. Pour 3 tablespoons wine vinegar into the pan and heat it, stirring to incorporate the sediment on the bottom of the pan. Spoon the hot vinegar over the skate.

Time ½ hour
Sufficient for 3 to 4 persons
Seasonable from August to April

INGREDIENTS
1 to 2 skate wings, total weight about 1½ lb (750 g)
½ pint (300 ml) vinegar
2 oz (60 g) salt
½ teaspoon peppercorns
1 onion, sliced
a small bunch of parsley
2 bay leaves
2 or 3 sprigs of thyme
Caper Sauce (page 203) to serve

Mrs Beeton writes

"Skate may also be served with onion sauce, or parsley and butter."

"THE SKATE – This is one of the ray tribe, and is extremely abundant and cheap in the fishing towns of England. The flesh is white, thick and nourishing, but we suppose, from its being so plentiful, it is esteemed less than it ought to be on account of its nutritive properties."

✐ *Sole with Cream Sauce*

Time ½ hour
Sufficient for 4 or 5 persons
Seasonable at any time

INGREDIENTS
2 sole
½ pint (300 ml) Fish Stock
  (page 336)
½ pint (300 ml) cream
salt, cayenne pepper and
  pounded mace to taste
the juice of ½ lemon

MRS BEETON DID NOT SPECIFY the type of sole to use, but there are two types – lemon sole and Dover sole. Lemon sole is probably the best choice for this recipe. Apart from being considerably less expensive than Dover sole, the fish tend to be larger so the fillets are less fiddly to roll up.

METHOD
Skin, wash and fillet the sole, and divide each fillet into 2 pieces. Roll up each piece of fish, skinned side inside, and secure by means of a skewer. Lay the rolls in a wide saucepan, pour in the fish stock and bring gradually to the boil. When the stock boils, take out the fish. Add the cream and seasonings to the stock and boil for a few minutes to reduce, then return the fish to the pan. Spoon the cream sauce over the rolls and simmer very gently for 5 minutes. Just before serving, put in the lemon juice.

NOTES
Sole Ask your fishmonger to skin and fillet the sole for you and to cut each fillet lengthways in half so that you will have 16 narrow pieces of fish altogether. Plaice can be used instead of sole.
Cream Use double cream.
Skewer Wooden cocktail sticks are more practical than skewers, which tend to be rather long. For an attractive presentation, they should be removed before the fish is served.

VARIATIONS
Mrs Beeton used salted water to poach the sole, but fish stock is used here for a better flavour. If you like, you can add a splash or two of dry white wine to the stock, and you could fold in a few cooked peeled prawns at the end, at the same time as the lemon juice.

Mrs Beeton writes

"This will be found a most delicate and delicious dish."

"THE SOLE – This ranks next to the turbot in point of excellence among our flat fish. It is abundant on the British coasts, but those of the western shores are much superior in size to those taken on the northern. The finest are caught in Torbay, and frequently weigh 8 or 10 lbs per pair. Its flesh being firm, white, and delicate, is greatly esteemed."

Sole à l'Italienne ❧

SOLE HAS A DELICATE TEXTURE, and here it is baked in the oven with a protective coating of egg and breadcrumbs, then served with a well-flavoured béchamel sauce. If you like the flavour of herbs with fish, you can easily substitute chopped parsley, dill or thyme, or a mixture of these, for the nutmeg seasoning. Choose a baking dish that is large enough for the fillets to cook in a single layer. To ensure a really crisp coating, put the coated fish in the dish and place it uncovered in the refrigerator for 1–2 hours before cooking.

METHOD

Skin, wash and fillet the soles. Brush them over with the white of the egg, sprinkle with bread crumbs and seasoning, and put them in a large baking dish. Place small pieces of butter over the fish and bake for 20 minutes. When they are done, squeeze the juice of a lemon over them and serve on a dish, with Italian Sauce.

The oven should be preheated to 375°F (190°C) Gas 5.

NOTES

Soles Buy lemon sole and ask your fishmonger to skin and fillet the fish for you. You should have a total of 8 fillets. You can buy fillets of sole in packets at supermarkets, but you will have to skin these yourself. For a less expensive dish, plaice fillets can also be used.

Italian Sauce is a béchamel sauce flavoured with shallots, mushrooms and ham. It goes very well with sole, but if you prefer a more simple dish, you can serve the fish without it.

Mrs Beeton writes

"Whiting may be dressed in the same manner,
and will be found very delicious."

"THE FLAVOUR OF THE SOLE – This, as a matter of course, greatly depends on the nature of the ground and bait upon which the animal feeds. Its natural food are small crabs and shell-fish. Its colour also depends on the colour of the ground where it feeds; for if this be white, then the sole is called white, or lemon sole; but if the bottom be muddy, then it is called the black sole. Small-sized soles, caught in the shallow water on the coasts, are the best in flavour."

Time ½ hour
Sufficient for 4 persons
Seasonable at any time

INGREDIENTS
2 sole
1 large egg white
about 3 oz (90 g) bread
  crumbs
salt, pepper and grated
  nutmeg to taste
2 oz (60 g) butter
the juice of 1 lemon
Italian Sauce (page 212) to
  serve

ᥒ *Mrs Beeton on giving and accepting invitations*

ENTERING WAS
INVARIABLY FORMAL IN
VICTORIAN DAYS, WITH
STRICT RULES TO BE
OBSERVED ON THE
MANNERS, ETIQUETTE
AND BEHAVIOUR OF THE
HOST, HOSTESS AND
GUESTS. TAKEN FROM
'THE MISTRESS', THE
FIRST CHAPTER
OF THE ORIGINAL BOOK,
THESE QUOTATIONS
PROVIDE A FASCINATING
INSIGHT INTO THE
CUSTOMS OF THE DAY.
ALTHOUGH SOME OF
THESE ARE STILL
OBSERVED, MOST ARE A
FAR CRY FROM OUR
CASUAL MODERN
MANNERS.

IN GIVING OR ACCEPTING an invitation for dinner, the following is the form of words generally made use of. They, however, can be varied in proportion to the intimacy or position of the hosts and guests:–

> Mr. and Mrs. A .... present their compliments to
> Mr. and Mrs. B ...., and request the honour (or
> hope to have the pleasure) of their company to dinner on
> Wednesday, the 6th of December next.
>
> A .... STREET,
> November 13th, 1859   R.S.V.P.

The letters in the corner imply 'Repondez, s'il vous plaît', meaning, 'an answer will oblige'. The reply, accepting the invitation, is couched in the following terms:–

> Mr. and Mrs. B .... present their compliments to
> Mr. and Mrs. A ...., and will do themselves the
> honour of (or will have much pleasure in) accepting their
> kind invitation to dinner on the 6th of December next.
>
> B .... SQUARE,
> November 18th, 1859

CARDS OR INVITATIONS for a dinner-party should be issued a fortnight or three weeks (sometimes even a month) beforehand, and care should be taken by the hostess, in the selection of the invited guests, that they should be suited to each other. Much also of the pleasure of a dinner-party will depend on the arrangement of the guests at table, so as to form a due mixture of talkers and listeners, the grave and the gay. If an invitation to dinner is accepted, the guests should be punctual, and the mistress ready in her drawing-room to receive them. At some periods it has been considered fashionable to come late to dinner, but lately *nous avons changé tout cela.*

AFTER-DINNER INVITATIONS may be given; by which we wish to be understood, invitations for the evening. The time of the arrival of these visitors will vary according to their engagements, or sometimes will be varied in obedience to the caprices of fashion. Guests invited for the evening are, however, generally considered at liberty to arrive whenever it will best suit themselves – usually between nine and twelve, unless earlier hours are specifically named. By this arrangement, many fashionable people and others, who have numerous engagements to fulfil, often contrive to make their appearance at two or three parties in the course of one evening.

IN PRIVATE PARTIES, a lady is not to refuse the invitation of a gentleman to dance, unless she be previously engaged. The hostess must be supposed to have asked to her house only those persons whom she knows to be perfectly respectable and of unblemished character, as well as pretty equal in position; and thus, to decline the offer of any gentleman present, would be tacit reflection on the master and mistress of the house.

⁓ Poached Trout

Time ½ hour
Sufficient for 4 persons
Seasonable from May to
   September

INGREDIENTS
4 middling-sized trout
½ onion, cut in thin slices
a little parsley
2 cloves
1 blade of mace
2 bay leaves
a little thyme
salt and pepper to taste
1 pint (600 ml) Medium
   Stock (page 334)
1 glass of port
thickening of ½ oz (15 g)
   each of butter and flour
   mixed to a paste

FARMED RAINBOW TROUT are sold at fishmongers and supermarkets at a very reasonable price. They are quick and easy to cook whole, but they often lack the flavour of wild trout. Although there was no farmed trout in Mrs Beeton's day, her recipe is just perfect for infusing the farmed fish with flavour.

METHOD
Wash the fish very clean, and wipe it quite dry. Lay it in a wide sauté pan or deep frying pan with all the ingredients but the butter and flour and simmer gently for about 15 minutes, or rather more should the fish be not quite done. Take the fish out and strain the liquid into a saucepan. Add the thickening, stir it over a high heat for 5 minutes, then pour it over the trout and serve.

NOTES
Middling-sized trout Most rainbow trout weigh about 10–12 oz (300–375 g), and one trout is enough for each person. They come ready cleaned and scaled, with their heads and tails left on. If you prefer to have these removed, the fishmonger will do it for you.
Medium stock is meaty, so you may prefer to use a fish stock, or just water. With the glass of port and all the other ingredients, there will be plenty of flavour.
Thickening is the English term for *beurre manié* or kneaded butter and flour. To avoid lumps, the paste should be added a little at a time and stirred or whisked vigorously until the sauce bubbles and thickens. If you prefer, you can omit the thickening and simply boil the liquid until reduced to the required consistency.

Mrs Beeton writes

"Trout may be served with anchovy or caper sauce, baked in buttered paper, or fried whole. Trout dressed *à la Genevese* is extremely delicate. For this proceed the same as with salmon (page 50)".

"THE TROUT – This fish, though esteemed by the moderns for its delicacy, was little regarded by the ancients. Although it abounded in the lakes of the Roman empire, it is generally mentioned by writers only on account of the beauty of its colours."

Whiting au Gratin ೫

Mrs Beeton described whiting as a delicate fish, by which she may have meant that it is rather bland in flavour. The topping of breadcrumbs, parsley and mushrooms in this recipe does a lot to improve the flavour of whiting, and the juices from the fish mingle with sherry or Madeira to make a delicious sauce. The recipe works equally well with other white fish fillets, such as cod or haddock.

METHOD

Grease the bottom of a baking dish with a knob of butter, and over it strew some of the finely chopped parsley and mushrooms. Scale, empty and wash the whiting, and wipe them thoroughly dry. Lay them in the dish, sprinkle them with bread crumbs and seasonings, adding a little grated nutmeg and also a little more parsley and mushrooms. Place small pieces of butter over the whiting, moisten with the sherry or Madeira and bake for 20 minutes in a hot oven. If there should be too much sauce, reduce it by boiling over a high heat for a few minutes, then pour it under the fish. Serve with a cut lemon, and no other sauce.

The oven should be preheated to 375°F (190°C) Gas 5.

NOTES

Whiting are from the same family as cod, but they are rather smaller and have softer flesh. This recipe is intended to be used for whole whiting, but you are more likely to see this fish sold as fillets, which can be used just as well – allow 2 to 3 fillets per person and arrange them in a single layer in 1 or 2 baking dishes depending on their size. **Bread crumbs** Fresh are best for this recipe, and you will need only 1 to 2 tablespoons.

Mrs Beeton writes

"THE WHITING – This fish forms a light, tender, and delicate food, easy for digestion. It appears in our seas in the spring, within three miles of the shores, where it arrives in large shoals to deposit its spawn. It is caught by line, and is usually between 10 and 12 inches long, and seldom exceeding a pound and a half. When less than six inches long, it is not allowed to be caught."

Time ½ hour
Sufficient for 4 persons
Seasonable all the year, but best from October to March

INGREDIENTS

butter
1 tablespoon finely chopped parsley
a few finely chopped mushrooms when obtainable
4 small whiting
bread crumbs
pepper, salt and grated nutmeg to taste
2 glasses of sherry or Madeira
a cut lemon to serve

✍ *Whiting aux Fines Herbes*

Time ½ hour

Sufficient for 4 persons

Seasonable all the year, but
   best from October to
   March

INGREDIENTS

4 small whiting

a bunch of sweet herbs

about 2 oz (60 g) butter

THIS VERY SIMPLE RECIPE is for whole whiting, but it can also be used for other small whole fish, such as rainbow trout, herring, red or grey mullet, red snapper and mackerel, or for white fish fillets such as cod, haddock, brill, plaice and sole. Ask your fishmonger what is best on the day. If you are using whole fish, you may find it a little tricky to fasten their tails in their mouths. Mrs Beeton suggested this for an attractive presentation, but you can simply lay them flat in the dish – this will not affect the way they cook.

METHOD

Clean and skin the fish, fasten the tails in the mouths and lay them in a baking dish. Chop the herbs very fine, strew them over the fish and place small pieces of butter over. Cover and bake for 15 to 20 minutes. Turn the fish once or twice, and serve with the cooking juices spooned over.

The oven should be preheated to 375°F (190°C) Gas 5.

NOTES

Sweet herbs   The most suitable herbs would be a mixture of finely chopped fresh dill and flat-leaf parsley. They should be very fresh and chopped at the last moment. If you like, you can sprinkle some extra chopped fresh herbs over the fish at the moment of serving.

Seasoning is not mentioned in the the original recipe, but the fish would benefit from a sprinkling of salt and pepper before baking.

Mrs Beeton writes

"THE WHITING, POUT AND POLLACK – About the mouth of the Thames, and generally all round the English coasts as well as in the northern seas, the pout is plentiful. It bears a striking resemblance to the whiting, and is esteemed as an excellent fish. The pollack is also taken all round our coasts, and likewise bears a striking resemblance to the whiting. Indeed, it is sometimes mistaken by the inexperienced for that fish; its flesh being considered by many as equally delicate."

Hot Crab ❧

When you buy a whole crab from the fishmonger it will have been boiled already, so this is a very simple dish to make. To save time, get the fishmonger to remove all the meat for you and ask him to pack it back in the cleaned shell. He will most likely do this at no extra charge, but he may need a little notice, especially on weekends and other busy periods.

METHOD

Pick the meat out from the shell and claws of the crab and mix it with the nutmeg and seasoning. Cut up the butter in small pieces and add the bread crumbs and vinegar. Mix altogether, put everything in the large shell and brown with a salamander.

NOTES

Vinegar was popular as a seasoning for fish and shellfish in Victorian times, and was used in larger quantities then than it is today. Add 1 tablespoon to start with, then taste and add more if you like. You can use freshly squeezed lemon juice if you prefer.

Salamander This is a long iron rod with a metal disc at the end, still used by chefs today. The disc is heated and used to brown food quickly, especially dishes topped with breadcrumbs and desserts like *crème brûlée*, before sending them to the table. To brown the crab without a salamander, put it in the grill pan and pop it under a hot grill for about 5 minutes until golden brown and bubbling. Many chefs use a blow torch instead of a salamander; you can buy small ones for kitchen use in hardware shops and by mail order.

Time ¼ hour
Sufficient for 2 to 3 persons
Seasonable all the year, but
    not so good in May, June
    and July

INGREDIENTS
1 cooked crab weighing
    about 3½ lb (1.6 kg)
grated nutmeg, salt and
    pepper to taste
3 oz (90 g) butter
¼ lb (125 g) bread crumbs
3 tablespoons vinegar

Mrs Beeton writes
─────────────

"THE CRAB TRIBE –
The most remarkable
feature in their history
is the changing of their
shells and the
reproduction of their
broken claws. The former
occurs once a year,
usually between
Christmas and Easter,
when the crabs retire to
cavities in the rocks, or
conceal themselves under
great stones."

✍ *Lobster Curry*

Time ¼ hour or rather more
Sufficient for 2 to 3 persons
Seasonable at any time

INGREDIENTS
1 cooked lobster weighing
   about 2 lb (1 kg)
2 onions
1 oz (30 g) butter
1 tablespoon curry powder
½ pint (300 ml) Fish Stock
   (page 336) or chicken
   stock
the juice of ½ lemon

THIS IS A VERY QUICK DISH when made with a ready-cooked lobster from a fishmonger or supermarket. To save time, you can ask for the meat to be removed from the shell, although it is quite simple to do this yourself. Mrs Beeton made the curry with a rich meaty stock, but you will find a light fish or chicken stock is more suited to the delicate flavour of lobster.

METHOD

Pick the lobster meat from the shell and cut it into nice square pieces. Finely chop the onions and fry them until pale brown in the butter. Stir in the curry powder and stock and simmer until it thickens, then put in the lobster and simmer gently for a few minutes until hot, stirring occasionally. Just before serving, put in the lemon juice. Serve with boiled rice, the same as for other curries.

NOTES

Lobster To remove the meat from the body, tail and claws, place the lobster on its back and cut it in half lengthways from head to tail. Remove the green liver, pink roe (the coral) and gravel sac (the stomach). Pull the white tail meat out from each side of the shell and discard the black intestinal vein. Crack the claws just below the pincers with a lobster cracker or a nutcracker and remove the meat from the base. Pull away the small pincer and the white membrane with it, then remove the meat from this part of the shell. Pull the meat from the large pincer shell.

Scalloped Oysters ⧎

Mrs Beeton gave many recipes for oysters because they were so plentiful and cheap. Nowadays oysters are expensive and highly prized, and reserved for special occasions. Here they are served in scallop shells, which makes a very pretty presentation, ideal for a winter dinner party. Native British oysters are among the best in the world, and they are in season when there is an 'r' in the month – from September to April, just as Mrs Beeton said.

Method

Scald the oysters in their own liquor, take them out, beard them and strain the liquor free from grit. Put the butter into a saucepan. When melted, dredge in sufficient flour to dry it up. Add the stock, cream and strained liquor and bring to the boil. Put in the oysters and seasoning and let them gradually heat through but not boil. Have ready 6 buttered scallop shells. Lay in the oysters and as much of the liquid as the shells will hold. Cover them with bread crumbs, over which drizzle a little melted butter. Brown them in the oven – about 10 minutes – and serve very quickly, and very hot.

The oven should be preheated to 375°F (190°C) Gas 5.

Notes

Oysters For this recipe the oysters need to be shelled or 'shucked'. Hold each oyster in a cloth with the rounded side of the shell down and the hinge facing you. Insert an oyster knife just below the hinge and twist it to prise the two shells apart. Work the knife between the two shells, severing the muscle, then lift off the top shell. Run the knife blade under the oyster to detach it from the bottom shell. Make sure not to spill any of the liquor, which is needed for the sauce. The beard is the dark frilly edge on the oyster. It can easily be cut off.
White stock is made from veal and poultry trimmings. You can equally well use fish or chicken stock.
Cream Use double cream.

Time ½ hour
Sufficient for 6 persons
  (3 to 4 oysters each)
Seasonable from September
  to April

INGREDIENTS
18 to 24 oysters
1 oz (30 g) butter
about 1 tablespoon flour
¼ pint (150 ml) White Stock
  (page 335)
¼ pint (150 ml) cream
pepper and salt to taste
about 8 heaped tablespoons
  bread crumbs
melted butter

✑ *Prawns in Cream Sauce*

Time ¼ hour

Sufficient for 2 persons

Seasonable at any time

INGREDIENTS

2 oz (60 g) butter

1 teaspoon flour

⅓ pint (200 ml) double
  cream

salt and cayenne pepper to
  taste

a small quantity of pounded
  mace or lemon juice,
  when liked

½ lb (250 g) shelled cooked
  prawns

SIMPLE AND QUICK, this dish makes the perfect after-work supper served on a bed of boiled rice. If you choose lemon juice as a flavouring rather than pounded mace, you could add a last-minute sprinkling of chopped fresh parsley, dill or snipped chives to enhance the flavour.

METHOD

Put the butter into a saucepan, dredge in the flour and keep shaking the pan around until the butter is melted. Add the cream and seasoning and bring to the boil, stirring. Let it simmer gently for 5 minutes, then add either pounded mace or lemon juice to give it flavour. Add the prawns and simmer gently for 3 minutes. Serve.

NOTES

Prawns You can use fresh or frozen prawns. If using frozen prawns, make sure they are thoroughly thawed before use and drain and dry them very well on kitchen paper. If they are wet, they will dilute the cream sauce and make it watery and insipid.

Mace is the outer lacy membrane of nutmeg. You can buy pieces of it, which are called blades, and pound them very fine, using a mortar and pestle, or you can get the spice ready ground. The flavour of mace is similar to that of nutmeg, but more subtle. You can use either mace or nutmeg in this or any other recipe, sweet or savoury.

SERVED WITH THIN SLICES of hot toast, potted shrimps are a superb first course, and they are very easy to make. Once the butter on top of the shrimps has cooled, put the pots to chill in the refrigerator, where they can remain for up to 2 days before being served.

METHOD

Put the shrimps into a saucepan with half of the butter and the other ingredients. Let them heat gradually in the butter, but do not let it boil. Pour into small pots and leave until cold. Melt and cool the remaining butter. When the shrimps are cold, pour the melted butter carefully over them to exclude the air.

NOTES

Shrimps are not as readily available as prawns. You can occasionally get them in fishmongers or at the coast in areas where they are netted. They are sold cooked, and the best shrimps for potting are the brown kind rather than the pretty pink ones. If they are sold by weight rather than volume, you should know that 1 pint (600 ml) shelled shrimps will weigh about 6 oz (175 g). Shrimps are very fiddly to peel because of their size, but they have more flavour than the larger prawns, which can be potted in the same way as shrimps.

Mrs Beeton writes

"THE SHRIMP – This shellfish is smaller than the prawn, and is greatly relished in London as a delicacy. It inhabits most of the sandy shores of Europe, and the Isle of Wight is especially famous for them."

Time ¼ hour
Sufficient for 3 to 4 persons
Seasonable at any time, but
    not in bad winter weather

INGREDIENTS
1 pint (600 ml) shelled
  cooked shrimps
½ lb (250 g) butter
1 blade of mace, pounded
cayenne pepper to taste
a little grated nutmeg, when
  liked

CHAPTER 3

Meat

Mrs Beeton began each section of her meat chapter with drawings of the different breeds of animal and a discussion of the merits of their meat. She spoke with great authority on the subject of man as a meat-eating animal.

'It is natural that man should seek to feed on flesh; he has too small a stomach to be supported alone by fruit, which has not sufficient nourishment to renovate him. It is possible he might subsist on vegetables, but their preparation needs the knowledge of art, only to be obtained after the lapse of many centuries.'

Individual methods of cooking were discussed in detail.

Baking was different from roasting 'in the fact that the fumes caused by the operation are not carried off in the same way'. This was in the days when meat was roasted on a spit or hook over an open fire.

Boiling was 'one of the easiest processes in cookery', but Mrs Beeton felt that it required 'skilful management'.

Broiling was the term used for grilling, and for this the cook must have 'a bright, clear fire so that the surface of the meat may be quickly heated'.

Frying was generally well received, for the reason that fried foods introduced 'an agreeable variety, possessing as they do, a peculiar flavour'.

Meat, which included offal, poultry and game, was always eaten at family dinners. It was usually served as a main course after the first course of either soup or fish. At formal dinners, two different meat dishes were served after the first course, one as an *entrée* and the other as a second course. The master of the house carved the meat.

It was fashionable to place all the dishes for the meal on the table together, in the style of dining called *service à la française*. Also coming into vogue at this time was a new and different style of formal dining known as *service à la russe*. It is best described in Mrs Beeton's own words.

'In a dinner *à la russe*, the dishes are cut up on a sideboard, and handed round to the guests, and each dish may be considered a course. Dinners *à la russe* are scarcely suitable for small establishments; a large number of servants being required to carve.'

✎ Baked Beef

Time 2½ hours
Sufficient for 5 or 6 persons
Seasonable at any time

INGREDIENTS
about 2 lb (1 kg) braising or
    stewing steak
2 small onions
1 large carrot or 2 small
    carrots
1 turnip
a small bunch of savoury
    herbs
pepper and salt to taste
½ pint (300 ml) gravy
½ pint (300 ml) ale
1½ lb (750 g) potatoes,
    boiled and mashed

Mrs Beeton writes
_____

"BEEF – The quality of
beef depends on various
circumstances; such as the
age, the sex, the breed of
the animal, and also on
the food upon which it
has been raised."

COLD ROAST BEEF was used in Mrs Beeton's original recipe. There
was always plenty of meat left from the Sunday joint, and she gave
readers lots of ideas for using up cold meat. Nowadays we rarely cook
large enough joints to have leftovers, but we can make just as good a
dish using fresh beef. For a decorative topping, mark the potatoes
with a fork and dot them generously with butter before baking.

METHOD
Cut the beef into slices or large squares. Place a layer of this in the
bottom of a pie dish with a portion of the onions, carrot and turnip,
which must also be sliced. Finely chop the herbs, sprinkle them over
the meat and season with pepper and salt. Put in another layer of
meat, vegetables, herbs and seasoning and proceed in this manner
until all the ingredients are used. Pour in the gravy and ale (water
may be substituted for the former, but it is not so nice), cover with a
lid and bake until the beef is tender – about 1½ hours. Remove the
dish from the oven, uncover, then spread the mashed potatoes over
the top. Increase the oven temperature and bake for ½ hour or rather
longer, until the potatoes are golden brown.

The oven should first be preheated to 325°F (160°C) Gas 3, then
increased to 375°F (190°C) Gas 5.

NOTES
Savoury herbs   Fresh parsley, thyme, marjoram, oregano and
rosemary are all suitable and you can use just one herb or a mixture
of several. If you don't have fresh herbs, use 1 to 2 teaspoons dried
mixed herbs. A combination of fresh and dried also works well.
Gravy Mrs Beeton had leftover gravy in mind, made with the juices
from roast meat so that it was very tasty. If you have no homemade
gravy, make it with gravy powder or use beef stock.
Ale   You can use pale or light ale, but for a richer flavour, use
Guinness or a sweet stout like Mackeson. If you are using stock rather
than gravy, this will help to boost the flavour.

VARIATIONS
The potato can be replaced with a puff pastry lid: let the meat
mixture go cold, then top with a sheet of puff pastry, glaze with
beaten egg and bake at 400°F (200°C) Gas 6.

Toad-in-the-Hole ❧

WE ALWAYS THINK OF toad-in-the-hole as sausages in batter, but as you will see from this recipe, this is not always the case. Steak and kidney are used here instead of sausages to make a variation on the steak and kidney pudding theme. It makes an excellent family supper, served with plenty of gravy and freshly cooked vegetables.

METHOD

Cut the steak into nice square pieces and divide the kidney into small pieces. Make a batter with the flour, eggs and milk. Pour a little of it into the bottom of a greased large pie dish, then put in the steak and kidney, which should be well seasoned with pepper and salt. Pour in the remainder of the batter and bake for 1 to 1¼ hours.

The oven should be preheated to 375°F (190°C) Gas 5.

NOTES

Lamb's kidney Mrs Beeton specified 1 kidney, but they are often very small, so you may want to buy 2 kidneys if you like their savoury flavour. Sometimes they are sold with white fat or suet around them, and this should be pulled off with your fingers. Next snip the thin membrane that surrounds the kidney with scissors and peel this off too. Cut the kidney in half and snip out any white core and tubes before cutting the kidney into small pieces.

Batter Put the flour in a bowl and make a well in the centre. Break the eggs into the well and whisk them, gradually drawing in some of the flour. Slowly start pouring in the milk and keep whisking, bringing more flour into the centre until all the ingredients are well mixed and a smooth batter is formed. A hand-held electric mixer is ideal for this.

VARIATIONS

The steak and kidney can be mixed with a chopped onion for extra flavour. Alternatively, instead of the steak and kidney, you can use your favourite sausages. They can be left whole or cut into large chunks.

Time 1½ to 1¾ hours
Sufficient for 4 or 5 persons
Seasonable at any time

INGREDIENTS
1½ lb (750 g) rump steak
1 lamb's kidney
6 oz (175 g) flour
4 eggs
1 pint (600 ml) milk
pepper and salt

Mrs Beeton writes
———————

"GOOD MEAT – Beef of the best quality is of a deep-red colour; and when the animal has approached maturity, and been well fed, the lean is intermixed with fat, giving it the mottled appearance which is so much esteemed.
It is also full of juice, which resembles in colour claret wine."

ᕲ *Steak Pie*

Time 1½ to 1¾ hours
Sufficient for 6 or 8 persons
Seasonable at any time

INGREDIENTS
1½ lb (750 g) rump steak
seasoning to taste of salt,
    black pepper and cayenne
    pepper
a sheet of puff pastry
the yolk of an egg

THIS RECIPE IS FOR A BASIC MEAT PIE, but as you will see in the variations below, there are lots of ways in which you can infuse it with extra flavour and so add interest. If you prefer short crust pastry, you can use this instead of the puff pastry suggested here, and if you want to make your own pastry, there are recipes on pages 337 and 338.

METHOD
Cut the steak into pieces about 3 inches (7.5 cm) long and 2 inches (5 cm) wide and arrange the meat in layers in a pie dish. Between each layer sprinkle a seasoning of salt and pepper, and a few grains of cayenne when liked. Fill the dish sufficiently with meat to support the crust and to give it a nice raised appearance when baked, not to look flat and hollow. Pour in sufficient cold water to half fill the dish, then border the dish with a strip of pastry. Brush the pastry strip with a little water and put on the cover. Slightly press down the edges with the thumb and trim off close to the dish. Ornament the pie with pastry leaves or with pieces of pastry cut in any shape you fancy, then brush it over with the beaten yolk of an egg and make a hole in the top of the crust. Bake for ¼ hour, then lower the oven temperature and bake for 1 hour.

The oven should be preheated to 400°F (200°C) Gas 6, then decreased to 350°F (180°C) Gas 4.

NOTES
Pastry sheet You can buy frozen ready rolled sheets of pastry measuring 280 x 229 mm. This size is just right for a 10 x 8 inch (25 x 20 cm) rectangular pie dish with a capacity of about 2 pints (1.2 litres), including the extra pastry you need for the strip that goes around the rim of the dish and to decorate the top. If the pastry shows signs of overbrowning, cover it loosely with foil.

VARIATIONS

Instead of water, use beef stock. Or use a combination of red wine, ale, stout or cider and water or beef stock.

Mix the steak with 1 chopped onion and a handful of chopped fresh herbs or 1 to 2 teaspoons dried mixed herbs.

Add a dash or two of Worcestershire sauce if you like a spicy flavour.

Cut 1 to 2 lamb's kidneys into small pieces and add to the steak.

Slice ¼–½ lb (125–250 g) mushrooms and add to the steak.

Mrs Beeton writes

"Have the steaks cut from a rump that has hung for a few days, that they may be tender, and be particular that every portion is perfectly sweet."

"BEEF-STEAK PIES – may be flavoured in various ways, with oysters and their liquor, mushrooms, minced onions, &c. For family pies, suet may be used instead of butter or lard for the crust, and clarified beef-dripping answers very well where economy is an object."

Grilled Steaks
with Potatoes à la Mode Française

Time ½ hour
Sufficient for 4 persons
Seasonable all the year

INGREDIENTS
8 potatoes
½ lb (250 g) butter
1 lb (500 g) steak
1 teaspoon finely chopped
   fresh herbs
salt and pepper to taste

BY GIVING THIS RECIPE the name *à la mode française* or 'in the French style', Mrs Beeton was referring to the way in which the potatoes were thinly sliced and sautéed in butter, which then had fresh herbs added to it. Sizzling herb butter is commonplace today, but in Victorian times it was considered very French and stylish. Flat-leaf parsley is the herb conventionally used in France for this dish, as in maître d'hôtel butter.

METHOD

Peel the potatoes and cut them into long thin slices. Put the butter into a frying or sauté pan, set it over a medium heat and let it get very hot. Put the potatoes into the hot butter and fry them, turning frequently, until they are a nice brown colour on all sides – about 20 minutes. Now grill the steaks under high heat for 5 minutes, turning them once or twice so that every part may be equally done. Put the herbs and seasoning in the butter the potatoes were fried in and pour it under the steak. Place the fried potatoes round as a garnish.

NOTES

Butter The quantity given here is the same as in the original recipe, but you may think it is too much, especially since the steak is grilled, a healthy cooking method in itself. You can use 4 to 6 tablespoons olive oil or groundnut oil (or half and half) instead of butter for a healthier way of frying the potatoes, or a combination of about 2 oz (60 g) butter and 3 tablespoons oil. Butter gives the potatoes a golden colour and flavour, and is still preferred by many French cooks.

Steak Choose sirloin, as Mrs Beeton suggested, or rump steak, with an edge of fat on it or a light marbling of fat through the meat. The quantity given here is for ¼ lb (125 g) per person, which is the average portion size, but you can increase or decrease this according to appetites. The ideal thickness is more like ½ to ¾ inch (1 to 2 cm) than the ⅓ inch (8 mm) Mrs Beeton suggested. If the steak is too thin it will dry out and be tough. As a safeguard against this, brush the steak with oil before grilling and season it with pepper. Do not sprinkle salt on steak before grilling as this tends to draw out the juices and toughen the surface of the meat. The cooking time given here is for rare meat; for medium, allow 8 minutes, for well-done, allow 12 minutes.

Mrs Beeton writes

"To have this dish in perfection, a portion of the fillet of the sirloin should be used, as the meat is generally so much more tender than that of the rump, and the steaks should be cut about ⅓ of an inch in thickness."

MEAT

MRS BEETON INSTRUCTED her readers to make these with the remains of cold roast beef, minced very finely. They were then served in a dish with gravy poured around. If we substitute raw minced beef for the cooked beef, and ketchup, mayonnaise and salad for the gravy, we have beefburgers, which can be served in seeded buns.

METHOD

Combine the beef with the bacon or ham, which must be chopped very small, and mix well together. Season and stir in the herbs, then bind with an egg, or 2 eggs should 1 egg not be sufficient. Make the mixture into small square cakes, about ½ inch (1 cm) thick, and fry them in hot dripping – about 5 minutes on each side or according to how you like your meat done.

NOTES

Minced beef Use the best quality you can buy. Ground steak, which is usually very finely minced, is the most expensive, but it tends to make dry beef cakes because it is so low in fat. A little fat (around 20 per cent) is essential for moist and juicy beef cakes, and one of the best ways to achieve this is to buy rump or chuck steak and either ask the butcher to mince it or chop it finely yourself – a food processor caan be used for this if you don't have a mincer, but take care not to chop it too finely.

Savoury herbs Parsley and basil both taste good in beef cakes.

Dripping If the liquid fat that exudes or drips from roasting meat is collected and left to go solid, it is called 'dripping'. Until recent years, it was widely used for frying, and for spreading on bread or toast. It is very tasty and can be heated to high temperatures without burning; for a healthier alternative, use groundnut oil.

Mrs Beeton writes

"A FRENCHMAN'S OPINION OF BEEF – This meat, which possesses in the highest degree the most nutritive qualities, is generally easily digested; stock is made from it, and it is eaten boiled, broiled, roasted, stewed, braised, and in a hundred other different ways. It is an exhaustless mine in the hands of a skilful artist, and is truly the king of the kitchen. Without it, no soup, no gravy; and its absence would produce almost a famine in the civilized world!"

Time 20 minutes
Sufficient for 4 persons
Seasonable at any time

INGREDIENTS

1 lb (500 g) minced beef
¼ lb (125 g) bacon or ham
seasoning to taste of pepper and salt
1 small bunch of finely chopped savoury herbs
1 or 2 eggs

∾ *Chargrilled Steaks*

Time ¼ hour
Sufficient for 1 steak for
   each person
Seasonable all the year

INGREDIENTS
suet
steaks
1 tablespoon good
   mushroom ketchup or
   Harvey's sauce
a little finely chopped
   shallot if liked
a piece of butter the size of
   a walnut
pepper and salt to taste
scraped horseradish or
   slices of cucumber to
   garnish

IN VICTORIAN TIMES a gridiron was used for cooking steaks over the fire. The cooking method was called broiling, a term that Americans still use, when speaking of grilling. A ridged cast iron pan is the modern equivalent of a gridiron and the cooking method, which we now call chargrilling, is just the same, so this recipe is a modern adaptation of the original. Mrs Beeton said, 'allow ½ lb to each person; if the party consist entirely of gentlemen, ¾ lb will not be too much' – a remark that would be rather contentious today.

METHOD
Put a ridged cast iron pan over a moderate to high heat for a few minutes to get thoroughly hot. Rub it with a piece of fresh suet to prevent the meat from sticking, then lay on the steaks, which should be cut of an equal thickness, about ¾ of an inch (2 cm) or rather thinner. Turn them frequently with steak-tongs (if these are not at hand, stick a fork in the edge of the fat, that no gravy escapes) and in 8 to 10 minutes they will be done. Have ready a very hot dish, put the ketchup into it, and a little finely chopped shallot if liked. Dish up the steaks, rub them over with butter and season with pepper and salt. Garnish with scraped horseradish or slices of cucumber. Oyster, tomato, onion, and many other sauces are frequent accompaniments to rump steak, but true lovers of this English dish generally reject all additions but pepper and salt.

NOTES
Steaks Use rump, sirloin or fillet steaks. Allow ¼–½ lb (125–250 g) per person according to individual appetites. Mrs Beeton suggested 'beating them as little as possible with a rolling-pin'. This was to make them all the same thickness so they would cook evenly, which is sound advice. The cooking time given is for medium to well-done steaks. For rare meat, cook for a total of 5 minutes.
Suet is the white solid fat that surrounds animal kidneys. It was used for frying for its rich tasty flavour and the fact that it can be heated to high temperatures without burning. It is high in saturated fat and cholesterol, so today we tend not to use it. To grease the pan, use a wad of kitchen paper dipped in groundnut oil.

MEAT

Mushroom ketchup and **Harvey's sauce** can be obtained at specialist food shops and delicatessens. It was traditional to put one of these savoury sauces under the steaks before serving, but instead you could serve the steaks with separate pots of either a smooth Dijon or grainy Meaux-style mustard. Bottled horseradish or horseradish cream would be equally delicious.

Mrs Beeton writes

"The exact time for broiling steaks must be determined by taste,
whether they are liked underdone or well done; more than
8 to 10 minutes for a steak ¾ inch in thickness, we think, would
spoil and dry up the juices of the meat. Great expedition is necessary
in sending broiled steaks to table; and, to have them in perfection,
they should not be cooked till everything else prepared for dinner
has been dished up, as their excellence entirely depends on their
being served very hot."

"ORIGIN OF THE WORD 'SIRLOIN' – The loin of beef is said
to have been knighted by King Charles II., at Friday Hall, Chingford.
The 'Merry Monarch' returned to this hospitable mansion from
Epping Forest literally 'as hungry as a hunter', and beheld, with
delight, a huge loin beef steaming upon the table. 'A noble joint!'
exclaimed the king. 'By St. George, it shall have a title!' Then drawing
his sword, he raised it above the meat, and cried, with mock dignity,
'Loin, we dub thee knight; henceforward be Sir Loin'!"

⌘ Bubble and Squeak

Time ½ hour
Sufficient for 4 persons
Seasonable at any time

INGREDIENTS
a few thin slices of cold beef
about ¾ lb (375 g) Brussels
   sprouts or cabbage
butter
1 sliced onion
pepper and salt to taste

THIS QUINTESSENTIALLY ENGLISH dish takes its name from the sound the ingredients make when cooking in the pan. Most people think of it as a dish for a Monday lunch or supper, made up of leftovers – roast meat from the Sunday joint, potatoes and greens – which are fried together in hot fat until crisp and golden brown. Mrs Beeton's version used boiled beef and did not include potatoes. Brussels sprouts are the correct green vegetable to use, with cabbage as the alternative when sprouts are not in season.

METHOD

Fry the slices of beef gently in a little butter, taking care not to dry them up. Lay them on a flat dish and cover with fried greens. The greens may be prepared from sprouts or green Savoy cabbage. They should be boiled until tender, well drained and finely chopped, then placed until quite hot in a frying pan with butter, a sliced onion and seasoning of pepper and salt. When the onion is done – after about 5 minutes – the greens are ready to place on the beef.

NOTES

Quantities are quite vague because this recipe is designed to use up leftovers – the amounts and proportions can be changed according to what you have to hand. There are no hard-and-fast rules.

VARIATIONS

If you have some leftover roast or boiled potatoes, mash or roughly chop them and cook them with the greens.
Although sprouts and cabbage are the traditional green vegetables for bubble and squeak, you can use any vegetable you like.

Mrs Beeton writes

"FRENCH BEEF – It has been all but universally admitted, that the beef of France is greatly inferior in quality to that of England, owing to inferiority of pasturage. M. Curmer, however, one of the latest writers on the culinary art, tells us that this is a vulgar error, and that French beef is far superior to that of England. This is mere vaunting on the part of our neighbours, who seem to want *la gloire* in everything."

Curried Beef ❧

LEFTOVER COLD MEAT was often curried to make it into a tasty hot meal. This recipe was originally made with cold beef, but fresh meat is used here. It is simple by today's standards, but delicious nevertheless. With very few ingredients, it has the added bonus of being quick to prepare.

METHOD

Cut the beef into pieces about 1 inch (2.5 cm) square and slice the onions. Put the butter into a saucepan with the onions and fry them until a light brown colour. Sprinkle in the curry powder, stir well, then add all the other ingredients and stir gently over a moderate heat for about 10 minutes. Cover and simmer gently for about 1½ hours or until the meat is tender. Should this curry be thought too dry, more beer, stock or water may be added, but a good curry should not be very thin. Place it in a deep dish with an edging of boiled rice, in the same manner as for other curries.

NOTES

Butter For an authentic Indian flavour use ghee, which is clarified butter (page 344) that has been simmered until it has a nutty aroma and taste. You can buy it in liquid form in cans, or in solid packets like ordinary butter, in Indian shops and large supermarkets. Once opened, it keeps for about 6 months in the refrigerator, so it is well worth buying. It can be heated to a high temperature without burning because it is so pure, which makes it an excellent fat for frying spices, and it gives homemade curries a glossy surface, the mark of an authentic Indian curry.

Beer Use a light or pale ale, or beef stock or water if you prefer not to use alcohol.

Curry powder Mrs Beeton gave a recipe for Indian Curry Powder (page 343), but nowadays there are many very good brands to buy. Garam masala, a ready mix of dry-roasted and ground spices, often has a better flavour than commercial curry powder. It is perfumed with cinnamon, cloves, mace and nutmeg, and is rarely overpoweringly hot.

Time 2 hours
Sufficient for 4 persons
Seasonable in winter

INGREDIENTS
1½ lb (750 g) braising or
    stewing steak
2 onions
3 oz (90 g) butter
2 teaspoons curry powder
1 wineglass of beer
½ pint (300 ml) beef stock
    or water
boiled rice to serve

❧ *Fricandeau of Beef*

Time 2¼ hours or rather
  longer
Sufficient for 6 persons
Seasonable at any time

INGREDIENTS
4–6 oz (125–175 g) streaky
  bacon
pepper and salt to taste
3 cloves
2 blades of mace
6 allspice berries
about 3 lb (1.4 kg) boned,
  rolled and tied joint
  of beef
1 pint (600 ml) Medium
  Stock (page 334) or water
1 glass of sherry
a bunch of savoury herbs
2 chopped shallots

ORIGINALLY MADE WITH FILLET OF BEEF that was larded with bacon to keep it moist, this pot roast is best made with a less prime cut that benefits from long slow cooking in liquid. Mrs Beeton suggested serving it with sorrel, but spinach will do just as well, or any other green vegetable such as broccoli or Brusssels sprouts. Mashed or boiled potatoes would make another good accompaniment, to soak up the delicious gravy.

METHOD

Cut the bacon into thin strips and put them into a saucepan or casserole with a seasoning of pepper and salt and the well pounded cloves, mace and allspice. Place the beef in the pan and add the stock or water, sherry, herbs and shallots. Bring slowly to boiling point, then cover the pan and cook the meat gently until tender – about 2 hours. Take out the meat, cover it closely and set aside. Skim off all the fat from the gravy, then strain it into a clean pan and boil it until it reduces and becomes glazed. Serve the beef sliced, with the gravy poured over.

NOTES

Beef The best joints for pot roasting are top rump, topside or brisket. These joints are often dry roasted, but they are more succulent and tender when cooked in liquid as in this recipe. The secret is to keep the heat very low so that the meat does not toughen. If you prefer, you can cook it in the oven at 325°F (160°C) Gas 3.

Savoury herbs In this case, a bouquet garni would be an ideal choice to go with the flavours of beef and bacon. You can buy ready made bouquets garnis, either fresh or dried, or make your own by tying together a bay leaf, a few sprigs each of parsley and thyme and a piece of celery.

Mrs Beeton writes

"MEMORANDA IN ROASTING – Some cooks always fail
in their roasts, though they succeed in nearly everything else.
A French writer on the culinary art says that anybody can learn
how to cook, but one must be born a roaster."

Beef Olives ❧

THE WORD 'OLIVE' IS USED to describe slices of meat that are rolled up around a stuffing into an olive shape. They are sometimes also called 'birds' because they look like little birds, and in France they are described as *paupiettes* or *roulades*. Mrs Beeton only used herbs for the stuffing, so they are not particularly plump. For a more substantial dish, you can substitute any forcemeat or stuffing you like for the herbs, and there are three recipes to choose from on pages 340 to 342. Your butcher will beat the steak thin and cut it for you if you tell him what you need it for. You can also buy ready-cut beef olives from some supermarkets.

METHOD

Have the steak cut rather thin and lightly beaten to make it flat, then cut it into 8 or 10 pieces. Brush over one side of the meat with beaten egg, sprinkle with herbs and season with pepper and salt. Roll up the pieces tightly and fasten each one with a small skewer. Put the stock in a saucepan that will exactly hold the rolls, for by being pressed together they will keep their shape better. Place the rolls of meat in the pan, cover them with the bacon, cut in thin slices, and over that put a piece of paper. Simmer very gently for a full 2 hours; the slower they are done the better. Take them out, remove the skewers and thicken the gravy with butter and flour. Bring to the boil, stirring, then pour over the meat and serve.

NOTES

Skewers Use wooden cocktail sticks or toothpicks.

Medium stock is a meaty stock, but it takes a long time to make. For speed and convenience, use a carton of fresh beef stock from the supermarket.

Paper Greaseproof paper or non-stick baking parchment is the ideal covering. It helps seal in the vapours and juices during long slow cooking. Mrs Beeton didn't mention it, but the pan should be tightly covered with the lid as well.

Light thickening This refers to *beurre manié*, but this would probably make the sauce unnecessarily heavy. A better option would be to take out the meat and boil the cooking juices rapidly until they are sufficiently reduced.

Time 2½ hours
Sufficient for 4 or 5 persons
Seasonable at any time

INGREDIENTS
2 lb (1 kg) rump steak
1 egg
1 tablespoon very finely
  chopped savoury herbs
pepper and salt to taste
1 pint (600 ml) Medium
  Stock (page 334)
2 or 3 slices of bacon
a light thickening of butter
  and flour

✎ Roast Ribs of Beef

Time 2 to 2½ hours
Sufficient for 6 or 8 persons
Seasonable all the year

INGREDIENTS
2 ribs of beef
3 tablespoons flour
salt and pepper
1 pint (600 ml) vegetable
  cooking water or stock
Yorkshire Pudding (page
  193) and Horseradish
  Sauce (page 211) to serve

RIBS ARE THE TRADITIONAL CUT for English roast beef, because the presence of the bones helps keep the meat moist and tender, but the same method can be used for boned and rolled joints such as sirloin and topside. See the variation at the end of the recipe for cooking times.

METHOD

Dust the ribs of beef with 1 tablespoon of the flour and sprinkle with salt and pepper. Stand the ribs upright in a roasting tin and place in a very hot oven. Roast for ¼ hour until the joint starts to brown, then lower the oven heat and roast for a further 1¾ to 2¼ hours, according to how you like your beef done. Baste the meat frequently during roasting. When done, lift the meat out, cover it and leave it in a warm place for about 10 minutes. During this time the gravy can be made with the juices in the roasting tin. Put the tin on top of the stove and sprinkle in the remaining flour. Stir over a low to moderate heat for a few minutes until brown, then gradually stir in the cooking water or stock and bring to the boil. Simmer, stirring, until reduced, then add seasoning and strain through a sieve if you like.

The oven should be preheated to 450°F (230°C) Gas 8, then decreased to 350°F (180°C) Gas 4.

NOTES

Ribs of beef The weight for 3 ribs is usually about 5½ lb (2.5 kg). Trim off excess fat, but leave a thin layer so that there is no need to add extra fat. If there is not enough fat for basting, add a few spoonfuls of stock or water to the tin during roasting.

Degrees of doneness It is very simple to calculate the roasting time according to how you like your beef cooked. If you like rare meat, the total roasting time should be 2 hours, for medium it will be 2¼ hours, for well-done meat 2½ hours.

Yorkshire Pudding and **Horseradish Sauce** have always been the traditional accompaniments to roast beef, and they are just as popular today as they ever were.

VARIATION

If you prefer a joint of beef that is not on the bone, choose sirloin or topside, both of which are sold boned, rolled and tied. For 6 to 8 people you need a joint weighing 4–4½ lb (1.8–2 kg). Weigh the meat and calculate the cooking time, allowing 20 minutes per 1 lb (500 g) plus 20 minutes for rare meat, 25 minutes for medium and 30 minutes for well-done. Follow the recipe left as for the ribs of beef, but keep the oven at a constant temperature of 350°F (180°C) Gas 4.

Mrs Beeton writes

"ROAST BEEF – has long been a national dish in England.
In most of our patriotic songs it is contrasted with the fricasseed
frogs, popularly supposed to be the exclusive diet of Frenchmen.
'O the roast beef of old England
And O the old English roast beef.'
This national chorus is appealed to whenever a song-writer wishes
to account for the valour displayed by Englishmen at sea or on land."

"BEEF CARVING – This joint will be the more easily cut
if the knife be first inserted between the bone and the meat,
before commencing to cut it into slices.
All joints of roast beef should be cut in even and thin slices.
Horseradish, finely scraped, may be served as a garnish;
but horseradish sauce is preferable for eating with the beef."

❧ Beef Stew

Time 2½ hours
Sufficient for 6 or 8 persons
Seasonable at any time

INGREDIENTS
1½–2 lb (750 g–1 kg) shin
    of beef
½ head of celery
4 carrots
2 turnips
1 onion
a bunch of savoury herbs
½ teaspoon allspice berries
½ teaspoon black
    peppercorns
pepper and salt to taste
thickening of butter and
    flour paste
3 tablespoons mushroom
    ketchup
2 tablespoons port

MEAT AND VEGETABLES simmered slowly together with herbs and spices make a flavoursome stew, and this one is very good. The addition of mushroom ketchup and port at the end makes it very special, but you can omit these for an everyday meal. Serve with mashed potatoes and a fresh seasonal vegetable, or with rice.

METHOD
Cut the beef into large squares. Roughly chop the celery, carrots, turnips, onion and herbs. Pound the allspice and peppercorns. Place the meat and vegetables in a saucepan or casserole with the herbs, spices and seasoning, then add 1 pint (600 ml) water and bring slowly to the boil. Cover and simmer very gently until the meat is tender – at least 2 hours. Lift out the beef, put it on a dish and keep hot. Thicken the gravy with the butter and flour and keep stirring until it boils, then strain and skim. Add the ketchup and port and bring to the boil again. Put the beef back in the pan and spoon the sauce over it. Serve the beef garnished with the carrots, turnips and onions.

NOTES
Shin of beef is a very good cut of meat for stews and casseroles. It is a gelatinous cut from the foreleg, and it literally melts in the mouth after long slow cooking. Ask your butcher for it by name or look for 'stewing beef' in the supermarket. Mrs Beeton does not brown the beef at the beginning of cooking, but this is a good idea to seal in the juices and give the finished stew richness and flavour. Heat 2 to 3 tablespoons groundnut oil in the pan and fry the pieces of meat in batches over a moderate to high heat until well browned on all sides. Lift each batch out with a slotted spoon, then return all the pieces to the pan, add the vegetables and proceed as in the recipe.
Savoury herbs Thyme, parsley and bay go well with the spices in this dish. You could also add a strip or two of pared orange rind, for a zesty flavour.
Thickening can be dispensed with. A better technique than this is to remove the meat and vegetables from the liquid, skim off any surface fat, then strain the liquid and boil it rapidly until reduced. It can be then be flavoured with mushroom ketchup and port. If you have no mushroom ketchup, use Worcestershire sauce.

Braised Leg of Lamb ❧

In classic French cookery there is a recipe called *Gigot de Mouton Braisé aux Haricots*, or Leg of Lamb with Haricot Beans, which this recipe resembles, especially as Mrs Beeton recommended serving it with 'a dish of white haricot beans boiled until tender, or with a garnish of glazed onions'. Some French cooks add cooked haricot beans to the lamb for the last half hour or so of cooking, and you can do this too if you wish.

METHOD

Line the bottom of a braising pan with a few slices of bacon. Roughly chop the carrots, onions, herbs and parsley and place these in the pan with seasoning to taste. Next place in the lamb, then cover with a few more slices of bacon. Pour in the stock, gravy or water, cover tightly with a lid and braise very gently for 4 hours, turning the lamb occasionally and adding more liquid if the level drops low. Strain the gravy into a clean pan and reduce it to a glaze over a high heat. Pour the glaze over the lamb and serve.

NOTES

Bacon Use smoked streaky rashers if you like a fairly strong, salty flavour, otherwise use unsmoked streaky bacon. About ½ lb (250 g) should be ample.

Savoury herbs In classic French cuisine a mixture of fresh rosemary, thyme and sage is traditional for this dish, but you can use just one or two of these herbs.

Stock/gravy You can buy lamb stock cubes, which would be appropriate here, but it isn't absolutely essential to use lamb stock. Beef stock can be used instead. A mixture of half stock and half red or white wine gives a very good flavour.

VARIATIONS

You can brown the lamb in 2 to 3 tablespoons hot groundnut oil before putting it on top of the bacon, vegetables and herbs in the pan. If you prefer, the lamb can be braised in a 325°F (160°C) Gas 3 oven for 3½ to 4 hours.

Time 4 hours
Sufficient for 6 or 8 persons
Seasonable at any time

INGREDIENTS
a few slices of bacon
4 carrots
3 onions
a bunch of savoury herbs
a bunch of parsley
seasoning to taste of pepper
and salt
1 leg of lamb weighing
about 4 lb (1.8 kg)
1 pint (600 ml) stock, gravy
or water, plus more if
necessary

Mrs Beeton writes

"Mutton is, undoubtedly, the meat most generally used in families; and, both by connoisseurs and medical men, it stands first in favour, whether its fine flavour, digestible qualifications, or general wholesomeness, be considered."

An Excellent Way
to Cook a Breast of Lamb

Time 1½ to 2 hours

Sufficient for 4 or 5 persons

Seasonable from June to
August

INGREDIENTS

a breast of lamb weighing
about 1½ lb (750 g)

2 onions

a piece of butter the size of
a walnut

a sprinkling of flour

a bunch of savoury herbs

salt and pepper to taste

about 2 pints (1.2 litres)
shelled young green peas

BREAST OF LAMB IS QUITE FATTY, but it is inexpensive and very tasty. This is an excellent way to cook it because it renders the fat down and the resulting meat is lean, succulent and tender. The addition of peas at the end of cooking is very French in style. Serve with boiled new potatoes tossed with a little butter and a handful of chopped fresh mint, which will complement the peas.

METHOD

Cut the lamb into pieces about 2 inches (5 cm) square, removing as much fat as you possibly can, so that it is tolerably lean. Slice the onions. Put the lamb into a saucepan with the butter and fry it until it is a nice brown. Dredge in a little flour, then add the onions, herbs and seasoning. Pour in sufficient water to just cover the meat, cover the pan and simmer gently until the lamb is tender – about 1 to 1½ hours. Take out the meat, strain and skim off all the fat from the gravy, then put both the meat and gravy back into the saucepan. Add the peas and let them boil gently until done – about 20 minutes.

NOTES

Savoury herbs Use mint, rosemary or parsley.

Peas The quantity of shelled peas given by Mrs Beeton was a huge amount. You will only need about 1 lb (500 g) peas in their pods to serve 4 to 5 persons, as this will give about half this weight in shelled peas. Only buy fresh peas at the very beginning of the season when they are young, or when you can be sure they are freshly picked. As they mature, peas become mealy and tough, and frozen peas are a better buy. If using frozen peas, allow ½ lb (250 g) and add them to the sauce while they are still frozen. Cook them for 3 to 5 minutes only. A pinch of sugar sprinkled over them while they are cooking greatly improves their flavour.

Mrs Beeton writes

———

" Two or three slices of bacon added and stewed with the lamb give additional flavour and, to ensure the peas being a beautiful green colour, they may be boiled in water separately, and added to the stew at the moment of serving."

Chargrilled Lamb Chops ❧

MRS BEETON USED A GRIDIRON to cook lamb chops. The modern equivalent is a ridged cast iron griddle, or you can use a non-stick frying pan if you haven't got a griddle. As long as the pan is thick and heavy, no extra fat is needed, which makes this a very healthy way to cook meat. In other recipes for lamb chops and cutlets Mrs Beeton recommended garnishing them with crisped (deep-fried) parsley, or placing them on mashed potatoes. She also said that asparagus, spinach and peas were favourite accompaniments to lamb chops. Tomato Sauce (page 229) is good with them too.

METHOD

Cut off any excess fat from the chops, trim them into a nice shape and lightly beat and level them. Put a ridged cast iron pan over a moderate to high heat for a few minutes to get thoroughly hot. Place the chops on the pan and cook them, turning frequently, for 6 to 8 minutes until they are done. Season with pepper and salt, arrange them on a very hot dish and rub a small piece of butter on each chop. Serve very hot.

NOTES

Lamb chops Loin chops are the best choice for this method of quick cooking because they are lean and tender with a succulent 'eye' of meat in the centre. They have a long bone, which makes it difficult to beat them as Mrs Beeton instructed, but this is not at all necessary. If you use chump chops, which come from the part of the animal between the loin and the leg, these are cut quite thick and are boneless. Beating them will flatten them and help make them cook quickly.

Serving It is important to serve lamb as soon as it is cooked because, unlike beef and pork, lamb quickly loses its flavour. This is why Mrs Beeton said to 'serve very hot'.

Time 6 to 8 minutes
Sufficient for 2 chops for
    each person
Seasonable at any time

INGREDIENTS
loin of lamb chops each
    about ¾ inch (2 cm) thick
pepper and salt
a little butter

✑ China Chilo

Time 1¼ hours

Sufficient for 6 persons

Seasonable from June to
August

INGREDIENTS

1½ lb (750 g) boneless leg,
loin or neck of lamb

1 lettuce

2 onions

about ¼ pint (150 ml) water

¼ lb (125 g) butter

1 teaspoon salt

1 teaspoon pepper

a little cayenne pepper
when liked

1 pint (600 ml) shelled
green peas

MRS BEETON SAID to serve China Chilo 'in a dish with a border of rice around, the same as for curry'. This, together with its rather strange oriental-sounding name, gives us the impression that this recipe might have come to Britain from the Far East, as many dishes did at the time Mrs Beeton was writing. The original recipe cooked the lamb and peas together for a total of 2 hours, which must have ruined the peas. Here the cooking time has been halved, making this a very quick supper dish. It is best made with the cayenne, and tastes delicious if it is sprinkled with chopped fresh mint or coriander just before serving.

METHOD

Mince the lamb, including a little of the fat. Put it into a saucepan with all the remaining ingredients except the peas, previously shredding the lettuce and onions rather fine. Tightly cover the pan after the ingredients have been well stirred, then simmer gently for ½ hour, adding more water as necessary. Add the peas, stir and simmer for another ½ hour.

NOTES

Lamb Mincing your own lamb is a good idea because then you can be sure of the cut and quality of meat, and the amount of fat to include, but you will need a mincer or food processor to do this. If you haven't got one of these machines, you can ask your butcher to mince one of the recommended cuts of lamb for you, or you can buy ready minced lamb at the supermarket. Lamb tends to be fatty, so check the fat content before buying it this way.

Peas You will need about 1 lb (500 g) fresh peas in their pods, or ½ lb (250 g) shelled peas or frozen peas.

VARIATION

If you omit the lettuce and add 1 to 2 tablespoons curry powder or garam masala with the cayenne, this dish becomes very like the Indian *keema* curry, which sometimes uses minced beef rather than lamb.

This is a real Irish stew, made with potatoes and onions only. You may see recipes with other vegetables and flavourings added, but these are not authentic. If you sprinkle the stew with chopped parsley and serve it with vegetables like carrots and broccoli, it will look colourful enough on the plate.

METHOD

Trim off the excess fat from the chops. Peel and thickly slice the potatoes and onions. Put a layer of potatoes in the bottom of a stewpan, then a layer of lamb and onions. Season with pepper and salt. Proceed in this manner until the pan is full, taking care to have plenty of vegetables at the top. Pour in the water, cover tightly and bring to the boil. Simmer very gently for 2½ hours, keeping the lid closely shut the whole time and occasionally shaking the pan to prevent the ingredients from burning on the bottom.

NOTES

Layering The top layer of ingredients should be potatoes, although this is not exactly specified in the original recipe.

Stewpan In Mrs Beeton's day, Irish stew would have been cooked in a stewpan, a pan with a close-fitting lid with a long handle, enabling it to be lifted off without burning the fingers. A flameproof casserole would be an ideal alternative.

Baking Mrs Beeton gave cooking in the oven as an alternative method to stewing on top of the stove. She suggested a moderate oven, which would be 350°F (180°C) Gas 4, for about 2 hours. This is the more usual method for a stew that takes so long to cook, and is further recommended because you can remove the lid for the last half hour and brown the top layer of potatoes.

Time 3 hours
Sufficient for 5 or 6 persons
Seasonable for a winter dish

INGREDIENTS
3 lb (1.4 kg) loin or neck of
    lamb chops of moderate
    thickness
about 2 lb (1 kg) potatoes
2 large onions
pepper and salt to taste
rather more than 1 pint
    (600 ml) water

&s Italian Lamb Cutlets

Time ½ hour or rather
   longer
Sufficient for 5 or 6 persons
Seasonable at any time

INGREDIENTS
3 lb (1.4 kg) best end of neck
   of lamb cutlets
clarified butter
the yolk of 1 egg
4 tablespoons bread crumbs
1 tablespoon finely chopped
   savoury herbs
1 tablespoon finely chopped
   parsley
1 teaspoon finely chopped
   shallot
½ teaspoon finely chopped
   lemon peel
pepper, salt and pounded
   mace to taste
a sprinkling of flour
½ pint (300 ml) hot stock or
   water
2 teaspoons Harvey's sauce
1 teaspoon soy sauce
2 teaspoons tarragon
   vinegar
1 tablespoon port

WITH THEIR HERB AND LEMON flavoured crumb coating, these crunchy-crisp cutlets are good served for an informal supper dish with boiled new potatoes. The sauce has an unusual mix of Eastern and Western flavours, almost like modern-day fusion cuisine. It can be simplified by adding fewer flavourings if you like. Harvey's sauce is a spicy bottled sauce made from anchovies, walnuts and shallots flavoured with vinegar and soy, so you could use this and omit the soy and tarragon vinegar, or vice versa.

METHOD
Trim off any excess fat from the cutlets, flatten them and dip them in clarified butter, then into the beaten yolk of an egg. Mix well together the bread crumbs, herbs, parsley, shallot, lemon peel and seasonings and cover the cutlets with these ingredients. Melt some clarified butter in a frying pan, lay in the cutlets and fry them until they are a nice brown – about 5 minutes on each side. Take them out and keep them hot. Dredge some flour into the pan and if there is not sufficient butter, add a little more. Stir until it looks brown, then pour in the hot stock or water and the remaining ingredients. Bring to the boil and pour around the cutlets. If the gravy is not thick enough, add a little more flour.

NOTES
Clarified butter (page 344) is used for frying these lamb chops because it has a high smoke point and does not burn at high temperatures like ordinary butter. If you don't have clarified butter, you can help to prevent ordinary butter from burning by melting it with 1 to 2 tablespoons groundnut or olive oil, both of which have high smoke points, or you can dispense with the butter altogether and use your favourite oil on its own.
Stock If you want to use stock rather than water, use lamb or chicken stock made with a stock cube. There are plenty of strong flavourings in the sauce, so the flavour of the stock is incidental.

Mrs Beeton writes
———————

"Mushrooms, when obtainable,
are a great improvement to this dish."

Mrs Beeton described these as a breakfast or supper dish, which is still true today, although for a supper you will need 2 to 3 kidneys per person. If you prefer, you can fry them in a little butter rather than grilling them. The preparation is the same, except that there is no need to thread them on skewers.

Method

Ascertain that the kidneys are fresh and cut them open very evenly lengthwise down to the root (should one half be thicker than the other, one would be underdone while the other would be dried). Do not separate them. Skin them and pass a skewer under the white part of each half to keep them flat. Grill them, inside facing uppermost, under high heat until they are done enough on one side – about 3 to 4 minutes. Turn them and cook them on the other side for the same length of time. Remove the skewers. Place the kidneys on a very hot dish, season with pepper and salt and put a tiny piece of butter in the middle of each. Serve very hot and quickly, on very hot plates.

Notes

Lamb's kidneys are small, with a sweeter flavour than pig's or ox (beef) kidneys. If they have hard white fat (suet) around them when you buy them, peel it off with your fingers before cutting the kidneys in half. Mrs Beeton referred to passing a skewer under 'the white part', meaning the central core of the kidney. The core helps hold the kidney together during grilling, but it is chewy and unpleasant to eat, so you may prefer to cut it out before skewering.

Time ¼ hour
Sufficient for 1 kidney for
each person
Seasonable at any time

INGREDIENTS
lamb's kidneys
pepper and salt to taste
a little butter

Mrs Beeton writes

"A prettier dish than this may be made by serving the kidneys each on a piece of buttered toast cut in any fanciful shape. In this case a little lemon juice will be found an improvement."

✍ *Roast Lamb*

Time 1¾ to 2 hours

Sufficient for 4 persons

Seasonable at any time

INGREDIENTS

3 lb (1.4 kg) piece of leg or
  shoulder of lamb
2 tablespoons oil
salt and pepper to taste
a few sprigs of rosemary
a little flour
½ pint (300 ml) hot stock or
  water

MRS BEETON'S INSTRUCTIONS for roasting a joint of lamb were very simple, consisting of little more than advice to make a 'brisk clear fire', dredge the meat well with flour and 'keep continually basting the whole time it is cooking'. This modern recipe for roasting either a leg or shoulder of lamb on the bone is equally simple, but more precise.

METHOD

Rub the meat all over with the oil and salt and pepper, then sprinkle with the leaves from the rosemary sprigs. Place the meat on a rack in a roasting tin and roast for 1½ hours. Take the meat from the tin, cover and set aside in a warm place for about 10 minutes. During this time, pour off almost all of the drippings from the tin and place the tin over a low to moderate heat. Sprinkle in enough flour to absorb the drippings and stir for 1 to 2 minutes. Pour in the hot stock or water and bring to the boil, stirring. Season well and serve very hot, with the carved lamb.

The oven should be preheated to 350°F (180°C) Gas 4.

NOTES

Lamb The roasting time given is for medium-rare lamb. You can decrease or increase the time by 10 minutes for rare or well-done meat. A roast joint is an excellent for serving a large group of people, so you may want to cook a larger piece of meat than the one specified here. To serve 6 to 8 people, you will need a joint weighing about 4 lb (1.8 kg). To calculate the cooking time, allow 20 minutes per 1 lb (500 g) plus 20 minutes for rare meat; 25 minutes for medium-rare and 30 minutes for well-done.

Flavour You can use groundnut or olive oil, depending on the flavour you like. The same goes for the stock, which can be any type you happen to have. Lamb, chicken or vegetable are the best choices. A few spoonfuls of port, sherry or wine can be used to flavour the gravy, with a little redcurrant jelly.

VARIATION

Make incisions all over the lamb with the point of a sharp knife and insert slivers of garlic into them. You can also do this with rosemary sprigs, letting them protrude out of the meat like little tufts. This looks very attractive on the finished roast.

Mrs Beeton writes

"See that the butcher joints the meat properly, as thereby much annoyance is saved to the carver, when it comes to table."

"HOW TO BUY MEAT ECONOMICALLY – If the housekeeper is not very particular as to the precise joints to cook for dinner, there is oftentimes an opportunity for her to save as much money in her purchases of meat as will pay for the bread to eat with it. It frequently happens with many butchers, that, in consequence of a demand for legs and loins of mutton, they have only shoulders left, and these they will be glad to sell at a reduction."

MRS BEETON WAS SAID
TO DISLIKE FORMAL
PARTIES, BUT SHE GAVE
THEM NEVERTHELESS.
THESE QUOTATIONS
REVEAL HOW DIFFICULT
SHE FOUND THEM,
WHICH IS SMALL
WONDER GIVEN THE
NUMBER OF RULES AND
REGULATIONS THAT HAD
TO BE OBSERVED.
IT IS INTERESTING TO
NOTE HOW CERTAIN
CUSTOMS HAVE
SURVIVED (EVEN LAST-
MINUTE APPREHENSIONS
AND NERVES) AND TO
SEE THAT IT WAS THE
HOSTESS RATHER THAN
THE HOST WHO PLAYED
THE MOST IMPORTANT
ROLE IN ENTERTAINING
AT HOME, WHICH IS WHY
THESE INSTRUCTIONS
CAME IN THE FIRST
CHAPTER OF MRS
BEETON'S ORIGINAL
BOOK.

THE HALF-HOUR BEFORE DINNER has always been considered as the great ordeal through which the mistress, in giving a dinner-party, will either pass with flying colours, or, lose many of her laurels. The anxiety to receive her guests – her hope that all will be present in due time – her trust in the skill of her cook and the attention of the other domestics, all tend to make these few minutes a trying time. The mistress, however, must display no kind of agitation, but show her tact in suggesting light and cheerful subjects of conversation, which will be much aided by the introduction of any particular new book, curiosity of art, or article of vertu [collector's item], which may pleasantly engage the attention of the company.

IN GIVING AN ENTERTAINMENT OF THIS KIND, the mistress should remember that it is her duty to make her guests feel happy, comfortable and quite at their ease; and the guests should also consider that they have come to the house of their hostess to be happy. Thus an opportunity is given to all for innocent enjoyment and intellectual improvement.

DINNER BEING ANNOUNCED, the host offers his arm to, and places on his right hand at the dinner-table, the lady to whom he desires to pay most respect, either on account of her age, position, or from her being the greatest stranger in the party. If this lady be married and her husband present, the latter takes the hostess to her place at table, and seats himself at her right hand. The rest of the company follow in couples, as specified by the master and mistress of the house, arranging the party according to their rank and other circumstances which may be known to the host and hostess.

IT WILL BE FOUND of great assistance to the placing of a party at the dinner-table, to have the names of the guests neatly (and correctly) written on small cards, and placed at that part of the table where it is desired they should sit. With respect to the number of guests, it has often been said that a private dinner-party should consist of not less than the number of the Graces, or more than that of the Muses. A party of ten or twelve is, perhaps, in a general way, sufficient to enjoy themselves and be enjoyed.

WHITE KID GLOVES are worn by ladies at dinner-parties, but should be taken off before the business of dining commences.

IT IS NOT USUAL, where taking wine is *en règle*, for a gentleman to ask a lady to take wine until the fish or soup is finished, and then the gentleman honoured by sitting on the right of the hostess may politely inquire if she will do him the honour of taking wine with him. This will act as a signal to the rest of the company, the gentleman of the house most probably requesting the same pleasure of the ladies at his right and left. At many tables, however, the custom or fashion of taking wine in this manner is abolished, and the servant fills the glasses of the guests with the various wines suited to the course in progress.

WHEN FRUIT HAS BEEN TAKEN, and a glass or two of wine passed round, the time will have arrived when the hostess will rise, and thus give the signal for the ladies to leave the gentlemen, and retire to the drawing-room. The gentlemen of the party will rise at the same time, and he who is nearest the door, will open it for the ladies, all remaining courteously standing until the last lady has withdrawn.

IN FORMER TIMES, when the bottle circulated freely amongst the guests, it was necessary for the ladies to retire earlier than they do at present, for the gentlemen of the company soon became unfit to conduct themselves with that decorum which is essential in the presence of ladies. Thanks, however, to the improvements in modern society, and the high example shown to the nation by its most illustrious personages, temperance is, in these happy days, a striking feature in the character of a gentleman. Delicacy of conduct towards the female sex has increased with the esteem in which they are now universally held, and thus, the very early withdrawing of the ladies from the dining-room is to be deprecated. A lull in the conversation will seasonably indicate the moment for the ladies' departure.

✑ Rolled Loin of Lamb

Time 3 hours plus
 marinating for a day
Sufficient for 5 or 6 persons
Seasonable at any time

INGREDIENTS

about 3½ lb (1.6 kg) boned
 double loin of lamb, with
 the bones
½ teaspoon black
 peppercorns
¼ teaspoon allspice berries
¼ teaspoon pounded mace
¼ teaspoon grated nutmeg
6 cloves
Forcemeat (page 340)
1 glass of port
2 tablespoons mushroom
 ketchup

Mrs Beeton writes

"Serve with redcurrant
jelly and, if obtainable, a
few mushrooms stewed
for a few minutes in the
gravy."

MRS BEETON DESCRIBED this recipe as 'very excellent' and
instructed her readers to bone the lamb themselves, but you can ask
your butcher to bone it for you. He should do this at no extra charge,
but will probably appreciate advance notice. Tell him not to roll and
tie it because it is to be stuffed, and that you need the bones for
making stock, or he may not save them for you.

METHOD

Sprinkle the lamb inside and out with the pepper, allspice, mace,
nutmeg and cloves, all of which must be pounded very fine. Let it
remain for a day, then cover the meat inside with the forcemeat and
roll and tie it. Put the lamb bones in a deep roasting tin and just cover
with about 1 pint (600 ml) water. Place the lamb in the tin and roast
for 2½ hours, basting occasionally and adding more water if it drops
below the level of the bones. Take the meat from the tin, cover and
set aside in a warm place for about 10 minutes. During this time,
pour the cooking liquid from the tin into a saucepan, skim off as
much fat as possible, then boil until reduced by about one-third. Add
the port and ketchup and bring to the boil again. Season and serve
very hot, with the carved lamb.

NOTES

Forcemeat is made with ham or bacon, breadcrumbs and suet,
generously flavoured with fresh herbs and lemon. Similar types,
usually described as stuffings, are sold ready made in supermarkets –
you will need 8–10 oz (250–300g).

Mushroom ketchup is a bottled sauce made from fresh mushrooms,
cayenne pepper, allspice and ginger. You can get it in delicatessens and
specialist food shops. It keeps for a long time and is well worth having
in your storecupboard to add a dash of spicy savouriness to sauces,
soups and stews.

Seasoning the lamb Mrs Beeton instructed her readers to leave the
lamb for a day before cooking so that the meat would take on the
flavour of the spices. To do this, cover it and keep it in the refrigerator
until about 1 hour before you are ready to cook.

THE FLAVOURING INGREDIENTS in this braise permeate the lamb to make it taste superb. Using new season's lamb, it would make an ideal lunch for Easter Sunday, served with Jersey new potatoes boiled in their jackets, then tossed in melted butter and chopped fresh mint. Mrs Beeton suggested serving it with peas or spinach, either of which would complement it well.

METHOD

Line the bottom of a pan with a few thin slices of fat bacon, then place the lamb in the pan. Roughly chop the vegetables and herbs and place them around the lamb. Sprinkle in the mace, cover the meat with a few more slices of bacon and pour in 1 pint (600 ml) stock. Simmer very gently for 2 hours, adding more stock if necessary. Remove the meat, cover and set aside. Strain and reduce the gravy to a glaze season, then use to glaze the meat.

NOTES

Stock can be made with the bones left after the butcher has boned the meat for you. Follow either the recipe for Medium Stock (page 334) or White Stock (page 335), using the lamb bones in place of some of the beef or veal bones. Alternatively, you can use a lamb stock cube, or even chicken stock if you prefer a less meaty flavour.

Glaze The meat needs to be set aside to rest for about 10 minutes before carving, during which time you can boil the gravy until reduced. Don't worry if it is not thick enough to coat the meat in a shiny glaze. Many people prefer runny gravy with roast meat rather than a glaze.

Mrs Beeton writes

"SHEPHERDS AND THEIR FLOCKS – In the Highlands of Scotland, where the herbage is scanty, the sheep-farm requires to be very large, and to be watched over by many shepherds. The farms of some of the great Scottish landowners are of enormous extent. 'How many sheep have you on your estate?' asked Prince Esterhazy of the duke of Argyll. 'I have not the most remote idea,' replied the duke; 'but I know the shepherds number several thousands'."

Time 2½ hours
Sufficient for 4 or 5 persons
Seasonable from Easter to
   Michaelmas

INGREDIENTS
a few thin slices of bacon
1½–2 lb (750 g–1 kg) boned
   and rolled single loin
   of lamb
a bunch of spring onions
5 or 6 young carrots
a bunch of savoury herbs
2 blades of mace, pounded
about 1 pint (600 ml) stock
salt to taste

‰ *Pan-fried Pork Chops*

Time 20 to 25 minutes
Sufficient for 4 persons
Seasonable from October
 to March

INGREDIENTS
4 pork loin chops
a beaten egg
6 tablespoons bread crumbs
1 tablespoon finely chopped
 sage
pepper and salt to taste
clarified butter

IN A BASIC RECIPE for pork chops Mrs Beeton instructed her readers to pan-fry plain chops with a simple seasoning of salt and pepper 'for about ¼ hour, turning them 3 or 4 times. She also advised them to be particular that they are thoroughly done, but not dry'. These simple instructions will produce good results, but the recipe given here is more detailed and more interesting.

METHOD
Trim the chops and scrape the top part of the bones. Brush them over with egg, then sprinkle them with bread crumbs, which have been mixed with the sage and a seasoning of pepper and salt. Drizzle a little clarified butter on them and press the crumbs well down. Put the frying pan on a moderate to high heat and put in some clarified butter. When this is hot, lay in the chops. Fry them, turning them frequently, until light brown on both sides – about 15 minutes altogether. Take them out, dry the greasy moisture from them, then dish them up on mashed potatoes. Serve with any sauce that may be preferred, such as Tomato Sauce or Sauce Piquante, or with pickled gherkins.

NOTES
Bread crumbs may be fresh or dried. If they are dried, the coating will be crisper. You will need about 2–3 oz (60–90 g) to coat the pork chops evenly.

Clarified butter (page 344) has a high smoke smoke point, so there is no risk of burning. Mrs Beeton used lard in her original recipe because this too can be heated to a high temperature without burning, but it is an unhealthy saturated fat. To pan-fry the chops in clarified butter, you will need about 2 to 3 tablespoons. As an alternative, use 1 to 2 tablespoons ordinary butter with 1 to 2 tablespoons groundnut or olive oil, or use 2 to 4 tablespoons oil and leave out the butter.

Tomato Sauce (page 229) is hot and spicy with cayenne pepper, while **Sauce Piquante** (page 228) is sweet, sour and spicy as its name suggests. Both go well with pork because their sharp flavours offset the richness of the meat.

Roast Leg of Pork ❧

Everyone loves succulent roast pork with traditional stuffing, crisp crackling and all the usual trimmings. This basic recipe provides all the information you need for superb results. Mrs Beeton used the knuckle or shank (bottom) end of a pork leg, but she was rather vague about the presence of the bone and where to put the stuffing. If you buy a leg of pork with the bone in, simply cook the stuffing in a separate baking dish. It will be crisper this way, which is how most people prefer it.

Method

Choose a small leg of pork and score the skin across in narrow strips about ¼ inch (5 mm) apart. Cut a slit in the knuckle, loosen the skin and fill it with a sage and onion stuffing. Brush the joint over with a little oil (this makes crisper crackling and a better colour). Roast for 2½ hours. Baste it well and serve with a little gravy made in the roasting tin. Do not omit to serve it with a well-made apple sauce.

The oven should be preheated to 350°F (180°C) Gas 4.

Notes

Crackling For an even crisper crackling, rub the oiled skin with salt before roasting. After roasting, strip off the crackling and cover the joint, then leave it to stand for 10 minutes. Increase the oven temperature to 400°F (200°C) Gas 6 and return the crackling to the oven while you make the gravy and carve the pork.

Sage and Onion Stuffing and **Apple Sauce** are the traditional accompaniments to roast pork. If you don't have the time to make them yourself, use good-quality bought stuffing and sauce. Instructions for making gravy are given on pages 197–199.

Time 2¾ to 3 hours
Sufficient for about
  6 persons
Seasonable from September
  to March

INGREDIENTS
a leg of pork weighing about
  4 lb (1.8 kg)
a little oil
Sage and Onion Stuffing
  (page 342)
Apple Sauce (page 200)
  to serve

✑ Roast Loin of Pork

Time 2¼ hours

Sufficient for 4 or 6 persons

Seasonable from September to March

INGREDIENTS

a boned, rolled and tied loin
of pork weighing about
2¾ lb (1.25 kg)

a little oil

a little salt

Apple Sauce (page 200) and
gravy (pages 197-199) to
serve

Mrs Beeton's instructions were for a loin of pork on the bone, but a boned and rolled loin is easier to cook and carve. Her recipe is very plain, although she did tell her readers that 'a stuffing of sage and onion may be made separately, and baked in a flat dish'. She added, 'this method is better than putting it in the meat, as many persons have so great an objection to the flavour'. If you would like to make your own sage and onion stuffing, you will find a very good recipe on page 342.

METHOD

Score the skin of the pork in strips rather more than ¼ inch (5 mm) apart. Place the joint on a rack in a roasting tin and rub the skin all over with a little oil and salt. Roast for 2 hours, keeping the joint well basted all the time it is in the oven. Serve with apple sauce and a little gravy made in the roasting tin.

The oven should be preheated to 350°F (180°C) Gas 4.

NOTES

Cooking times To roast a loin of pork that is a different size from the one in this recipe, allow 30 minutes per 1 lb (500 g) plus 30 minutes. To test for doneness, insert a skewer into the centre of the joint: the juices should run clear, not pink or red.

Crackling Skin is not always left on a boned, rolled and tied joint, so check when buying. For a really crisp crackling, increase the oven temperature to 425°F (220°C) Gas 7 for the last 20 minutes of the cooking time.

Apple Sauce and **gravy** are the traditional accompaniments for roast pork.

Mrs Beeton writes

"Pork should be very thoroughly cooked, but not dry. Be careful never to send it to table the least underdone, as nothing is more unwholesome and disagreeable than underdressed white meats."

THE LEARNED PIG – That the pig is capable of education, is a fact long known to the world; and though, like the ass, naturally stubborn and obstinate, that he is equally amenable with other animals to caresses and kindness, has been shown from very remote time; the best modern evidence of his docility, however, is the instance of the learned pig, first exhibited about a century since, but which has been continued down to our own time by repeated instances of an animal who will put together all the letters or figures that compose the day, month, hour, and date of the exhibition, besides many other unquestioned evidences of memory."

✎ To Boil a Ham
to Give it an Excellent Flavour

Time 2½ hours plus cooling
    if serving cold
Sufficient for 8 persons
Seasonable all the year

INGREDIENTS

a gammon joint weighing
    about 4½ lb (2 kg)
1–2 celery hearts
2 turnips
3 onions
a large bunch of savoury
    herbs
2 tablespoons vinegar
fine bread raspings

THESE INSTRUCTIONS ARE FOR a classic ham on the bone, which is traditionally served at Christmas and on other special occasions. Gammon is the name given to raw cured pork from the hind legs of the pig. Once the gammon is cooked, it is known as ham. Sizes of gammon joints range from fairly small to very large – for cooking times for different-sized joints, see the notes opposite. If the gammon is unsmoked (sometimes referred to as 'green'), soaking is not necessary. For smoked gammon joints, cover the joint with cold water and leave to soak for 3 hours, then drain, rinse and drain again before starting the recipe.

METHOD

Wash the gammon thoroughly clean and put it into a large saucepan with the celery, turnips, onions and herbs, all roughly chopped. Pour in sufficient cold water to cover the gammon, and add the vinegar. Bring the liquid gradually to the boil and, as the scum rises, carefully remove it. Keep it simmering very gently until tender – 1¾ hours – and be careful that it does not stop boiling, nor boil too quickly. When done, take it out of the pan, strip off the skin and sprinkle over it a few fine bread raspings. Put a frill of cut paper round the knuckle and serve. If it is to be eaten cold, let the ham remain in the water until nearly cold. By this method the juices are kept in and it will be found infinitely superior to one taken out of the water hot (it should, however, be borne in mind that the ham must not remain in the pan all night). When the skin is removed, sprinkle over bread raspings or, if wanted particularly nice, glaze it. Place a paper frill round the knuckle and garnish with parsley or cut vegetable flowers.

NOTES

Savoury herbs A bouquet garni made up of fresh bay leaves, parsley and celery would be appropriate, or you can use a ready made dried bouquet garni. For additional flavour, you can also add a few black peppercorns and/or cloves to the water.

Bread raspings are bread crumbs that have been dried in the oven until browned. You will need about 2 oz (60 g). To make them extra fine, work them through a sieve with the back of a spoon.

Cooking Time For joints of under 10 lb (4.5 kg), allow 20 minutes per 1 lb (500 g) plus 20 minutes. For joints over this weight, allow 15 minutes per 1 lb (500 g) plus 15 minutes. Start timing from the moment when the water comes to the boil.

Glaze For a simple shiny glaze, melt together a few tablespoons each of clear honey and Dijon mustard, then brush over the ham.

Mrs Beeton writes

"HOW TO SILENCE A PIG. ANECDOTE OF CHARLES V. –
When the emperor Charles V. was one day walking in the
neighbourhood of Vienna he was much annoyed by the noise
of a pig, which a country youth was carrying a little way
before him. 'Have you not learned how to quiet a pig?'
demanded the imperial traveller tartly. 'Noa,' replied the ingenuous
peasant, ignorant of the quality of his interrogator. 'Noa,
and I should very much like to know how to do it.'
'Why take the pig by the tail,' said the emperor, 'and you
will see how quiet he will become'.
Struck by the novelty of the suggestion, the countryman at once
dangled his noisy companion by the tail, and soon discovered that
the pig had indeed become silent. Looking with admiration on his
august adviser, he exclaimed, 'Ah, you must have learned the trade
much longer than I, for you understand it a great deal better'."

ᏔᎣ *Pork Cheese*

Time 1½ hours plus cooling
Sufficient for about 10
 persons
Seasonable from October to
 March

INGREDIENTS
2 lb (1 kg) minced pork
pepper and salt to taste
2 blades of mace
nutmeg
a few sprigs of parsley
4 leaves of sage
a very small bunch of
 savoury herbs
peel from ¼ lemon
about ½ pint (300 ml) good
 strong gravy or sufficient
 to fill the mould

IN OLD COOKERY BOOKS recipes for 'cheeses' described potted foods that were used as spreads, rather like modern-day pâtés. Meat cheeses like this one were popular, so too were mixtures of cheese and butter flavoured with spices or mustard, and sweet fruit cheeses, which were like very thick, spreadable purées. This pork cheese was described by Mrs Beeton as an excellent breakfast dish, but we are more likely to serve it as a pâté or meat loaf for supper, accompanied by toast or bread and a salad garnish.

METHOD
Season the pork with pepper and salt. Pound the mace and grate about ¼ teaspoon nutmeg. Finely chop the parsley, sage, herbs and lemon peel and mix everything nicely together. Put it into a 2 pint (1.2 litre) mould, fill up with strong well-flavoured gravy and bake for rather more than one hour. When cold, turn it out of the mould.

The oven should be preheated to 350°F (180°C) Gas 4.

NOTES
Pork The orginal recipe was made with cold roast pork, allowing ¼ lb (125 g) fat to each 1 lb (500 g) lean meat, but it is quicker and more practical to make it with raw minced pork.
Gravy was always to hand in a Victorian kitchen, but as this is rarely the case these days, chicken stock can be used instead.
Testing for doneness After 1 hour, insert a skewer in the centre of the meat. When the meat is sufficiently cooked, the juices should run clear, not red or pink.

Mrs Beeton writes

"THE UNIVERSALITY OF THE HOG – A singular circumstance
in the domestic history of the hog, is the extent of its distribution
over the surface of the earth; being found even in insulated places,
where the inhabitants are semi-barbarous, and where the wild species
is entirely unknown."

Sausagemeat Cakes ❧

THESE ARE LIKE HOMEMADE sausage burgers, although Mrs Beeton described them as shortcut way to make sausagemeat. They taste good served in burger buns with a tangy pickle, relish or sauce, plus a few thin slices of gherkin or some fresh salad leaves.

METHOD
Remove all skin, gristle and bone from the pork and chop the meat finely with the bacon. Add the remaining ingredients except the flour and carefully mix everything together. Pound it well in a mortar, then make it into convenient-sized cakes. Flour these and fry them in hot oil for about 10 minutes until they are a nice brown.

NOTES
Pork Mrs Beeton specified lean meat, but the cakes will be dry if it is too lean. A good cut to use is boneless sparerib. It has a light marbling of fat, which helps keep the meat moist and juicy.
Bacon Rindless streaky bacon rashers are best and you can choose from smoked or unsmoked, whichever you prefer. If using smoked bacon, you will only need ¼ teaspoon salt.
Mortar A food processor can be used to chop all the ingredients together instead of a mortar and pestle. Do not to overwork the meat or it will become like a paste. It should have a fairly coarse texture.

Mrs Beeton writes

"This is a very simple method of making sausagemeat, and on trial will prove very good, its great recommendation being that it is so easily made."

"THE HOG IN ENGLAND – From time immemorial, in England, this animal has been esteemed as of the highest importance. In the Anglo-Saxon period, vast herds of swine were tended by men, who watched over their safety, and who collected them under shelter at night. At that time, the flesh of the animal was the staple article of consumption in every family, and a large portion of the wealth of the rich freemen of the country consisted of these animals."

Time ½ hour
Sufficient for 4 to 6 persons
Seasonable from September to March

INGREDIENTS
1 lb (500 g) lean pork
¾ lb (375 g) fat bacon
½ oz (15 g) salt
¼ teaspoon pepper
¼ teaspoon grated nutmeg
1 teaspoon finely chopped parsley
flour for coating
oil for frying

✌ Veal à la Maintenon

Time 15 to 18 minutes
Sufficient for 4 persons
Seasonable from March to
  October

INGREDIENTS
1 lb (500 g) veal escalopes
1 or 2 egg yolks
bread crumbs
2 tablespoons finely
  chopped savoury herbs
a little grated nutmeg
salt and pepper to taste
oil for frying

THESE ARE VERY LIKE *wienerschnitzel*, although the recipe originally used veal cutlets, ¾ inch (2 cm) thick. The success of *wienerschnitzel* depends on the use of very thin veal that literally melts in the mouth. You will probably prefer to serve this dish with lemon wedges for squeezing rather than the melted butter or gravy suggested by Mrs Beeton.

METHOD
Flatten the veal and brush the pieces over with egg yolk. Dip them into bread crumbs mixed with the herbs and grated nutmeg and seasoned with salt and pepper. Fry them in in batches in very hot oil for 3 minutes on each side. Serve with melted butter or a good gravy.

NOTES
Veal Tell the butcher what you are making and he will pound the veal very thin with a meat mallet. If you need to do it yourself, put the veal between two sheets of cling film and pound it with the flat bottom of a saucepan.

Bread crumbs For the very crisp coating that is typical of *wienerschnitzel*, the breadcrumbs should be dried, and you will need about 3 oz (90 g). They should also be as fine as possible, so if you have made them yourself in the food processor, rub them through a sieve after processing.

Savoury herbs Veal has rather a bland flavour, so choose a pungent herb like basil, dill, marjoram or sage. All of these herbs go well with veal, but it is better to use a single variety, rather than the mixture Mrs Beeton appeared to advocate.

Loin of Veal à la Daube ∽

A LOIN OF VEAL IS AN EXPENSIVE CUT, so this recipe is best reserved for special occasions. In Mrs Beeton's recipe she reduced the gravy right down to a glaze, but here it is reduced rather less and served as a sauce, which seems a better option with a prime veal cut that is very lean and has a tendency to dryness. Mrs Beeton recommended serving the meat with a tomato, mushroom or sorrel sauce, but this is not necessary if you are serving it with the gravy.

METHOD
Fill the cavity in the veal where the bone was taken from with forcemeat. Tie the veal up and lay it in a casserole with the bones and trimmings. Cover it with a few slices of bacon and add the herbs, mace, peppercorns, onions and stock or water. Cover the pan with a closely fitting lid and simmer for 1¾ hours, shaking the pan occasionally. Take out the veal, cover and set aside. Strain the cooking liquid and boil to reduce to a gravy.

NOTES
Veal chump end is the leg end of a loin of veal. It is a tricky joint to carve with the bone in, so it is often sold ready boned. If your joint is a different size from the one used here, calculate the cooking time after stuffing, allowing 30 minutes per 1 lb (500 g) plus 30 minutes.

Forcemeat is a breadcrumb-based stuffing flavoured with lemon, herbs and cayenne pepper. If you don't have the time to make it yourself, there are similar ready made stuffings available in the chilled cabinets at supermarkets. Packet sizes are about 10 oz (300 g). Any stuffing that does not fit in the veal can be baked in a separate dish.

Savoury herbs Parsley is used in the forcemeat, so it is a good herb to use here.

Time 2¼ hours
Sufficient for 4 or 5 persons
Seasonable from March to October

INGREDIENTS
the boned chump end of a loin of veal, weighing about 2½ lb (1.25 kg)
Forcemeat (page 340)
a few slices of bacon
a bunch of savoury herbs
2 blades of mace
½ teaspoon white peppercorns
5 or 6 spring onions
1 pint (600 ml) veal stock or water

ᔕᗡ Calf's Liver aux Fines Herbes

Time ¼ hour
Sufficient for 4 or 6 persons
Seasonable from March to
   October

INGREDIENTS
1 lb (500 g) calf's liver
flour
butter
a bunch of savoury herbs
   including parsley
2 finely chopped shallots
   when liked
1 tablespoon vinegar
1 tablespoon lemon juice
pepper and salt to taste
¼ pint (150 ml) water

FRESH HERBS AND A TANGY lemon and vinegar sauce suit calf's liver very well. Their flavours cut the richness of the meat and the whole dish tastes quite superb. Take care not to overcook calf's liver: it is delicate and tender and is best served slightly rare. Serve with boiled new potatoes and freshly cooked vegetables, such as broccoli, beans and carrots.

METHOD
Cut the liver into slices of a good and equal shape (if this has not already been done by the butcher). Dip them in flour and fry them in a little butter until they are a good colour – about 2 minutes on each side according to the thickness of the liver. When they are done, put them on a dish and keep hot. Chop the herbs very fine, put them in the frying pan with a little more butter and 1 teaspoon flour, stir well, then add the remaining ingredients. Stir and simmer gently until the herbs are done, then pour over the liver.

NOTES
Calf's liver Mrs Beeton said to 'procure a calf's liver as white as possible', by which she meant that it should be very pale in colour. The palest and best liver is from very young calves which have only been fed on milk. Its flavour is sweet and delicate and it has a melt-in-the-mouth texture. If calves have been fed on grass, their livers are darker and not so sweet. You can use the less expensive lamb's liver for this dish, but it will have a stronger flavour.
Savoury herbs Sage is the traditional herb to use with liver, and it goes well with the parsley that is also mentioned.

Mrs Beeton writes

"A VERY VEAL DINNER – At a dinner given by Lord Polkemmet,
a Scotch nobleman and judge, his guests saw, when the covers were
removed, that the fare consisted of veal broth, a roasted fillet of veal,
veal cutlets, a veal pie, a calf's head, and calf's foot jelly.
The judge, observing the surprise of his guests, volunteered
an explanation: 'Ou, ay, it's a cauf; when we kill a beast, we just
eat up ae side, and doun the tither'."

Calf's Liver and Bacon ⌒

CLASSIC FRIED LIVER AND BACON is given a special touch by being served with a tangy lemon sauce and stuffing balls. For a substantial evening meal, mashed potatoes go well with this dish, plus a simple fresh vegetable like carrots, cabbage or green beans.

METHOD

Cut the liver into 8 or 12 slices. Fry the bacon first, put it on a hot dish and keep hot. Fry the liver in the fat which comes from the bacon, after seasoning it with pepper and salt and dredging over it a very little flour. Turn the liver occasionally to prevent it burning. When done – after about 4 minutes – lay it round the dish with a piece of bacon between each. Pour away the bacon fat, put in a small piece of butter, dredge in a little flour and add the lemon juice and water. Bring to the boil and pour it in the middle of the dish. It may be garnished with slices of cut lemon or forcemeat balls.

NOTES

Forcemeat balls These are very easy to make with Forcemeat (page 340), a breadcrumb-based stuffing flavoured with lemon, herbs and cayenne. If you don't want to make your own forcemeat, buy ready made fresh stuffing or use a plain pork sausagemeat, which also goes well with liver and bacon, and add these flavourings to it yourself. To make the balls, roll large walnut-sized pieces of forcemeat, stuffing or sausagemeat in wet hands, dust them lightly with flour and fry in hot oil until golden brown and crisp on all sides. Drain on kitchen paper before serving.

Time 5 to 10 minutes
Sufficient for 4 or 6 persons
Seasonable from March to
    October

INGREDIENTS
1 lb (500 g) calf's liver
8 or 12 slices of bacon
pepper and salt to taste
flour
a small piece of butter
2 tablespoons lemon juice
¼ pint (150 ml) water

CHAPTER 4

Poultry & Game

Mrs Beeton included poultry and game under the general heading of 'Meat Cookery'. Any one of these meats might be served as a main course at 'family dinners', after a first course of either soup or fish and before a hot pudding or pastry. At formal dinners, poultry or game was served after the first course, either as an *entrée* or a second course.

In 'Fowl as Food', on the opening page of the chicken recipes in the original book, Mrs Beeton sang the praises of chicken.

'Well-fattened and tender, a fowl is to the cook what the canvas is to the painter; for do we not see it served boiled, roasted, fried, *fricasséed*, hashed, hot, cold, whole, dismembered, boned, broiled, stuffed, on dishes and in pies - always handy and ever acceptable?'

Nowadays, chicken is chicken, and different breeds are seldom sold as such. This was not the case in Victorian times.

'The common or barn-door fowl is one of the most delicate varieties, and at Dorking in Surrey the breed is brought to great perfection. The English counties most productive in poultry are Surrey, Sussex, Norfolk, Herts, Devon and Somerset.'

Nowadays we choose chicken because it is a widely available and inexpensive source of low-fat protein. It is also quick and easy to cook and extremely versatile. In Mrs Beeton's day it was appreciated for its versatility, and for another reason as well.

'It has been the opinion of the medical faculty of all ages and all countries that the flesh of the young chicken is the most delicate and easy to digest of all animal food. It is less alkalescent than the flesh of any other animal, and its entire freedom from any irritating quality renders it a fit dish for the ailing, or those whose stomachs are naturally weak.'

Mrs Beeton gave recipes for a huge variety of poultry and game and they were often accompanied by handsome illustrations of specific breeds, including many birds and animals that are seldom seen or sent to table these days. Guinea fowl and pigeon were more popular then than now, so too were blackcock, landrail, plover, ptarmigan, teal, snipe, widgeon, woodcock, leveret, rabbit, hare and venison. There were even recipes for larks and wheatears.

She drew the line at guinea pigs.

'Their flesh, although eatable, is decidedly unfit for food. They have been tasted, however, we presume by some enthusiast eager to advance the cause of science, or by some eccentric epicure in search of new pleasure for his table.'

Chicken with Mushroom Sauce

Time about 1 hour

Sufficient for 4 or 5 persons

Seasonable all year round

INGREDIENTS

1 large chicken weighing
  about 4 lb (1.8 kg)
2 to 3 tablespoons melted
  butter or oil
seasoning to taste of pepper
  and salt
FOR SAUCE
2 handfuls of button
  mushrooms
1 slice of lean ham
a small piece of butter the
  size of a walnut
¾ pint (450 ml) thickened
  gravy
1 teaspoon lemon juice
½ teaspoon caster sugar

IN THE ORIGINAL RECIPE the chicken was first roasted, then broiled over the fire, but this seems unnecessarily complicated and time-consuming, so the method has been simplified. For more flavour, add a little crushed garlic to the mushrooms, and for a more modern presentation, sprinkle the chicken and sauce with finely chopped chervil or flat-leaf parsley.

METHOD

Cut the chicken into quarters and place them on a rack in a roasting tin. Brush the chicken with melted butter or oil and season with pepper and salt. Roast for about 40 minutes, keeping the chicken well basted. Have ready some mushroom sauce made in the following manner. Chop the mushrooms and ham and put them into a saucepan with a small piece of butter, a seasoning of pepper and salt and the gravy. Simmer these gently for ½ hour, then add the lemon juice and sugar. Serve the chicken with the sauce poured over and around.

The oven should be preheated to 375°F (190°C) Gas 5.

NOTES

Chicken You can buy joints instead of a whole chicken, and both legs and wings are suitable. If you prefer chicken breasts, make sure they are on the bone, or the tender flesh will dry out.

Mushrooms 2 small handfuls weigh about ¼ lb (125 g). You can use ordinary button mushrooms, but chestnut mushrooms or one of the exotic varieties like shiitake will have more flavour.

Thickened gravy A Cheap Gravy (page 197) would be suitable, or you could use a well-reduced chicken stock and a few tablespoons double cream, which will thicken the mushroom juices as they reduce during cooking.

Mrs Beeton writes

"STOCKING THE FOWL-HOUSE – Crowing hens, and those
that have large combs, are generally looked on with mistrust,
but this is mere silliness and superstition – though it is possible that
a spruce young cock would as much object to a spouse with such
peculiar addictions, as a young fellow of our own species would
to a damsel who whistled and who wore whiskers."

Curried Chicken ೨

COMPARED TO MODERN RECIPES with their long and daunting lists of spices, this recipe is very simple, but it tastes very good nevertheless – and there is less work to do. If you want to embellish it a little, you can add finely chopped garlic and chillies with the onions and sprinkle the curry with fresh coriander before serving. Boiled rice is the best accompaniment, with sweet and spicy side dishes of mango chutney and lime pickle, two condiments which were very popular during the days of the Raj.

METHOD

Cut up the chicken into joints. Slice the onions. Peel, core and finely chop the apple. Put the butter into a pan with the chicken, onions and apple. Fry until pale brown, add the gravy and cook gently for 20 minutes. Mix the curry powder and flour with a little of the gravy until quite smooth and stir this into the other ingredients in the pan. Simmer for rather more than ½ hour. Just before serving, add the hot cream and lemon juice. Serve with boiled rice, which may be heaped lightly on a dish by itself or put around the curry as a border.

NOTES

Chicken To cut down on fat, remove the skin from the chicken before cooking. If you prefer curry 'off the bone', use boneless skinless chicken thighs, cut into large chunks. You can also use chicken breasts, but they will only need cooking for a total of 20 minutes.

White veal gravy Use chicken stock.

Curry powder was often a hand-ground mix of different spices in Victorian times – Mrs Beeton gives a recipe for Indian Curry Powder on page 343 – but you can buy good ready made blends now. Indian brands are usually excellent. If you like a hot curry, go for a Madras curry powder; a north Indian garam masala is milder and perfumed with scented spices like cinnamon, nutmeg and cloves. It is a good idea to stir the curry powder and flour into the fried chicken mixture and cook it briefly before adding the stock.

Cream Double cream is used to enrich curries and to temper the fieriness of chillies and other spices.

Time 1 to 1¼ hours
Sufficient for 3 or 4 persons
Seasonable in the winter or
at any time

INGREDIENTS

1 chicken weighing about
4 lb (1.8 kg)
3 onions
1 apple
2 oz (60 g) butter
1½ pints (900 ml) white veal
gravy
1 tablespoon curry powder
1 tablespoon flour
4 tablespoons hot cream
1 tablespoon lemon juice

Mrs Beeton writes
———
"This curry may be made
of cold chicken, but
undressed meat will be
found far superior."

✆ Chicken Fricassée

Time 2 hours
Sufficient for 4 to 6 persons
Seasonable at any time

INGREDIENTS
2 small chickens weighing
   about 2½ lb (1.2 kg) each
   or 1 large one weighing
   about 4 lb (1.8 kg)
a bunch each of parsley and
   spring onions, chopped
a strip of lemon peel
1 clove
2 blades of mace
1 chopped shallot
1 bay leaf
salt and white pepper to
   taste
3 oz (90 g) butter
a little flour
¼ pint (150 ml) cream
pounded mace and cayenne
   pepper to taste
the yolks of 3 eggs

THIS IS A CLASSIC French recipe that begins by using the trimmings from the chicken to make a proper stock. This may seem a little complicated, but it doesn't take long and the flavour of the finished dish makes it well worthwhile, particularly for a special occasion. If you are short of time, you can cut corners by using chicken breast joints and ready made chicken stock.

METHOD
Remove the skin from the chickens, cut them into joints and blanch in boiling water for 2 or 3 minutes. Take them out and immerse them in cold water to render them white. Put the trimmings from the chicken into a saucepan with the parsley, onions, lemon peel, clove, mace, shallot, bay leaf and a seasoning of salt and pepper. Add to these the water that the chicken was blanched in and simmer gently for rather more than 1 hour. Have ready another saucepan and put in the joints of chicken with the butter. Dredge them with flour and let them get hot, but do not brown them much. Moisten the fricassée with the stock made from the trimmings and cook very gently for ½ hour. Lift the chicken into another saucepan, skim the sauce, reduce it quickly over a high heat by letting it boil fast, then strain it and add the cream and a seasoning of pounded mace and cayenne. Bring to the boil, pour over the chicken and cook gently for another 10 minutes. When ready to serve, stir the well beaten yolks of 3 eggs into the sauce. These should not be put in until the last moment, then the sauce should not boil or it will instantly curdle.

NOTES
Cream Double cream can be used for a very rich sauce. Crème fraîche is an alternative with a lower fat content and a tangy flavour.
Egg yolks With no thought for their fat content, Mrs Beeton used 3 egg yolks to enrich and thicken the sauce. You can use just 1 or 2 egg yolks, if you prefer.

Mrs Beeton writes

"A few button mushrooms stewed with the fowl
are by many persons considered an improvement."

Fried Chicken ᔰ

Mrs Beeton gave two recipes for fried chicken using 'the remains of cold roast fowls'. Her recipe works just as well with fresh chicken pieces, especially drumsticks and thighs, and the version here uses them in a modern adaptation of the original dish. Fried parsley – sprigs of parsley lowered into hot oil and deep-fried until dark green and crisp – is a classic French garnish for fried chicken. It can be omitted, however.

Method

Steep the chicken for an hour in a little vinegar with salt, cayenne and the chopped shallots. Dip the pieces into the egg yolk, sprinkle over the bread crumbs mixed with the mace and lemon peel and a good pinch each of salt and cayenne. Fry in hot deep oil until light brown – about 15 to 20 minutes. Pile them high in the dish and garnish with fried parsley or rolled bacon. When approved, a sauce or gravy may be served with them.

Notes

Chicken For a less fatty dish, remove the skin before steeping the chicken pieces. The vinegar (white wine vinegar for preference) is used to tenderize and whiten the flesh and to get rid of impurities. You can omit it if you like or use lemon juice instead – you will need 2 to 3 tablespoons. To make a marinade, add the same quantity of olive oil.

Bread crumbs Fresh or dried crumbs can be used.

Rolled bacon This refers to bacon rolls, made by stretching rindless streaky bacon rashers with the flat of a large knife blade, then rolling them up and threading them on skewers. They should be grilled for 5 to 10 minutes, turning them once or twice, until they are crisp and cooked through.

Sauce or gravy American-style Southern fried chicken is traditionally served with a gravy made from chicken stock and cream, so Mrs Beeton's suggestion is a good one. You may prefer the easier option of serving the fried chicken more simply, with lemon wedges for squeezing. It is good served hot or cold.

Time ½ hour plus steeping
Sufficient for 4 to 6 persons
Seasonable at any time

INGREDIENTS
8 to 12 chicken pieces, preferably drumsticks
a little vinegar
salt and cayenne pepper to taste
4 finely chopped shallots
the yolks of several eggs
6 oz (175g) bread crumbs
1 blade of mace, pounded
½ teaspoon grated lemon peel
oil for deep-frying
fried parsley or rolled bacon to garnish

Poulet à la Marengo

Time 1 hour
Sufficient for 4 persons
Seasonable at any time

INGREDIENTS

1 chicken weighing 3–3½ lb
   (1.4–1.6 kg)
4 tablespoons oil
1 tablespoon flour
about 1 pint (600 ml)
   Medium Stock (page 334)
   or water
about 20 button mushrooms
a very small piece of garlic
1 teaspoon caster sugar
salt and pepper to taste

THIS CLASSIC FRENCH DISH was created for Napoleon in 1800, to celebrate his successful defeat of the Italians in the Battle of Marengo. Mrs Beeton claimed she was faithful to his chef's original, but there are many more fanciful interpretations in other cookery books, most of which include tomatoes, cognac and freshly caught crayfish, which are not in this recipe. Mrs Beeton also omitted wine from her recipe, despite stressing its importance when talking about the origins of the dish. It is interesting to note that Napoleon's French chef was forced to use oil instead of the butter he was accustomed to. This would have been olive oil.

METHOD

Cut the chicken into 8 or 10 pieces. Put them with the oil into a pan and brown them over a moderate heat. Dredge in the flour and when that is browned, pour in 1 pint (600 ml) stock or water. Bring it slowly to the boil and skim off any fat as it rises to the top. Add the mushrooms, crushed garlic and sugar and season with salt and pepper. Simmer very slowly for 30 to 40 minutes, adding more stock or water if necessary. Take out the chicken and mushrooms and arrange pyramidically on a dish, with the inferior joints at the bottom. Reduce the sauce by boiling it quickly over a high heat, keeping it stirred until sufficiently thick to coat the back of a spoon. Pour the sauce over the chicken and serve.

NOTES

Chicken You can use chicken pieces instead of a whole chicken. Skinless thighs are a good choice, and the cooking time will be the same. If you prefer to use chicken breasts, choose ones with the bone in, and cook them for 20 minutes.

Medium stock is very meaty. Chicken stock can be used instead, preferably homemade or one of the good-quality fresh stocks sold in the chiller cabinets at supermarkets.

VARIATIONS

Flambé the chicken in about 4 tablespoons brandy before dredging it with flour.

Use half dry white wine and half stock.

Add about ½ lb (250 g) tomatoes, peeled and chopped, with the mushrooms.

Finish off the dish by adding about ½ lb (250 g) crayfish or prawns in their shells to the sauce at the end.

Mrs Beeton writes

"A LA MARENGO – On the evening of the battle
the first consul was very hungry after the agitation of the day,
and a fowl was ordered with all expedition. The fowl
was procured, but there was no butter at hand, and unluckily
none could be found in the neighbourhood.
There was oil in abundance, however; and the cook having
poured a certain quantity into his skillet, put in the fowl,
with a clove of garlic and other seasoning, with a little
white wine, the best the country afforded; he then
garnished it with mushrooms, and served it up hot.
Every since, a fowl à la Marengo is a favourite dish
with all lovers of good cheer."

✑ Chicken Ragoût

Time 1 hour
Sufficient for 4 persons
Seasonable at any time

INGREDIENTS

2 small chickens weighing
about 2½ lb (1.25 kg) each
or 1 large one weighing
about 4 lb (1.8 kg)
3 chopped shallots
2 blades of mace
a bunch of savoury herbs
2 or 3 slices of lean ham
1 chopped onion
1 pint (600 ml) stock or
water
1 oz (30 g) butter
about 2 teaspoons flour
1 tablespoon lemon juice
½ teaspoon caster sugar
pepper and salt to taste
Croûtons (page 344) to
serve

THE FRENCH WORD *ragoût* is used to describe a light stew. It comes from the verb *ragoûter (re-à-gouter)*, which means to stimulate or bring back the appetite. When a dish is described as *ragoûtant* it means it is appetizing and very delicious. Mrs Beeton's original recipe used leftover cold roast chicken, but most classic French *ragoûts* are based on fresh meat, poultry, fish or vegetables. Fresh chicken is used here, and the original recipe has been adapted accordingly.

METHOD

Remove the skin from both chickens, cut them into joints and blanch these in boiling water for 2 or 3 minutes. Take them out and immerse them in cold water to render them white. Put the chicken into a pan with the shallots, mace, herbs, ham, onion and the stock or water. Simmer gently for 40 minutes, then strain off the cooking liquid. Put a small piece of butter into a pan. When melted, dredge in sufficient flour to dry up the butter and stir it over a moderate heat. Whisk in the strained liquid, then boil for a few minutes, stirring frequently. Squeeze in the lemon juice, add the sugar and a seasoning of pepper and salt and heat through without boiling.

Arrange the pieces of chicken on a dish and strain the sauce over them. Garnish with croûtons and serve.

NOTES

Chicken Blanching is a method used to rid the chicken of any impurities, but it is not strictly necessary, especially as the skin is removed. Simply rinse the skinned pieces under the cold tap, then pat them dry with kitchen paper. If you prefer, you can use ready cut joints rather than jointing whole chickens yourself. Legs, wings and thighs are best suited to a stew of this kind.

Savoury herbs Use flat-leaf parsley, chervil or tarragon.

Croûtons are the classic garnish for a *ragoût*. For an attractive presentation, make large triangular ones, which the French call *croûtes*, and dip one of their points in finely chopped parsley. Stand them around the edge of the dish with the parsley points facing upwards.

Chicken à la Mayonnaise ∞

THIS IS A VERY SIMPLE SALAD, but good nevertheless, especially if you use a homemade mayonnaise. You can buy whole chickens ready roasted from the supermarket, or you could use breast pieces. It is also a good recipe for chunks of cooked chicken, which can be tossed in the mayonnaise and sprinkled with herbs.

METHOD

Cut the chicken into neat joints and lay them in a deep dish, piling them high in the centre. Sauce the chicken with mayonnaise and garnish the dish with young lettuces cut in halves, watercress, endive and hard-boiled eggs. The eggs may be sliced in rings or laid on the dish whole, cutting off a piece of the white at the bottom to make the egg stand upright. The sauce should not be poured over the chicken until the moment of serving.

NOTES

Mayonnaise Mrs Beeton's recipe on page 231 is rich and thick, and perfectly plain. If you like, you can add chopped fresh tarragon or other herbs to it, and/or finely grated lemon peel.

Young lettuces Use small lettuces, such as Little Gem, or lettuce hearts.

Endive is sometimes confused with chicory, because the French and the Americans use the name endive for the bitter tasting bullet-shaped vegetable that is known as chicory in England. In this recipe Mrs Beeton was referring to the curly, loose-leaved vegetable which she variously described as 'beautiful in appearance' and 'remarkably pretty'.

Time ¼ hour to assemble
  the dish
Sufficient for 4 to 6 persons
Seasonable from April to
  September

INGREDIENTS
a cold roast chicken
Mayonnaise (page 231)
2 young lettuces
a bunch of watercress
1 endive
4 hard-boiled eggs

Mrs Beeton writes

"All kinds of cold meat
and solid fish may be
dressed *à la mayonnaise*,
and make excellent
luncheon or
supper dishes."

❧ Roast Chicken

Time 1½ to 1¾ hours
Sufficient for 4 or 6 persons
Seasonable all the year

INGREDIENTS
1 chicken weighing 3–3½ lb
  (1.4–1.6 kg)
about 1 oz (30 g) softened
  butter
a little flour
salt and pepper to taste
good brown gravy and Bread
  Sauce (page 202) to serve

MRS BEETON SAID TO ROAST OVER 'a bright clear fire' in her basic recipe for 'Roast Fowls', so this recipe has been brought up to date, but it is still very simple, like the original. She recommended mushroom, oyster or egg sauce as 'very suitable accompaniments' in addition to gravy and bread sauce. She also gave another recipe for roast chicken called *Poulet aux Cressons*, in which a simple roast chicken was served on a bed of watercress sprinkled with a little salt and vinegar. A little gravy was poured over and the rest was served in a gravy boat.

METHOD

Put the chicken in a roasting tin, brush it all over with butter and sprinkle with a little flour and salt and pepper. Cover the breast with a sheet of buttered paper. Roast the chicken for 1¼ to 1½ hours, basting it frequently. Ten minutes before serving, remove the paper, dredge the chicken with a little more flour and baste well with the cooking juices, adding a little more butter if necessary. Serve with good brown gravy, a little of which should be poured over the chicken, and a bowl of well-made bread sauce.

The oven should be preheated to 400°F (200°C) Gas 6.

NOTES

Trussing Detailed instructions were given in the original recipe. A well-trussed bird keeps its shape better than an untrussed bird during roasting, but most chickens that are sold these days have a very good shape, with their legs tied or clipped together ready for the oven. Trussing is only necessary if you have to untie the bird to stuff the breast end (see Variations opposite).

Testing for doneness To be sure that the bird is properly cooked by the end of the roasting time, insert a fork between the inner thigh and body, pulling the leg slightly away from the bird. The juices will run clear, not pink or red, when the bird is done. If they are pink or red, return the bird to the oven for a further 5 to 10 minutes, then test again.

Gravy Use the recipe for A Cheap Gravy on page 197.

Bread sauce is a traditional accompaniment to English roast chicken.

VARIATIONS

If you like, you can stuff the breast end of the chicken or bake some stuffing in a separate dish. For stuffing recipes, see pages 340-342.

For more succulent, tasty meat, insert a few lemon or onion quarters in the cavity of the bird before cooking. Roast the bird upside down for the first 30 minutes, then for a further 30 minutes on each side and finally breast side up.

To make the breast meat moist, insert softened butter between the skin and the flesh of the breast and roast the bird breast side up. The butter can be plain, seasoned with salt and black pepper or flavoured with chopped herbs, garlic or grated lemon rind.

Mrs Beeton writes

"The wings, breast and merrythought [wishbone] are esteemed the prime parts of a fowl, and are usually served to the ladies of the company, to whom legs, except as a matter of paramount necessity, should not be given."

"GRAVY-KETTLE – This is a utensil which will not be found in every kitchen; but it is a useful one where it is necessary to keep gravies hot for the purpose of pouring over various dishes as they are cooking. It is made of copper, and should, consequently, be heated over the hot plate, if there be one, or a charcoal stove."

✍ Croquettes of Chicken

Time ½ hour plus chilling
Sufficient for 2 to 3 persons
Seasonable at any time

INGREDIENTS
about 6 oz (175 g) cooked
 chicken
3 or 4 chopped shallots
1 oz (30 g) butter
1 teaspoon flour
½ teaspoon caster sugar
pepper, salt and pounded
 mace to taste
about ¼ pint (150 ml) thick
 White Sauce (page 230)
the yolks of 2 eggs
a whole egg
about 2 oz (60 g) bread
 crumbs
oil for frying

MRS BEETON'S RECIPE USED 'the remains of cold roast fowls' and you can use leftover roast chicken or turkey if you have any, or buy ready cooked chicken breasts from the supermarket. Mrs Beeton suggested serving them 'on a border of mashed potatoes, with gravy or sauce in the centre', but you may prefer to serve them with a salad or French fries. Made into bite-sized balls, they are very good as a pre-dinner nibble with drinks, or as an appetizer.

METHOD

Mince the chicken, carefully removing all the skin and any bones. Fry the shallots in the butter, add the minced chicken, dredge in the flour and add the sugar, pepper, salt and mace and sufficient white sauce to moisten. Stir in the well-beaten yolks of 2 eggs and set it to cool. Make the mixture into balls, coat them in the whole egg and bread crumbs and fry them in hot oil until a nice brown colour – about 5 minutes on each side.

NOTES

White sauce This needs to be thick enough to bind the other ingredients together. Follow the recipe given on page 230, but use 1 oz (30 g) each of butter and flour and ¼ pint (150 ml) milk.

Mincing If you don't have a mincer, the chicken can be finely chopped using a food processor or by hand. The skin should not be included.

Chilling The mixture will benefit from being chilled in the refrigerator after cooling and before shaping. Chill for 30 minutes to 1 hour. When the croquettes have been coated in egg and breadcrumbs, arrange them on a plate and chill them again. This will help to ensure that the coating is crisp after the croquettes have been fried in hot oil.

Chicken Sauté with Peas ∾

ALTHOUGH MRS BEETON USED 'the remains of cold roast fowl', this is an excellent recipe for boneless breasts of fresh chicken. The combination of succulent nuggets of chicken and new season's peas is excellent. For the very best flavour, buy organic or free-range chicken. A sauté is meant to be a simple pan-fried dish (it comes from the French verb *sauter* meaning to jump or toss), but if you prefer more sauce than is suggested here, increase the flour by another teaspoon and use more stock.

METHOD

Cut the chicken into nice pieces, removing all of the skin and any bones. Melt the butter in a sauté pan and sauté the chicken until it is a nice brown colour, previously sprinkling it with pepper, salt and pounded mace. Dredge in the flour and shake the ingredients well round, then add the stock and peas and simmer until both the chicken and peas are tender, which will be in about 20 minutes. Stir in the sugar and serve, placing the chicken around the edge of the dish and the peas in the middle.

NOTES

Weak stock Use chicken stock, either homemade or a good-quality brand from the chiller cabinet at the supermarket. There are very few other ingredients in this recipe, which makes the flavour of the stock quite important. If you like, you can use some dry white wine instead of some of the stock.

Peas Shelled peas were usually measured by volume in Mrs Beeton's day. For this amount, you will need about 1¼ lb (625 g) peas in their pods. If you prefer to use frozen peas or petits pois, it is easy enough to pour these into a measuring jug. They should be added to the chicken for the last 10 minutes.

Serving suggestion Sprinkle a little chopped fresh flat-leaf parsley over the dish at the end of cooking.

Mrs Beeton writes

"When liked, mushrooms may be substituted for the peas."

Time ½ hour
Sufficient for 4 persons
Seasonable from June to
August

INGREDIENTS
4 chicken breasts
2 oz (60 g) butter
pepper, salt and pounded
mace to taste
2 teaspoons flour
½ pint (300 ml) weak stock
1 pint (600 ml) shelled
green peas
1 teaspoon caster sugar

๛ *Chicken Pillau*

Time 1¾ to 2 hours
Sufficient for 6 persons
Seasonable at any time

INGREDIENTS

1 chicken weighing 3–3½ lb
   (1.4–1.6 kg)
4 pints (2.4 litres) chicken
   stock
1 tablespoon cardamom
   pods
2 tablespoons coriander
   seeds
1 tablespoon cloves
2 teaspoons allspice berries
1 tablespoon mace blades
3 cinnamon sticks
4 teaspoons whole
   peppercorns
1 lb (500 g) best Patna rice
2 oz (60 g) butter
4 onions
oil for deep-frying
6 thin slices of bacon
2 hard-boiled eggs

DESCRIBED BY MRS BEETON as an Indian dish 'based on M. Soyer's Recipe', we might expect this recipe to be Franco-Indian, along the lines of today's fusion cuisine, but French-born Alexis Soyer was the chef at the Reform Club in London and had worked for the British government and the army during the Crimean War. This recipe was therefore influenced more by Raj-style cooking than French *haute cuisine*. Originally, the rice was cooked with the whole chicken – but the recipe has been adapted to make the dish more manageable – and easier to serve. The onion, egg and bacon garnish was traditional in Victorian times, but this can be omitted and a simple garnish of chopped fresh coriander used instead.

METHOD

Put the chicken into a saucepan with the stock. Pound the spices thoroughly in a mortar, tie them in a piece of muslin and put them in with the chicken. Bring to the boil, cover and simmer slowly until the chicken is done – about 1 hour. Remove the chicken from the pan. Well wash the rice and put it into a large saucepan with the butter. Keep stirring over a low heat until the rice is lightly browned, then add to it 1½ pints (900 ml) of the liquid in which the chicken was cooking. Cook until the rice is quite tender and almost dry – about 20 minutes. Cut the onions into slices, sprinkle them with flour and fry them in hot oil without breaking them until they are a nice brown colour. Have ready the slices of bacon curled and grilled and the eggs boiled hard. Remove the chicken meat from the carcass and cut it into bite-sized pieces. When the rice is done, add the chicken and toss to mix the rice and chicken together. Arrange the rice and chicken on a dish in the form of a pyramid. Garnish with the fried onions and bacon, and the hard-boiled eggs cut into quarters. Serve very hot.

NOTES

Patna rice is long grain rice, named after Patna in India. You can still buy it by name in some shops, but basmati, the 'king of rice' will make a better pillau. The best basmati comes from the foothills of the Himalayas. It has delicate, slender grains that are slightly perfumed.

Bacon Mrs Beeton's 'slices of bacon curled and grilled' are what we know simply as bacon rolls. These can be made by stretching rindless streaky bacon rashers with the flat of a large knife blade, rolling them up, threading them on skewers and then grilling them for 5 to 10 minutes, turning them once or twice until the bacon rolls are crisp and cooked through.

Mrs Beeton writes

"VARIETIES OF RICE – Of the varieties of rice
brought to our market, that from Bengal is chiefly
of the species denominated cargo rice, and is of a coarse
reddish-brown cast, but peculiarly sweet and large-grained;
it does not readily separate from the husk, but it is preferred
by the natives to all others. Patna rice is more esteemed in Europe,
and is of very superior quality; it is small-grained, rather long
and wiry, and is remarkably white. The Carolina rice is considered
as the best, and is likewise the dearest in London."

✆ *Duck Ragoût*

Time 1¾ hours
Sufficient for 3 to 4 persons
Seasonable from November
  to February; ducklings
  from April to August

INGREDIENTS
1 large duck weighing about
  4 lb (1.8 kg)
pepper and salt to taste
good beef gravy
2 onions
4 sage leaves
a few leaves of lemon thyme

THE COOKING METHOD HERE is an unusual one – first the duck is roasted, then it is stewed. Duck is a fatty bird, and the idea behind this method is to pour the excess fat off the duck after roasting, so that when the stew is cooked the sauce will not be too fatty. Mrs Beeton thickened the sauce with butter and flour before serving, but this would add more fat, so the thickening has been omitted here. For an attractive presentation, quarter the duck after roasting and serve it on individual plates with the sauce spooned over. A slice of lemon on each serving and a few sprigs of lemon thyme would make an attractive garnish.

METHOD

Season the duck inside and out with pepper and salt. Roast it on a rack in a roasting tin for about 20 minutes until it acquires a nice brown colour. Put the duck into a pan with sufficient well-seasoned beef gravy to cover it. Slice the onions and finely chop the sage and lemon thyme. Fry the onions in a little of the duck fat and add these to the gravy with the sage and thyme. Simmer gently until the duck is tender – about 1¼ hours. Remove the duck, strain and skim the gravy, then boil until thickened. Pour over the duck and serve.

The oven should be preheated to 425°F (220°C) Gas 7.

NOTES

Duck fat To help rid the duck of excess fat, prick the breast all over with a fork or skewer and roast the duck upside down on the rack. At

the end of roasting, the liquid fat in the tin can be poured off, cooled, then saved in the refrigerator for future frying if you like. It is very popular in France, where its flavour is much appreciated.

Good beef gravy In Victorian times there would have been a pot of gravy on or near the kitchen stove at all times. A Cheap Gravy (page 197) can be used, although you may prefer a chicken stock. To make your own chicken stock, use the recipe for White Stock (page 335).

Lemon thyme Thyme is a highly aromatic herb that helps with the digestion of fatty foods like duck. Lemon thyme is just one of the many varieties that you can grow (it is unlikely that you will see it in the shops). Its citrus flavour also helps to offset the fattiness of duck, so it is most appropriate here.

Mrs Beeton writes

"When in season, about 1½ pints of young green peas, boiled separately and put in the *ragoût*, very much improve this dish."

"VARIETIES OF DUCKS – In connection with their value for table, light-coloured ducks are always of milder flavour than those that are dark-coloured, the white Aylesbury's being general favourites. Ducks reared exclusively on vegetable diet will have a whiter and more delicate flesh than those allowed to feed an animal offal; while the flesh of birds fattened on the latter food, will be firmer than that of those which have only partaken of food of a vegetable nature."

ᦂ *Roast Duck*

Time 2¼ hours
Sufficient for 6 or 7 persons
Seasonable ducklings from
    April to August; ducks from
    November to February

INGREDIENTS
Sage and Onion Stuffing
    (page 342)
2 ducks, each weighing
    about 4 lb (1.8 kg)
a little flour
gravy and Apple Sauce
    (page 200) to serve

MRS BEETON WAS VERY SENSIBLE to recommend roasting two birds for 6 or 7 servings of duck. The amount of meat to bone and fat on a duck is far less than on a chicken. Duck is a very rich meat, however, so portion sizes need not be large. She also recommended a dish of green peas as an accompaniment, but you may prefer mangetout or sugarsnaps. Other suitable side dishes are roast potatoes and carrots.

METHOD

Make a stuffing of sage and onion sufficient for one duck. Leave the other duck unstuffed, as the flavour of stuffing is not liked by everybody. Roast the ducks on a rack in a roasting tin for 1¾ hours, keeping them well basted the whole time they are cooking. A few minutes before serving, dredge them lightly with flour to make them froth and look plump. Serve hot and quickly, with a good brown gravy poured around the ducks but not over them, and a little of the same in a small tureen or sauce boat.

The oven should be preheated to 375°F (190°C) Gas 5.

NOTES

Sage and onion stuffing is traditionally served with fatty meats like duck, geese and pork because sage is known to help with their digestion. Put some stuffing in the neck end of the bird and secure it with a small metal skewer, then bake the rest in a separate dish for 30 to 40 minutes while the ducks are roasting. If you prefer you can bake all the stuffing separately; you can also buy it ready made, in which case, follow the cooking instructions on the packet.

Prick the duck breasts all over with a fork or skewer and sprinkle the skin liberally with salt (this will help make it crisp). Drain off the excess fat once or twice during roasting, to reduce the likelihood of it spitting and making the oven dirty.

Gravy Mrs Beeton's recipe for A Cheap Gravy (page 197) is suitable, or you may prefer to make your own favourite gravy.

Apple sauce is traditional with roast duck in England, but nowadays duck is often served with cranberry sauce instead.

THE PAIRING OF DUCK AND PEAS has been popular for a long time in this country. Recipes like this one appeared in seventeenth and eighteenth century cookery books, and the dish was said to be a favourite of Queen Anne's. Mrs Beeton's recipe called for cold roast duck, but here fresh duck is used with a slight change of method to make the dish less fatty and rich. Spring onions and peas help to offset the richness of duck, and if you serve the finished dish sprinkled with chopped fresh herbs at the end, this will serve the same purpose. Parsley or coriander are the best herbs to use.

METHOD

Cut up the duck into joints. Roughly chop the ham or bacon and the spring onions. Put the duck in a pan with the ham or bacon and cook until the duck is brown – about 10 minutes. Pour off the excess fat, then dredge the duck in the flour and stir this well in before adding the stock. Put in the onions, parsley and cloves and when it has simmered for 15 minutes, add the young green peas. Cook gently for about ½ hour or until the duck is tender. Season with cayenne, salt and sugar. Take out the duck and serve it round the edge of a dish with the peas in the middle.

NOTES

Stock   In the original recipe a 'thin gravy' was specified. Chicken stock would be the best substitute, because it is light. If you make your own stock, make sure to skim off all the fat before using.

Peas   Buy 1¼ lb (625 g) peas in their pods to give you about ½ lb (250 g) shelled peas. If you prefer, you can use ½ lb (250 g) frozen peas or petits pois and add them to the duck for the last 10 minutes.

Mrs Beeton writes

"THE AYLESBURY DUCK – The white Aylesbury duck is, and deservedly, a universal favourite. In parts of Buckinghamshire, this member of the duck family is bred on an extensive scale; not on plains and commons, however, as might be naturally imagined, but in the abodes of the cottagers. Round the walls of the living-rooms, and of the bedroom even, are fixed rows of wooden boxes, lined with hay; and it is the business of the wife and children to nurse and comfort the feathered lodgers, to feed the little ducklings, and to take the old ones out for airing."

Time 1¼ hours
Sufficient for 3 to 4 persons
Seasonable from June to
   August

INGREDIENTS
1 duck weighing about 4 lb
   (1.8 kg)
3 or 4 slices of lean ham or
   bacon
a small bunch of spring
   onions
1 tablespoon flour
2 pints (1.2 litres) stock
3 sprigs of parsley
3 cloves
1 pint (600 ml) shelled
   young green peas
cayenne pepper and salt
   to taste
1 teaspoon caster sugar

Mrs Beeton on the arrangement and economy of the kitchen

KITCHENS WERE INVARIABLY LARGE IN VICTORIAN DAYS AND STAFF WERE EMPLOYED EVEN IN MODEST MIDDLE CLASS HOMES. COOKING WAS DONE ON A COAL-FIRED RANGE AND THERE WERE NO REFRIGERATORS OR FREEZERS, SO MUCH OF MRS BEETON'S ADVICE ON KITCHEN MANAGEMENT AND CLEANING DOES NOT APPLY IN A MODERN KITCHEN. THE FOLLOWING QUOTATIONS FROM THE THIRD CHAPTER OF THE ORIGINAL BOOK, ENTITLED 'ARRANGEMENT AND ECONOMY OF THE KITCHEN' ARE INTERESTING FROM A HISTORICAL POINT OF VIEW; THEY ALSO ILLUSTRATE THE SOUND AND SENSIBLE ADVICE THAT MRS BEETON GAVE HER READERS, SOME OF WHICH IS STILL PERTINENT TODAY.

IT MUST BE REMEMBERED that it [the kitchen] is the great laboratory of every household, and that much of the 'weal or woe' as far as regards bodily health, depends upon the nature of the preparations concocted within its walls. A good kitchen, therefore, should be erected with a view to the following particulars.
1. Convenience of distribution in its parts, with largeness of dimension.
2. Excellence of light, height of ceiling, and good ventilation.
3. Easiness of access, without passing through the house.
4. Sufficiently remote from the principal apartments of the house, that the members, visitors, or guests of the family, may not perceive the odour incident to cooking, or hear the noise of culinary operations.
5. Plenty of fuel and water, which, with the scullery, pantry and storeroom, should be so near it, as to offer the smallest possible trouble in reaching them.

AMONGST THE MOST ESSENTIAL REQUIREMENTS of the kitchen are scales or weighing-machines for family use. The modern English weights were adjusted by the 27th chapter of Magna Charta, or the great charter forced, by the barons, from King John at Runnymede, in Surrey. Therein it is declared that the weights, all over England, shall be the same, although for different commodities there were two different kinds, *Troy* and *Avoirdupois*. The origin of both is taken from a grain of wheat gathered in the middle of an ear. The standard of measures was originally kept at Winchester, and by a law of King Edgar was ordained to be observed throughout the kingdom.

ACCOMPANYING THE SCALES, or weighing-machines, there should be spice-boxes, and sugar and biscuit canisters. The covers of these should fit tightly, in order to exclude the air, and if necessary, be lettered in front, to distinguish them.

AS NOT ONLY HEALTH but life may be said to depend on the cleanliness of culinary utensils, great attention must be paid to their condition generally, but more especially to that of the saucepans, stewpans, and boilers. Inside they should be kept perfectly clean, and where an open fire is used, the outside as clean as possible. Care should be taken that the lids fit tight and close, so that soups or gravies may not be suffered to waste by evaporation.

WHEN FUEL AND FOOD are procured, the next consideration is, how the latter may be best preserved, with a view to its being suitably dressed [cooked]. More waste is often occasioned by the want of judgment, or of necessary care in this particular, than by any other cause; and the utmost skill in the culinary art will not compensate for the want of proper attention to this particular. Great care should be taken that nothing is thrown away, or suffered to be wasted in the kitchen, which might, by proper management, be turned to a good account. Roast beef bones or shank bones of ham make excellent stock for pea soup. When the whites of eggs are used for jelly, confectionery or other purposes, a pudding or a custard should be made that the yolks may be used. All things likely to be wanted should be in readiness: sugars of different sorts; currants washed, picked, and perfectly dry; spices pounded, and kept in very small bottles closely corked, or in canisters. Much waste is always prevented by keeping every article in the place best suited to it. Vegetables keep best on a stone floor, if the air be excluded; meat, in a cold dry place; as also salt, sugar, sweet-meats, candles, dried meats, and hams. Rice, and all sorts of seed for puddings, should be closely covered to preserve them from insects; but even this will not prevent them from affected by these destroyers, if they are long and carelessly kept.

✦ Roast Turkey

Time 4 hours
Sufficient for 10 to 12
  persons
Seasonable from December
  to February

INGREDIENTS
1 oven-ready turkey
  weighing about 10 lb
  (4.5 kg)
Forcemeat (page 340)
butter
gravy and Bread Sauce
  (page 202), to serve

MRS BEETON HAD LOTS TO SAY about accompaniments for the Christmas turkey. She said that fried sausages were a favourite addition, both as a pretty garnish and for adding to the flavour. If these were not to hand, she suggested that a few forcemeat balls should be placed around the dish as a garnish, or that the turkey might be stuffed with sausagemeat or a chestnut forcemeat. Her roasting times and temperatures were rather vague; this recipe provides all the information you need.

METHOD

Stuff the neck end of the turkey with forcemeat and secure it with a skewer. Weigh the bird and calculate the cooking time, allowing 20 minutes per 1 lb (500 g) plus 20 minutes. Put the bird in a roasting tin, brush it well with butter and place a sheet of buttered paper over the breast. Roast for the calculated cooking time, keeping the bird well basted the whole of the time it is cooking. Serve with a jug of good brown gravy and a bowl of bread sauce.

The oven should be preheated to 350°F (180°C) Gas 4.

NOTES

Forcemeat made with ham or bacon, breadcrumbs, suet and egg flavoured with lemon, fresh herbs and spices is the stuffing recommended by Mrs Beeton. If you don't want to make your own, there are many ready made fresh stuffings available at Christmas time, so you can choose according to personal preference. Chestnut stuffing goes very well with turkey, so too does a herb stuffing like parsley, sage and thyme, and stuffings based on pork sausagemeat and fruits such as apricots, apples and cranberries.

Testing for doneness It is important that turkey is cooked properly. To be absolutely sure, roast the turkey with a meat thermometer inserted into the thickest part of a thigh (away from the bone) from the beginning of cooking. When the turkey is done, it should register 90°C. Without a thermometer, check by inserting a skewer into the thickest part of a thigh. If the juices run clear, not red or pink, the turkey is cooked. After removing the bird from the oven, wrap it in foil and leave it in a warm place while making the gravy in the roasting tin.

Gravy Use A Cheap Gravy (page 197).

Bread sauce is the traditional accompaniment for roast turkey. Cranberry sauce and cranberry jelly are also popular now.

Mrs Beeton writes

"A noble dish is a turkey, roast or boiled. A Christmas dinner, with the middle classes of this empire, would scarcely be a Christmas dinner without its turkey; and we can hardly imagine an object of greater envy than is presented by a respected portly *pater-familias* carving, at the season devoted to good cheer and genial charity, his own fat turkey, and carving it well."

"ENGLISH TURKEYS – These are reared in great numbers in Suffolk, Norfolk and several other counties, whence they were wont to be driven to the London market in flocks of several hundreds; the improvement in our modes of travelling now, however, enable them to be brought by railway. Their drivers used to manage them with great facility, by means of a bit of red rag tied to the end of a long stick, which, from the antipathy these birds have to that colour, effectually answered the purpose of a scourge."

✍ *Croquettes of Turkey*

Time ½ hour plus cooling
Sufficient for 4 or 6 persons
Seasonable at
  Christmastime

INGREDIENTS
½ lb (250 g) cold roast
  turkey
2 oz (60 g) ham or bacon
2 shallots
½ pint (300 ml) stock made
  from turkey bones and
  trimmings
salt and pepper to taste
1 oz (30 g) butter
1 tablespoon flour
the yolks of 2 eggs
egg
bread crumbs
oil for frying

THIS IS AN EXCELLENT WAY to use up the dark leg meat of leftover Christmas turkey once all the nice white breast meat has been eaten. Indeed, as Mrs Beeton said, 'the smaller pieces that will not do for a *fricassée* or hash answer very well for this dish'. The quantities can be adjusted according to how much turkey you have (see *Mrs Beeton writes*, below).

METHOD
Mince the meat finely with the ham or bacon. Chop the shallots very finely. Season the stock well with salt and pepper. Put the shallots into a pan with the butter. Heat until the butter melts, add the flour and mix well, then put in the minced mixture and the stock. When just boiled, remove from the heat and turn the mixture into a bowl to cool. Add the yolks of 2 eggs and then shape the mixture into croquettes. Cover the croquettes with egg and bread crumbs and fry them in hot oil until a delicate brown – 5 minutes on each side.

NOTES
Shaping the croquettes The orginal instructions were to shape the mixture 'in a wineglass', which is rather vague. It could mean to fill the glass with the mixture and then turn it out to make large balls, but an easier method would be to use the rim of a glass like a cutter to stamp out round shapes. Either way, the mixture will be easier to shape if it is first chilled in the refrigerator for 30 minutes to 1 hour.
Egg and bread crumbs Use 1 large whole egg, well beaten, and 2–3 oz (60–90 g) fresh or dried bread crumbs. If you have the time, chill the coated croquettes, uncovered, in the refrigerator for 30 minutes to 1 hour before frying. This will make them more crisp.

Mrs Beeton writes

"To every ½ lb of meat, allow 2 oz of ham or bacon.
The proportion of the butter must be increased or diminished according to the quantity of mince."

"THE DISPOSITION OF THE TURKEY – Among themselves, turkeys are extremely furious, whilst amongst other animals they are usually both weak and cowardly."

Fricasséed Turkey ๑

THIS IS A SIMPLE WAY TO USE UP both the leftover white breast meat from the Christmas turkey and the carcass. Mrs Beeton recommended 'celery or cucumbers, cut into small pieces, put into the sauce; if the former, it must be boiled first'. Either of these additions would be good. The traditional accompaniment for a *fricassée* is boiled rice (page 345).

METHOD

Cut some nice slices from the remains of a cold turkey and set aside. Put the bones and trimmings into a pan with the lemon peel, herbs, onion, pepper, salt and water. Bring to the boil and simmer for about 1 hour, then strain to make a tasty stock. Warm the turkey slices through in the stock, remove from the heat and lay them on a hot dish. Add the cream and the yolk of an egg to the stock, stir it well round until thick, then pour the sauce over the turkey. Garnish the *fricassée* with sippets of toasted bread.

NOTES

Cream and egg yolk This classic French thickening for sauces is known as a *liaison*. Use double cream and take care not to boil the stock or the egg yolk will curdle. A way to help to prevent this is to mix the cream and egg yolk together in a bowl, then mix in a little of the hot stock and pour it back into the pan, whisking constantly.

Sippets are fried pieces of bread used for garnishing. They resemble French *croûtes*.

Mrs Beeton writes

"THE TURKEY – The turkey, for which fine bird
we are indebted to America, is certainly one of the most glorious
presents made by the New World to the Old."

Time 1½ hours
Sufficient for 2 to 3 persons
Seasonable at
    Christmastime

INGREDIENTS
the remains of cold roast
    turkey
a strip of lemon peel
a bunch of savoury herbs
1 sliced onion
pepper and salt to taste
1 pint (600 ml) water
4 tablespoons cream
the yolk of an egg
Sippets (page 344) to
    garnish

✍ *Roast Goose*

Time 3¾ to 4½ hours

Sufficient for 6 or 8 persons

Seasonable from September
to March; in perfection
from Michaelmas to
Christmas

INGREDIENTS

1 goose weighing 10–12 lb
(5–6 kg)

Sage and Onion stuffing
(page 342)

gravy and Apple Sauce
(page 200) to serve

MRS BEETON WAS VAGUE about the weight of the bird and gave a very short cooking time. She simply said 'a large goose, 1¾ hours; a moderate-sized one 1¼ to 1½ hours'. The roasting time for this recipe has been calculated on the weight of the bird after stuffing, allowing 20 minutes per 1 lb (500 g). Before carving, tent the goose with foil and let it rest in a warm place for about 10 minutes. During this time you can make the gravy in the roasting tin.

METHOD

Stuff the goose and secure it firmly with skewers so that the stuffing will not escape. Put the goose in the preheated oven, then immediately lower the temperature and roast the goose for 3¼ to 4 hours according to the size, keeping it well basted. Remove the skewers and serve with a good gravy, and well-made apple sauce.

The oven should be preheated to 450°F (230°C) Gas 8, then decreased to 350°F (180°C) Gas 4.

NOTES

Sage and onion stuffing should be used for the neck end of the bird only, and you will probably find that 1 short metal skewer is sufficient to secure the neck flap over the stuffing so that it does not burst out during roasting. Any leftover stuffing can be baked in a separate dish, allowing 30 to 40 minutes. Mrs Beeton said of the stuffing: 'a very highly flavoured seasoning be preferred, the onions should not be parboiled, but minced raw: of the two methods, the mild seasoning is far superior'.

Gravy Use the recipe for A Cheap Gravy on page 197.

Apple sauce is the traditional accompaniment to roast goose in England. Goose is a very rich meat and a sharp and tangy apple sauce helps offset this richness. Red cabbage has the same effect, so Sweet and Sour Red Cabbage (page 197) would make a suitable vegetable dish to serve with the goose.

Mrs Beeton writes

"A *ragoût*, or pie, should be made of the giblets, or they may be stewed down to make gravy. Be careful to serve the goose before the breast falls, or its appearance will be spoiled by coming flattened to table. As this is rather a troublesome joint to carve, a large quantity of gravy should not be poured round the goose, but sent in a tureen."

ONLY ROAST YOUNG PHEASANTS. Older birds are not suitable for roasting because it tends to make them dry and tough. They should only be used in casseroles, in which they can cook slowly and gently in plenty of liquid. Ask your poulterer or game dealer for advice. Mrs Beeton made no reference to fact that the breast of the pheasant is very tender and should be protected, so in this recipe it has been smeared with softened butter, but you could equally well cover it with streaky bacon rashers – or do both. Other game birds, such as pigeon, partridge and grouse, can be roasted in the same way.

METHOD

Wipe the birds very dry and season them inside with pepper and salt. Put about ¾ oz (20 g) of the butter into the body of each: this makes them moist. Smear the remaining butter over the breasts of the birds, then put them in a roasting tin. Roast the pheasants for ¾ to 1 hour, basting frequently. Ten minutes before serving, dredge the pheasants with a little flour and baste well. Serve with brown gravy, a little of which should be poured round the birds, and a bowl of bread sauce.

The oven should be preheated to 400°F (200°C) Gas 6.

NOTES

Pheasants are in season from 1 October to 31 January, but you can get inexpensive frozen pheasants all year round.
Gravy for roast game birds is traditionally thin. Use the recipe for A Cheap Gravy on page 197.
Bread sauce is the usual accompaniment to roast game birds. Game chips are another traditional trimming, made by deep-frying wafer thin slices of raw potato in hot oil until crisp and golden brown. You can cheat by warming through some plain potato crisps in the oven for a few minutes.

Time 1 to 1¼ hours according to the size of the birds
Sufficient for 4 persons
Seasonable from the 1st of October to the beginning of February

INGREDIENTS
1 brace of oven-ready pheasants
pepper and salt to taste
3 oz (90 g) butter
flour
gravy and Bread Sauce (page 202) to serve

Mrs Beeton writes

"Two or three of the pheasant's best tail-feathers are sometimes stuck in the tail as an ornament, but the fashion is not much to be commended."

"THE PHEASANT – This beautiful bird has long been naturalized in the warmest and most woody counties of England. It is very common in France; indeed so common as to be esteemed a nuisance by the farmers."

∾ Rabbit à la Minute

Time ¾ hour
Sufficient for 4 or 5 persons
Seasonable from September
 to February

INGREDIENTS
¼ lb (125 g) butter
1 rabbit, jointed
salt and pepper to taste
2 blades of mace, pounded
2 teaspoons flour
3 dried mushrooms
2 glasses of sherry
1 pint (600 ml) water
2 tablespoons finely
 chopped parsley

As its name suggests, this is a quick dish to make – even more so now than in Mrs Beeton's day, because we can make it with ready prepared rabbit joints from the supermarket. Mrs Beeton said that chicken or hare could be cooked 'in the same manner'. In fact, this is a very good recipe for chicken breasts, either on or off the bone.

Method

Put the butter into a pan with the pieces of rabbit and salt, pepper and pounded mace. Cook, stirring frequently, over a moderate heat until the rabbit is three parts done – about 20 minutes. Add the flour and stir for 1 to 2 minutes, then put in the remaining ingredients and simmer for about 10 minutes until the rabbit is tender. It will then be ready to serve.

Notes

Rabbit Mrs Beeton said to 'empty, skin, and wash the rabbit thoroughly, cut it into joints'. Instead, buy about 1¼ lb (625 g) boneless skinless rabbit meat, which is sold in the chiller cabinets at some large supermarkets and butchers. There is absolutely no need to start with a whole rabbit. Rabbit meat looks very like chicken, but it is slightly darker and has a stronger, more gamey, taste.

Dried mushrooms Use porcini or shiitake, both of which are widely available in supermarkets and delicatessens. Soak them in hot water for 20 to 30 minutes, drain and rinse, then slice or chop.

Sherry Chicken stock can be used for a stronger flavour and red or white wine or cider instead of sherry. You will need to use about 4 fl oz (120 ml).

Mrs Beeton writes

"THE RABBIT – Though this animal is an inhabitant of most temperate climates, it does not reach so far north as the hare. The wild rabbit is a native of Great Britain, and is found in large numbers in the sandy districts of Norfolk and Cambridgeshire. Its flesh by some is considered to have a higher flavour than that of the tame rabbit, although it is neither so white nor so delicate. The animal becomes larger and fatter in the tame than in the wild state, but it is not desirable to have it so fat as it can be made."

Ragoût of Rabbit ∽

Mrs Beeton gave quite a few recipes for rabbit *ragoûts* and stews, all with similar ingredients to this one, which was also recommended for hare. Forcemeat balls (page 340) are suggested in one recipe, and they go very well with the gamey flavour of rabbit. This dish is real comfort food, good in winter as Mrs Beeton suggested, and absolutely delicious with mashed potatoes and a dish of red cabbage.

Method

Slice the onions and put them into a pan with the flour and butter. Put the pan over a low heat and stir well as the butter melts, then cook until the onions become a rich brown colour, adding by degrees a little water or gravy until the mixture is the consistency of cream. Lay the thin slices of bacon in the pan with the rabbit. Add a seasoning of pepper and salt, the lemon and bay leaf, then simmer until tender – about 40 minutes. Pour in the port, bring to the boil and serve.

Notes

Rabbit Use 1½ lb (750 g) boneless skinless rabbit, which you can get in some large supermarkets and butchers. If you can't get rabbit, use chicken thigh meat. The cooking time will be the same.
Water or gravy Use a homemade or good-quality bought chicken stock to give the *ragoût* flavour. You will need about ¾ pint (450 ml).
Bacon Unsmoked or sweetcure streaky bacon would be a good choice here. If smoked bacon is used, the *ragoût* may taste too salty at the end and there will be no way of correcting this.

Time 1 hour
Sufficient for 4 or 5 persons
Seasonable from September to February

INGREDIENTS
3 onions
3 teaspoons flour
2 oz (60 g) butter
a few thin slices of bacon
1 rabbit cut into neat joints
pepper and salt to taste
2 slices of lemon
1 bay leaf
1 glass of port

Mrs Beeton writes

"VARIETIES IN RABBITS – Almost everybody knows that a rabbit is a furry animal that lives on plants and burrows in the ground; that it has its varieties as well other animals, and that it is frequently an especial favourite with boys."

∽ Game Casserole

Time rather more than ¾
   hour
Sufficient for 4 persons
Seasonable from April to
   September

INGREDIENTS

2 small oven-ready game
   birds
2 tablespoons finely
   chopped parsley
3 oz (90 g) butter
a few slices of bacon
sufficient rich strong stock
   to cover the birds
thickening of butter
   and flour
1 tablespoon mushroom
   ketchup
1 tablespoon port

THIS RECIPE WAS ORIGINALLY called 'Stewed Pigeons', but it can be used for any game birds, such as pheasant, partridge and grouse, as well as for pigeons. These birds are in season during the winter months, but you can get them frozen all year round, and thawed frozen birds are good enough for a casserole. Mrs Beeton suggested mincing the livers of the birds and working them into the butter. You can do this too if the livers are supplied with the giblets.

METHOD

Empty and clean the birds thoroughly. Mix the parsley and butter together and put it into the insides of the birds. Tie the legs together, and put the birds into a pan with a few slices of bacon placed under and over them. Add the stock and simmer gently for 30 to 40 minutes. Dish up the birds, strain the gravy, then thicken it with butter and flour. Add the ketchup and port and bring to the boil, then pour over the pigeons and serve.

NOTES

Rich strong stock If you don't have game stock, use Medium Stock (page 334) made with beef, veal, ham and vegetables. If you don't have time to make it, use a good-quality beef or chicken stock. You will need about ¾ pint (450 ml). To boost the flavour, add a splash or two of a full-bodied red wine and/or the finely grated rind and juice of 1 large orange.

Thickening Make a paste of ½ oz (15 g) each of butter and flour and add it a little at a time to the boiling gravy. Whisk constantly over a high heat until all the paste has been added and the gravy has thickened. Add the ketchup and port.

Mushroom ketchup is a bottled sauce with a spicy flavour. If you don't have any, simply increase the quantity of port or add a dash of Worcestershire sauce to give the gravy more flavour.

Venison Stew ❧

LOW IN FAT, VENISON BENEFITS from moist pot roasting, otherwise it can be a very dry meat. Mrs Beeton's recipe is as fitting today as it was over a hundred years ago. This dish would be ideal for a special Sunday lunch, served with roast, boiled or mashed potatoes and Sweet and Sour Red Cabbage (page 000). If you find it more convenient, the venison can be cooked in a tightly covered casserole dish in the oven at 325°F (170°C) Gas 3. The cooking time will be the same as it is on top of the stove.

METHOD

Soak the pork fat or bacon slices in half of the port seasoned with pepper and allspice for 2 or 3 hours, then place them over the venison and tie securely. Put the joint into a pan, add the stock, whole allspice and peppercorns, the remaining port and any remaining marinade. Cover very tightly with the lid and simmer very gently for 3 to 3½ hours. When quite tender, remove the joint and set it aside for about 10 minutes. Strain the gravy and reheat it, letting it boil until reduced if you like. Unwrap the joint and carve the meat into neat slices. Spoon some of the gravy over the meat and the remainder in a sauce boat. Serve with redcurrant jelly.

NOTES

Seasons for game The seasons when game may be shot are today very clearly delineated. The season for red deer stags, for instance, extends from August 1st to April 30th, whereas hinds are seasonable only from November 1st to the end of February. This applies to England and Wales; in Scotland, the dates are slightly different.

Flavourings For extra flavour, finely chop 1 large onion, 1 carrot and 1 stick of celery and fry them in about 2 tablespoons oil before putting the venison in the pan.

Stock or gravy Game stock would be ideal. Failing that, you could use beef stock.

Mrs Beeton writes

"Unless the joint is very fat, the above is the best mode of cooking it."

Time 3½ to 4 hours plus marinating

Sufficient for 10 or 12 persons

Seasonable Buck venison, from June to Michaelmas; doe venison, from November to the end of January (see Notes)

INGREDIENTS

a few thin slices of pork back fat or streaky bacon

2 glasses of port

ground pepper and allspice to taste

a boneless joint of venison (shoulder or haunch) weighing about 3½ lb (1.6 kg)

1½ pints (900 ml) stock or gravy

½ teaspoon allspice berries

½ teaspoon black peppercorns

redcurrant jelly to serve

CHAPTER 5

Vegetables

In her 'General Observation on Vegetables', Mrs Beeton made no mention of vegetables as food, nor did she give them much prominence in 'Bills of Fare' later on in the book. She seldom listed specific vegetables in her sample menus, but simply called for 'vegetables' to be served with the meat, poultry or game.

This might give the mistaken impression that vegetables were not much valued by the Victorians. On the contrary, the vegetable chapter was both long and comprehensive. It included basic cooking instructions for all the well-known vegetables, plus an interesting mix of British, French and German recipes. The vegetables appeared in alphabetical order and were supported by illustrations and paragraphs providing useful information. Some of this had nothing to do with cooking, but it made fascinating reading.

'Uses of the Jerusalem Artichoke - The fibres of the stems may be separated by maceration and manufactured into cordage or cloth.'

The origin of vegetables was a common theme.

'The Origin of the Onion - This vegetable is thought to have orginally come from India, through Egypt, where it became an object of worship. Thence it was transmitted to Greece, thence to Italy, and ultimately it was distributed throughout Europe, in almost every part of which it has, from time immemorial, been cultivated.'

Another favourite topic was the medicinal property of vegetables.

'Asparagus - This plant not only acts as a wholesome and nutritious vegetable, but also as a diuretic, aperient and deobstruent.'

'The Horseradish has been highly recommended in chronic rheumatism, palsy, dropsical complaints, and in the case of enfeebled digestion. Its principle use, however, is as a condiment to promote appetite and excite the digestive organs.'

Mrs Beeton's serious and authoritative tone was often amusing.

'The cauliflower possesses a most agreeable flavour, and is sufficiently delicate to be served at the tables of the wealthy. It is a wholesome vegetable, but should be eaten moderately, as it induces flatulence. Persons of weak constitution and delicate stomachs should abstain from cauliflower as much as possble.'

'The Parsnip - In its wild state, the root is white, mucilaginous, aromatic and sweet, with some degree of acrimony. When old, it has been known to cause vertigo. Willis relates that a whole family fell into delirium from having eaten of its roots, and cattle never touch it in its wild state.'

✺ *Globe Artichokes with Melted Butter*

Time ½ to ¾ hour according
to size
Sufficient for 4 persons
Seasonable from July to the
beginning of September

INGREDIENTS

4 globe artichokes

4 pints (2.4 litres) boiling
water

about 1 heaped teaspoon
salt to taste

2 tablespoons white wine
vinegar or lemon juice

melted butter to serve

GLOBE ARTICHOKES MAKE an easy first course. The leaves are pulled off one at a time and dipped into melted butter, then the fleshy base is nibbled off and the rest of the leaf discarded. Provide plenty of napkins and finger bowls.

METHOD

Wash the artichokes well in several changes of water, checking that no insects remain. Trim away the leaves at the bottom and cut off the stems. Put the artichokes into the boiling water to which the salt and vinegar or lemon juice have been added. Keep the saucepan uncovered and let the artichokes boil quickly until tender – 20 to 35 minutes according to size. To ascertain when they are done, pierce a fork into one of them, or try to remove one of the leaves – it should come out easily. Take the artichokes out and let them drain upside down for a minute or two before serving. A sauce boat of melted butter should accompany them.

NOTES

Weighting down Artichokes float to the surface of the water during boiling. To keep them submerged, weight them down with a plate.
Removing the choke Mrs Beeton did not mention this, but the hairy choke in the centre of each artichoke needs to be removed before they are served. After draining the artichokes upside down, pull out the the central cone of leaves from each artichoke with your fingers, then dig out the choke with a sharp-edged teaspoon.

VARIATIONS

For the dipping sauce, serve the melted butter with a squeeze or two of lemon juice added, or instead of melted butter, serve with a vinaigrette dressing or Hollandaise sauce.

Mrs Beeton writes

"This vegetable, unlike any other, is considered better for being gathered two or three days; but they must be well soaked and washed previous to dressing."

Jerusalem Artichokes with Cream Sauce ∽

JERUSALEM ARTICHOKES ARE knobbly-looking vegetables which are difficult to peel – one of the reasons why they are not as popular as they might be (the other is that they have a reputation for causing flatulence, something Mrs Beeton failed to mention). It is a pity that more people do not try them, because they have a delicious nutty flavour and tender flesh, and they can be cooked with their skins on, just like potatoes.

METHOD

Wash, peel and shape the artichokes into rounds or ovals and put them into a saucepan with sufficient salted cold water to cover them. Let them boil gently until tender – about 20 minutes. Drain them and serve them with cream sauce, a little of which may be poured over the artichokes.

NOTES

Buying artichokes Varieties of Jerusalem artichokes are now being cultivated which are straighter than before, and therefore easier to clean, Look for these in the shops. If you can't get them, choose the cleanest looking specimens and brush them well under the cold tap. They can then be cooked without being peeled. The nutrients lie just under the skin, so this is better for you than eating peeled artichokes.

Cream sauce is very simple, flavoured with mace or lemon juice, either of which would go well with the nutty flavour of the artichokes. Alternatively, toss the cooked artichokes in melted butter and chopped fresh herbs or coarse sea salt, freshly ground black pepper and pinch or two of cayenne pepper. Walnut and hazelnut oil can be used in place of butter to accentuate the nutty flavour of Jerusalem artichokes.

VARIATION

Mashed Jerusalem Artichokes Boil the artichokes as above until tender. Drain and press the water from them, then beat them with a fork. When thoroughly mashed and free from lumps, put them into a saucepan with 1 oz (30 g) butter and a seasoning of white pepper and salt. Keep stirring over a moderate heat until the artichokes are quite hot, then serve.

Time ½ hour
Sufficient for 6 persons
Seasonable from September
  to June

INGREDIENTS
10 Jerusalem artichokes
about 1 teaspoon salt to
  taste
about 4 pints (2.4 litres)
  water
Cream Sauce (page 206) to
  serve

Asparagus with Melted Butter

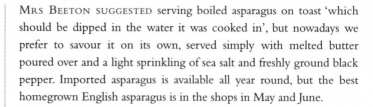

Time ¼ hour
Sufficient for 4 or 5 persons
Seasonable Forced
  asparagus from January,
  but cheapest in May, June
  and July

INGREDIENTS
about 50 heads of asparagus
about 1 teaspoon salt to
  taste
4 pints (2.4 litres) boiling
  water
melted butter to serve

MRS BEETON SUGGESTED serving boiled asparagus on toast 'which should be dipped in the water it was cooked in', but nowadays we prefer to savour it on its own, served simply with melted butter poured over and a light sprinkling of sea salt and freshly ground black pepper. Imported asparagus is available all year round, but the best homegrown English asparagus is in the shops in May and June.

METHOD

Scrape the white part of the stems, beginning from the heads, and throw them into cold water as you work. Hold them together in bundles, keeping the heads all one way, then cut the stems evenly so they are all the same length. Put the asparagus into a saucepan of salted boiling water and keep them boiling quickly, with the pan uncovered, until tender – about 5 to 7 minutes. Drain and serve with melted butter.

NOTES

Asparagus steamers are tall, narrow stainless steel pans which cook the asparagus standing upright. This is a good technique because the delicate tips steam above the water and do not become overcooked. If you don't have one of these pans, another good way to cook asparagus is to lay the spears flat in a sauté pan or deep frying pan, pour over boiling water to cover, then cook for the time suggested above.

Mrs Beeton writes

"Asparagus should be dressed as soon as possible after it is cut, although it may be kept for a day or two by putting the stalks into cold water, yet to be good, like every other vegetable, it cannot be cooked too fresh."

"ASPARAGUS – Asparagus is a native of Great Britain, and is found on various parts of the seacoast, and in the fens of Lincolnshire. At Kynarve Cove, in Cornwall, there is an island called 'Asparagus Island', from the abundance in which it is there found."

French-style Beans

It is interesting to note that Mrs Beeton wrote this recipe for runner beans, not French beans. In fact it can be used for any type of green bean. Bicarbonate of soda was added to the water in the original recipe, to help preserve the green colour of the beans. This used to be common practice, but now we know that it leaches out vitamins and minerals and it is no longer used.

Method

Cut off the heads and tails and a thin strip on each side of the beans, to remove the strings. Then divide each bean into 4 or 6 pieces, according to size, cutting them lengthways in a slanting direction. As they are cut, put them into cold water with a small quantity of salt dissolved in it. Have ready a saucepan of salted boiling water, put in the beans and keep them boiling quickly, uncovered, until tender – about 5 minutes. Drain the beans, put them into a saucepan and shake over a moderate heat to dry away the moisture. When quite dry and hot, add the butter, pepper, salt and lemon juice. Shake the pan to keep it moving, but do not use a spoon, as that would break the beans. When the butter is melted and all is thoroughly hot, serve. If the butter does not mix well, add a tablespoonful of stock and serve very quickly.

Notes

French beans do not have 'strings' running down their sides like runner beans and so are less fiddly to prepare. Simply top and tail them and leave them whole or cut them diagonally in half .

Mrs Beeton writes

"This vegetable should always be eaten young. When allowed to grow too long, it tastes stringy and tough when cooked. When they are very young, beans are sometimes served whole; when they are thus dressed, their colour and flavour are better preserved, but the more general way of dressing them is to cut them into thin strips."

Time ¼ hour
Sufficient for 4 or 5 persons
Seasonable from the middle of July to the end of September

INGREDIENTS
1 lb (500 g) beans
salt and pepper to taste
3 oz (90 g) butter
the juice of ½ lemon

✒ Broad Beans à la Poulette

Time 10 minutes
Sufficient for 6 to 8 persons
Seasonable in July and
    August

INGREDIENTS
about 2 lb (1 kg) broad
    beans
about 1 teaspoon salt to
    taste
4 pints (2.4 litres) boiling
    water
½ pint (300 ml) hot stock
a small bunch of finely
    chopped savoury herbs
    including parsley
a small lump of sugar
pepper to taste
the yolk of an egg
¼ pint (150 ml) cream

POULETTE IS THE FRENCH WORD FOR a young chicken or pullet. When dishes are described as 'à la poulette' they have a cream sauce flavoured with parsley, and sometimes with lemon juice or white wine. The sauce was originally served with chicken (*poulet*), hence its name, but now it is also served with vegetables, fish, shellfish and offal. Broad beans are delicious with it but, as Mrs Beeton suggested in another recipe, they can also be plainly served with parsley and butter, and are an excellent accompaniment to boiled bacon or ham.

METHOD
Procure some young and freshly gathered beans and shell them. Put them into salted boiling water and let them boil rapidly until nearly done – 5 to 15 minutes. Drain them well into a colander, then return them to the pan with the stock, herbs, sugar and pepper. Simmer the beans until perfectly tender and the liquor has dried away a little – about 3 minutes. Beat the yolk of an egg with the cream, add this to the beans and let everything get thoroughly hot. When on the point of simmering, serve.

NOTES
Stock The flavour of chicken stock goes very well with broad beans, but if you are cooking for vegetarians, use vegetable stock.
Cooking time varies according to the age and freshness of the beans. To test for doneness, lift a bean out on a slotted spoon and pinch it between a finger and thumb to see if it is tender.
Cream Double cream or crème frîche can be used without risk of curdling. You can use single cream or soured cream, but they will curdle if allowed to boil.

Mrs Beeton writes

"This is a favourite vegetable with many persons,
but to be nice should be young and freshly gathered.
Should the beans be very large or very old, the skin should be
removed before boiling. Boiled bacon should always accompany this
vegetable, but the beans should be cooked separately. It is usually
served with the beans laid round, and the parsley and butter in a
tureen. Beans also make an excellent garnish to a ham."

VEGETABLES

MRS BEETON GAVE INSTRUCTIONS for cooking a whole head of broccoli, but this is rather impractical. It is much easier to divide the head into individual florets for cooking.

METHOD

Put the broccoli florets into a saucepan of salted boiling water and keep them boiling quickly over a high heat, with the pan uncovered, for 4 minutes. Take them out of the water the moment they are done, drain them well and serve with a jug of melted butter, a little of which should be poured over the broccoli.

NOTES

Preparing broccoli You can buy ready prepared florets, but they are more expensive than buying a whole head. Cut the florets off the thick central stalk, then divide them into smaller florets if they seem large and cut off the individual stalks. Peel off the tough and discoloured outer layer of the central stalk, then slice the stalk into thin sticks about 2 inches (5 cm) long. Boil the stalks for 2 minutes before adding the florets.

Mrs Beeton writes

"If left in the water
after it is done, it will break,
its colour will be spoiled,
and its crispness gone."

Time 10 minutes
Sufficient for 6 persons
Seasonable from October to March; plentiful in February and March

INGREDIENTS
1 lb (500 g) broccoli florets
about 1 teaspoon salt to taste
4 pints (2.4 litres) boiling water
melted butter to serve

ᴥ Brussels Sprouts à la Maître d'Hôtel

Time 20 minutes
Sufficient for 4 persons
Seasonable from November to March

INGREDIENTS

1 lb (500 g) Brussels sprouts
about 1 teaspoon salt to taste
4 pints (2.4 litres) boiling water
Maître d'Hôtel Sauce (page 214) to serve

MRS BEETON SAID THAT Brussels sprouts could be boiled and served very simply with melted butter, which is true, but this way of serving them is a little more special. 'Allow between 40 and 50 for 5 or 6 persons' was her rather quaint way of expressing the quantity of sprouts. Here this quantity has been translated into an actual weight.

METHOD

Clean the sprouts from insects, nicely wash them and pick off any dead or discoloured leaves from the outsides. Put them into a saucepan of salted boiling water. Keep the pan uncovered and let them boil quickly over a high heat until tender – about 9 to 12 minutes. Drain and serve with a maître d'hôtel sauce poured over.

NOTES

Maître d'hôtel sauce is made from melted butter, parsley, lemon juice and shallots. It is very quick and easy to make, but if you prefer something even more simple, toss the sprouts in melted butter and a light sprinkling of freshly grated nutmeg.

Mrs Beeton writes

"Another mode of serving is, when they are dished, to stir in about 1½ oz butter and a seasoning of pepper and salt. They must, however, be sent to table very quickly, as, being so small, this vegetable soon cools. Where the cook is very expeditious, this vegetable, when cooked, may be arranged on the dish in the form of a pineapple, and, so served, has a very pretty appearance."

Sweet and Sour Red Cabbage ❧

THE ORIGINAL NAME FOR this delicious dish was 'Stewed Red Cabbage', which does not do it justice. It is an excellent side dish for all rich meats, such as pork, duck and goose, especially when these are roasted, and Mrs Beeton's suggestion at the end of the recipe is also a very good one. For a traditional touch, add a sliced cooking apple to the cabbage with the other ingredients.

METHOD

Cut the cabbage into very thin slices and put it into a pan with the ham cut in dice, the butter, ½ pint (300 ml) stock and the vinegar. Cover the pan closely and let it simmer for 1 hour. When the cabbage is very tender, add the remainder of the stock, a seasoning of salt and pepper and the sugar. Mix everything well together, stir over the heat until nearly all the liquor is dried away, and serve.

NOTES

Ham Use a smoked or honey roast ham for flavour, or use bacon if you prefer. For a vegetarian dish, omit the ham.

Weak stock Chicken or vegetable stock can be used.

Vinegar The original recipe specified ¼ pint (150 ml) vinegar, but this would make the dish very sharp. Red or white wine vinegar is milder than malt vinegar, and is therefore a better choice.

Sugar Mrs Beeton specified 'pounded sugar', which would have been white. A soft brown sugar or demerara sugar adds flavour as well as sweetness.

Mrs Beeton writes

"Fried sausages are usually sent to table with this dish; they should be laid round and on the cabbage, as a garnish."

"THE CABBAGE TRIBE – On the cliffs of Dover, and in many places on the coasts of Dorsetshire, Cornwall, and Yorkshire, there grows a wild plant, with variously-indented, much-waved, and loose spreading leaves, of a sea-green colour, and large yellow flowers. In spring, the leaves of this plant are collected by the inhabitants, who, after boiling them in two waters, to remove the saltness, use them as a vegetable along with their meat. This is the *Brassica oleracea* of science, the Wild Cabbage, or Colewort, from which have originated all the varieties of Cabbage, Cauliflower, Greens, and Brocoli."

Time rather more than 1 hour
Sufficient for 4 persons
Seasonable from September to January

INGREDIENTS
1 small red cabbage or
  ½ large red cabbage
a small slice of ham
½ oz (15 g) butter
1 pint (600 ml) weak stock
2 tablespoons vinegar
salt and pepper to taste
1 tablespoon sugar

To Cook Carrots in the German Way

Time ½ hour

Sufficient for 6 or 7 persons

Seasonable young carrots
   from April to June, old
   ones at any time

INGREDIENTS

8 large carrots

3 oz (90 g) butter

salt to taste

a very little grated nutmeg

1 tablespoon finely chopped
   parsley

2 teaspoons very finely
   chopped onion

rather more than 1 pint
   (600 ml) weak stock

about 1 tablespoon flour

MRS BEETON CREDITED the Germans with this method of cooking carrots and said it was 'a favourite accompaniment of roast pork, sausages, &c'- meats that are very popular in German cuisine. Other writers describe this method as the Flemish way, but no matter who lays claim to the original method, this remains one of the best ways to cook carrots.

METHOD

Wash and scrape the carrots and cut them into rings of about ¼ inch (5 mm) in thickness. Put the butter into a saucepan. When it is melted, lay in the carrots with salt, nutmeg, parsley and onion. Toss the pan over the heat for a few minutes until the carrots are well saturated with the butter, then pour in the stock and boil until they are nearly tender – about 10 minutes. Put a small piece of butter into another saucepan, dredge in about a tablespoonful of flour, stir this over the heat and when it is a nice brown colour, pour in the liquid that the carrots have been cooking in. Bring this just to the boil, pour it over the carrots in the other pan and let them finish simmering until quite tender – about 5 minutes. Serve very hot.

NOTES

Weak stock   Use chicken or vegetable stock. To bring out the natural sweetness of carrots, add 1 teaspoon white or brown sugar after adding the stock.

Mrs Beeton writes

"ORIGIN OF THE CARROT – In its wild state, this vegetable is found plentifully in Britain, both in cultivated lands and by waysides, and is known by the name of birds-nest, from its umbels of fruit becoming incurved from a hollow cup, like a birds-nest. In this state its root is whitish, slender, and hard, with an acrid, disagreeable taste, and a strong aromatic smell, and was formerly used as an aperient. When cultivated, it is reddish, thick, fleshy, with a pleasant odour, and a peculiar, sweet, mucilaginous taste. The carrot is said by naturalists not to contain much nourishing matter, and, generally speaking, is somewhat difficult of digestion."

MRS BEETON CALLED THESE 'Sliced Carrots' and described the recipe as an '*entremets*, or to be served with the second course as a side dish'. It is very like the classic French dish; *carottes Vichy*, an excellent way of cooking this everyday vegetable.

METHOD

Scrape and wash the carrots, cut them into slices of an equal size and boil them in salted water until half done – about 5 minutes. Drain them well, put them into a saucepan with the sugar and stock and let them simmer until reduced to a glaze – about 10 minutes. Add the butter and a seasoning of salt and shake the pan well. When the butter is well mixed with the carrots and the sauce all adheres to the carrots, serve.

NOTES

Weak stock Chicken stock is very good with glazed carrots unless you want the dish to be vegetarian, in which case you will need to use vegetable stock or water.

VARIATIONS

Replace up to half of the stock with dry cider.

Add about 4 tablespoons double cream with the butter.

Toss in 1 to 2 tablespoons chopped fresh parsley, chives or chervil just before serving.

Mrs Beeton writes

"NUTRITIVE PROPERTIES OF THE CARROT – It is used in winter and spring in the dairy to give colour and flavour to butter; and it is excellent in stews, haricots, soups, and, when boiled whole, with salt beef."

Time ½ hour
Sufficient for 4 people
Seasonable young carrots
   from April to June, old
   ones at any time

INGREDIENTS
5 or 6 large carrots
salt to taste
a large lump of sugar
1 pint (600 ml) weak stock
3 oz (90 g) butter

✺ Cauliflower with Parmesan Cheese

Time ½ hour
Sufficient for 4 to 6 persons
**Seasonable from the
  beginning of June to the
  end of September**

INGREDIENTS
1 cauliflower
4 pints (2.4 litres) boiling
  water
about 1 teaspoon salt to
  taste
rather more than ½ pint
  (300 ml) White Sauce
  (page 230)
2 tablespoons grated
  Parmesan cheese
3 tablespoons bread crumbs
2 oz (60 g) butter

Mrs Beeton gave the following advice for preparing whole cauliflowers. 'Choose cauliflowers that are close and white. Trim off the decayed outside leaves, and cut the stalk off flat at the bottom. Open the flower a little in places to remove the insects, which generally are found about the stalks, and let the cauliflowers lie in salt and water for an hour previous to cooking them, with their heads downwards; this will effectually draw out all the vermin.' Taking such action is not necessary with most store-bought cauliflowers, but the procedure is useful when preparing homegrown or organic cauliflowers.

Method

Separate the cauliflower into florets and put them into fast boiling water with the addition of salt. Let them boil briskly over a high heat, keeping the saucepan uncovered. The water should be well skimmed. When the cauliflower is tender – after about 6 minutes – take the florets out with a slotted spoon and let them drain. Put them with the flowers standing upright in a dish and pour sufficient hot white sauce over them just to cover the top. Sprinkle over this some grated Parmesan cheese and bread crumbs, and drizzle on these the butter, which should be melted, but not oily. Brown under the grill. Mix a small quantity of grated Parmesan cheese with the remainder of the sauce, then pour round, but not over, the cauliflower.

Notes

White sauce is described by Mrs Beeton as the French *sauce blanche*, a kind of Béchamel Sauce (page 201), which you could use instead.
Bread crumbs can be fresh or dried.
Grilling is a quick method of browning, but you will have to watch that the top of the cauliflower does not burn. An easier method is to brown it in a hot oven for 10 to 15 minutes. Before baking, pour all the sauce over the cauliflower, sprinkle with the Parmesan and bread crumbs and drizzle over the melted butter.

Celery with White Sauce ⌒

HEADS OF CELERY must have been smaller in Victorian times than they are today, because 6 heads of celery were originally listed in this recipe – to serve 5 or 6 persons. This version uses celery hearts, which are white and tender with no unpleasant 'strings'.

METHOD
Wash the celery, strip off any outer leaves and remove any bruised stalks. Put the hearts into a saucepan with the stock and simmer until tender, which will be after 30-45 minutes. Add the remaining ingredients, simmer for 4 or 5 minutes, then· pour into a dish and serve. It may be garnished with sippets of toasted bread.

NOTES
White stock is made from veal or chicken and vegetables. You could also use chicken or vegetable stock, whichever you prefer.

Cream Double cream gives a rich result and will not curdle when the sauce is simmered.

Sippets are fried or toasted pieces of bread and resemble the French *croûtes*. They make an excellent garnish.

Mrs Beeton writes

"By cutting the celery into smaller pieces, by stewing it
a little longer and, when done, by pressing it through a sieve,
the above stew may be converted into a purée of celery."

"ORIGIN OF CELERY – In the marshes and ditches
of this country there is to be found a very common plant,
known by the name of Smallage. This is the wild form of celery;
but, by being subjected to cultivation, it loses its acrid nature,
and becomes mild and sweet."

Time 1 hour
Sufficient for 5 or 6 persons
Seasonable from October
to April

INGREDIENTS
3 heads of celery hearts
½ pint (300 ml) White Stock
(page 335)
4 tablespoons cream
1 blade of mace, pounded
a very little grated nutmeg
pepper and salt to taste
Sippets (page 344) to
garnish when liked

❧ Sautéed Courgettes

Time 20 minutes
Sufficient for 4 persons
Seasonable in July, August
   and September

INGREDIENTS
6 medium-sized courgettes
salt and pepper
1 egg
about 2 oz (60 g) dried bread
   crumbs
oil for frying

MRS BEETON CALLED this recipe 'Fried Vegetable Marrow', and the marrows were boiled before being fried in hot lard. The recipe suits courgettes very well, but oil is used instead of lard as a healthier option.

METHOD
Slice the courgettes and blanch them in salted boiling water. Drain them thoroughly, dip them in seasoned beaten egg and sprinkle them with bread crumbs. Have ready some hot oil in a large frying pan and fry the courgettes in this until a nice brown. Serve hot, sprinkled with a little salt and pepper.

NOTES
Blanch means 'to whiten'. It is a culinary technique which varies according to the ingredient being blanched. In this case it is used to remove any bitterness from the courgettes. To blanch the courgettes, plunge them into salted boiling water, bring the water back to the boil, then immediately drain the courgettes into a colander and cool them under the cold tap. Dry them well on a tea towel or kitchen paper before continuing with the recipe.
Oil Olive oil is a good choice with courgettes, which tend to be bland. Use 4 to 6 tablespoons and make sure it is very hot before frying the courgettes.

Dressed Cucumber ~

THIS IS MORE OF A SALAD than a vegetable dish. Mrs Beeton described it as 'a favourite accompaniment to boiled salmon, a nice addition to all descriptions of salads, and a pretty garnish to lobster salad'. Cool and refreshing, it tastes exceedingly good with all kinds of fish, both hot and cold. It also goes well with chicken and lamb.

METHOD
Pare the cucumber and cut it equally into very thin slices. Put the slices into a dish, sprinkle over salt and pepper, then pour over the oil and vinegar. Turn the cucumber about and it is ready to serve.

NOTES
Salad oil and vinegar Sunflower oil and white wine vinegar are delicate enough not to mask the subtle flavour of cucumber, and you could add a little chopped fresh dill as a garnish just before serving. Or you could use tarragon vinegar with a sprinkling of fresh tarragon if you like the taste of this herb. Sesame oil and lemon juice are another good combination.

Mrs Beeton writes

"Generally speaking, delicate stomachs should avoid this plant, for it is cold and indigestible.'"

Time 10 minutes
Sufficient for 6 persons
Seasonable Forced
    cucumber from the
    beginning of March to the
    end of June; in full season
    in July, August and
    September

INGREDIENTS
1 cucumber
salt and pepper to taste
3 tablespoons salad oil
4 tablespoons vinegar

Haricots Blancs à la Maître d'Hôtel

**Time 1¼ to 1¾ hours plus
overnight soaking**
Sufficient for 4 or 5 persons
Seasonable in winter

INGREDIENTS
½ lb (250 g) white haricot
  beans
¼ lb (125 g) butter
1 tablespoon finely chopped
  parsley
pepper and salt to taste
the juice of ½ lemon

BUTTER AND PARSLEY MAKE Maître d'Hôtel, a classic French sauce for white haricot beans, traditionally used in France to accompany roast lamb. If you like, add 1 to 2 crushed garlic cloves with the butter, plus more chopped parsley.

METHOD

Soak the beans in cold water overnight. Drain, then simmer them slowly in fresh water until perfectly tender, 1 to 1½ hours. If the water should boil away, replenish it with a little more cold water, which makes the skin of the beans tender. Let them be very thoroughly done. Drain the beans well, then add to them the butter, parsley and a seasoning of pepper and salt. Keep moving the pan over the heat, but do not use a spoon, as this would break the beans. When the various ingredients are well mixed with the beans, squeeze in the lemon juice and serve very hot.

NOTES

Salt   Never add salt to the water when boiling dried beans. Salt toughens the skins and the beans will not become tender.

Mrs Beeton writes

"HARICOT AND LENTILS – Although these vegetables are
not much used in this country, yet in France and other Catholic
countries, from their peculiar constituent properties, they form an
excellent substitute for animal food during Lent and *maigre* days.
At the time of the prevalence of the Roman religion in this country
they were probably much more generally used than at present."

MRS BEETON DESCRIBED THIS AS a breakfast, luncheon or supper dish. She called open cup mushrooms 'mushroom-flaps' and said, 'for this mode of cooking, the mushroom flaps are better than the buttons, and should not be too large'. This is a simple way to cook field or wild mushrooms, which are full of flavour and need little embellishment.

METHOD

Cut off a portion of the mushroom stalks, peel the tops and wipe them carefully with a cloth dipped in a little fine salt. Put them into a baking dish, place a very small piece of butter on each mushroom and sprinkle over a little pepper. Bake for about 20 minutes, or longer should the mushrooms be very large. Have ready a very hot dish and pile the mushrooms high in the centre. Pour the cooking juices round and serve quickly, on very hot plates.

The oven should be preheated to 400°F (200°C) Gas 6.

NOTES

Field or meadow mushrooms (*Agaricus campestris*) are the ones that Mrs Beeton had in mind for this recipe. They are from the same family as the white button cultivated mushroom (*Agaricus bisporus*), but they have more flavour and their white caps open out as they mature. Look for them in specialist greengrocers, where you will also find wild mushrooms like ceps, chanterelles, horn of plenty and *pied de mouton* in season. These are all suitable for this recipe.

Time 20 to 30 minutes
Sufficient for 5 or 6 persons
Seasonable in September
and October (meadow
mushrooms)

INGREDIENTS
16 to 20 open cup
mushrooms
salt and pepper to taste
about 2 oz (60 g) butter

✌ *Mushrooms in a Cream Sauce*

Time ½ hour

Sufficient for 5 or 6 persons

Seasonable in September
and October if meadow
mushrooms are used;
cultivated mushrooms may
be had at any time

INGREDIENTS

1 lb (500 g) button
    mushrooms

lemon juice

3 oz (90 g) butter

white pepper and salt
    to taste

1 teaspoon flour

about ¼ pint (150 ml) cream
    or cream and milk

¼ teaspoon grated nutmeg

THE RECIPE WAS GIVEN the rather unappetizing name of 'Stewed Mushrooms' by Mrs Beeton, and yet she charmingly described the mushrooms themselves as 'mushroom-buttons'. This is an excellent way of cooking cultivated button mushrooms, which tend to have very little flavour. Garlic tastes very good with mushrooms and cream, so if you like its flavour, add 1 to 2 crushed garlic cloves with the butter. A sprinkling of finely chopped chervil or flat-leaf parsley would make a tasty garnish.

METHOD

Cut off and discard the ends of the mushroom stalks, and pare the mushrooms neatly. As they are done, put them into a basin of water with a little lemon juice. When all are prepared, take them from the water with the hands, to avoid the sediment, and put them into a saucepan with the butter, white pepper, salt and the juice of ½ lemon. Cover the pan closely and let the mushrooms simmer gently for 20 to 25 minutes. Stir in the flour to thicken the mixture, then gradually add sufficient cream or cream and milk to make the sauce a proper consistency. Put in the grated nutmeg and serve.

NOTES

Cleaning mushrooms   Mrs Beeton's instructions for soaking the mushrooms in acidulated water may be good for freshly gathered mushrooms from the field, but cultivated mushrooms are now grown in sterile soil and this is not necessary. Simply trim off any dirty stalk ends and wipe the caps with wet kitchen paper.

Cream   Double cream or crème fraîche can be used with equally good results.

Mrs Beeton writes

"LOCALITIES OF THE MUSHROOM – Mushrooms
are to be met with in pastures, woods, and marshes, but are
very capricious and uncertain in their places of growth, multitudes
being obtained in one season where few or none were to be found
in the preceding. They sometimes grow solitary, but more frequently
they are gregarious, and rise in a regular circular form. Many species
are employed by man as food; but, generally speaking, they are
difficult of digestion, and by no means very nourishing.
Many of them are also of suspicious qualities."

Baked Spanish Onions ∾

SPANISH ONIONS ARE LARGE, mild and sweet-fleshed. They taste absolutely delicious cooked in this simple way, which is an ideal method if you are cooking a roast in the oven at the same time. Red onions, which are also mild and sweet, can be cooked like this, but they are smaller than Spanish onions and will only need to be baked for one hour.

METHOD

Put the onions, with their skins on, into a saucepan of lightly salted boiling water and let them boil quickly for ½ hour. Take them out, wipe them thoroughly dry, then wrap each one separately in a piece of paper. Bake them for 2 hours, or longer should the onions be very large. They may be served in their skins and eaten with a piece of cold butter and a seasoning of pepper and salt, or they may be peeled and served with a good brown gravy poured over them.

The oven should be preheated to 350°F (180°C) Gas 4.

NOTES

Paper You can use a large sheet of greaseproof paper for each onion and twist it at the top like a money bag or tie it with string. An alternative method would be to use foil, which can be moulded around each onion with ease.

Good brown gravy If you are serving the onions with roast meat, you can pour a little of the meat gravy over them just before serving.

Mrs Beeton writes

"PROPERTIES OF THE ONION – Onions are not suited to all stomachs; there are some who cannot eat them either fried or roasted, whilst others prefer them boiled, which is the best way of using them, as, by the process they then undergo, they are deprived of their essential oil."

Time 2½ to 3 hours or
longer if very large
Sufficient for 4 persons
Seasonable from September
to January

INGREDIENTS
4 Spanish onions
salt and pepper
butter

IN A CHAPTER OF HER BOOK ENTITLED 'INTRODUCTION TO COOKERY', MRS BEETON TRACED THE HISTORY OF MANKIND THROUGH ITS CULINARY ADVANCES AND BLUNTLY TOLD HER READERS THAT IT WAS THE COOK WHO HELD THE KEY TO CIVILIZATION AND GENERAL HAPPINESS. SHE ALSO POINTED OUT THAT THE COOKS IN PRIVATE HOMES WERE WOMEN, WHEREAS IT WAS ALWAYS A 'MAN COOK' WHO PRESIDED OVER THE KITCHENS OF LARGE ESTABLISHMENTS LIKE HOTELS AND CLUBS – A PHENOMENON THAT IS STILL LARGELY TRUE TODAY.

AS IN THE FINE ARTS, the progress of mankind from barbarism to civilization is marked by a gradual succession of triumphs over the rude materialities of nature, so in the art of cookery is the progress gradual from the earliest and simplest modes, to those of the most complicated and refined. The object, then, is not only to live but to live economically, agreeably, tastefully, and well. Accordingly, the art of cookery commences; and although the fruits of the earth, the fowls of the air, the beasts of the field, and the fish of the sea, are still the only food of mankind, yet these are so prepared, improved, and dressed [cooked] by skill and ingenuity, that they are the means of immeasurably extending the boundaries of human enjoyments. Everything that is edible, and passes under the hands of the cook, is more or less changed, and assumes new forms. Hence the influence of that functionary is immense upon the happiness of a household.

IN ORDER THAT THE DUTIES of the Cook may be properly performed, and that he may be able to reproduce esteemed dishes with certainty, all terms of indecision should be banished from this art. All those indecisive terms expressed by a bit of this, some of that, a small piece of that, and a handful of the other, shall never be made use of, but all quantities be precisely and explicitly stated.

EXCELLENCE IN THE ART OF COOKERY, as in all other things, is only attainable by practice and experience. In proportion, therefore, to the opportunities which a cook has had of these, so will be his excellence in the art. It is in the large establishments of princes, noblemen, and very affluent families alone, that the man cook is found in this country. He, also, superintends the kitchens of large hotels, clubs, and public institutions. To be able to do this, therefore, it is absolutely necessary that he should be a judge of the season of every dish, as well as know perfectly the state of every article he undertakes to prepare. He must also be a judge of every article he buys; for no skill, however great it may be, will enable him to make that good which is really bad. He, therefore, holds a high position in a household, being inferior in rank only to the house steward, the valet, and the butler.

TO BE AQUAINTED with the periods when things are in season, is one of the most essential pieces of knowledge which enter into the 'Art of Cookery'.

Explanations of French terms

Mrs Beeton's 'Introduction to Cookery' concluded with the comment that 'Modern Cookery stands so greatly indebted to the gastronomic propensities of our French neighbours, that many of their terms are adopted and applied by English artists to the same as well as similar preparations'. A glossary of French terms followed, some of which have been retained in this book. They are reproduced here with Mrs Beeton's original explanations as to their meaning.

au bleu	Fish dressed in such a manner as to have a blueish appearance.
bain-marie	An open saucepan or kettle of nearly boiling water, in which a smaller vessel can be set for cooking and warming.
blanch	To whiten poultry, vegetables, fruit &c., by plunging them into boiling water for a short time, and afterwards plunging them into cold water, there to remain until they are cold.
compôte	A stew, as of fruit or pigeons.
croquette	Ball of fried rice or potatoes.
croutôns	Sippets of fried bread.
entremets	Small side or corner dishes, served with the second course
escalopes	Small, round, thin pieces of tender meat, or of fish, beaten with the handle of a strong knife to make them tender.
maigre	Broth, soup or gravy, made without meat.
menu	Bill of fare.
purée	Vegetables, or meat reduced to a very smooth pulp, which is afterwards mixed with enough liquid to make it of the consistency of very thick soup.
ragoût	Stew of hash.
vol-au-vent	A rich crust of fine puff-paste, which may be filled with various delicate ragouts or fricassées, of fish, flesh or fowl. Fruit may also be enclosed in a vol-au-vent.

✑ Green Peas à la Française

Time ¾ hour

Sufficient for 4 or 5 persons

Seasonable from June to the
    end of August

INGREDIENTS

about 2 lb (1 kg) fresh green
    peas in their shells

a bunch of parsley

6 spring onions

3 oz (90 g) butter

½ teaspoon flour

a small lump of sugar

½ teaspoon salt

THE CLASSIC FRENCH DISH, *petits pois à la française*, is cooked with lettuce, but Mrs Beeton preferred just spring onions and parsley, which are just as nice. She thickened the peas with a *beurre manié* paste of butter and flour, but this is not traditional and they are better served *au naturel*.

METHOD

Shell the fresh-gathered peas. Chop the parsley and spring onions. Put the peas into a saucepan with the butter, parsley and onions and stir them over a low heat until they are well covered with the butter. Dredge the flour over them, stir the peas well and moisten them with boiling water. Cook the peas quickly over a moderate heat for 20 minutes or until they are tender and there is no liquid remaining. Add a small lump of sugar and ½ teaspoon salt and shake the pan until the sugar has melted. Serve the peas piled high in the dish.

NOTES

Frozen peas may be substituted for fresh and cooked as above, but the cooking time will be shorter. Check the instructions listed on the packet.

VARIATION

To make the classic *petits pois à la française*, simply add a finely shredded lettuce with the parsley and onions. A Little Gem lettuce is the ideal size.

Mrs Beeton writes

"ORIGIN OF THE PEA – All the varieties of garden peas which are cultivated have originated from the *Pisum sativum*, a native of the south of Europe; and field peas are varieties of *Pisum arvense*. The Everlasting Pea is *Lathyrus latifolius*, an old favourite in flower-gardens. It is said to yield an abundance of honey to bees, which are remarkably fond of it. In this country the pea has been grown from time immemorial; but its culture seems to have diminished since the more general introduction of herbage, plants, and roots."

IN THE ORIGINAL RECIPE, two large potatoes were recommended for each person, so appetites must have been heartier in Victorian times than they are now. It is interesting to note how much the skin of a baked potato was valued. As we know today, the vitamins and minerals lie just below the skin, which should not be wasted.

METHOD

Choose large potatoes as much the same size as possible. Wash them and scrub them well, for the browned skin of a baked potato is by many persons considered the better part of it. Bake them for 1 to 1½ hours, turning them three of four times whilst they are cooking. Serve them immediately they are done (if kept a long time in the oven, they have a shrivelled appearance). Do not forget to serve with them a piece of cold butter.

The oven should be preheated to 425°F (220°C) Gas 7.

NOTES

Varieties of potato suitable for baking should have a floury texture. The best are Cara, Maris Piper and King Edward.
Piercing To speed up baking time, before putting the potatoes in the oven, pierce them all over with the tines of a fork or with a skewer. You can also thread them on a long metal skewer and bake them like kebabs.

Mrs Beeton writes

"THE POTATO AS AN ARTICLE OF HUMAN FOOD – This valuable esculent [edible substance], next to wheat, is of the greatest importance in the eye of the political economist. From no other crop that can be cultivated does the public derive so much benefit; and it has been demonstrated that an acre of potatoes will feed double the number of people that can be fed from an acre of wheat."

Time 1 to 1½ hours
Sufficient allow 1 potato to each person
Seasonable all the year, but not good just before and whilst new potatoes are in season

INGREDIENTS
potatoes
butter to serve

Mrs Beeton gave her readers the choice of two methods for boiling potatoes, both with and without skins, and she gave separate instructions for cooking new potatoes. Although the methods of all three are similar, she was right to distinguish between them.

New Potatoes

Allow 3 lb (1.4 kg) potatoes for 5 or 6 persons Do not have the potatoes dug long before they are cooked, as they are never good when they have been out of the ground some time. Wash them well, rub off the skins with a coarse cloth and put the potatoes into salted boiling water. Let them boil until tender − 15 to 20 minutes. When done, pour the water away from them and let them stand in a warm place with the lid of the pan partially uncovered. When the potatoes are thoroughly dry, put them into a hot vegetable dish with a piece of butter the size of a walnut.

Old Potatoes

Choose potatoes of equal size, allowing 10 or 12 potatoes for 6 persons. Peel them and take out all the eyes and specks. If they are large, cut them in half or in quarters. As they are prepared, throw them into cold water. Put them into a saucepan with sufficient cold water to cover them, add salt and bring them to the boil. Let them boil gently until tender − 20 to 30 minutes. Ascertain when they are done by probing them with a fork, and take them off the heat the moment they feel soft through, for if they are left in the water afterwards they become waxy or watery. Drain away the water, put the pan in a warm place with the lid partially uncovered to allow the steam to escape and let the potatoes get thoroughly dry. Their superfluous moisture will evaporate. Serve them quickly and very hot, and with an opening in the cover of the dish so that the steam may evaporate and not fall back on the potatoes.

POTATOES IN THEIR JACKETS

Choose potatoes of equal size, allowing 10 or 12 small potatoes for 6 persons. Wash the potatoes well and, if necessary, use a clean scrubbing brush to remove the dirt from them. When thoroughly cleansed, fill the saucepan half full with them and just cover the potatoes with cold water. They are more quickly boiled with a small quantity of water and are more savoury than when drowned in it. Bring them to boil, then let them simmer gently until tender – about 20 to 25 minutes. Ascertain when they are done by probing them with a fork. Pour off the water, uncover the pan and let the potatoes dry in a warm place for 5 minutes. Peel them quickly, put them in a very hot vegetable dish and serve very quickly.

NOTES

Salt Mrs Beeton suggested 1 heaped tablespoon salt for each 4 pints (2.4 litres) water. These days, 1 teaspoon salt is considered sufficient.

Varieties Old potatoes best for boiling include Cara, Desirée, Maris Piper and Romano. Best new potatoes seasonable from May to July are Arran Comet, Jersey, Maris Bard, Pentland Javelin, Rocket and Wilja.

Mrs Beeton writes

"In Ireland, where, perhaps, the cooking of potatoes is better understood than in any country, they are always served with the skins on, and a small plate is placed by the side of each guest."

"USES OF THE POTATO – It is generally supposed that the water in which potatoes are boiled is injurious; and as instances are recorded where cattle having drunk it were seriously affected, it may be well to err on the safe side, and avoid its use for any alimentary purpose. Potatoes which have been exposed to the air and become green, are very unwholesome."

✐ *Mashed Potatoes*

Time ½ hour
Sufficient for 4 to 6 persons
Seasonable at any time

INGREDIENTS
about 2 lb (1 kg) potatoes
salt
½ pint (300 ml) hot milk
3 oz (90 g) butter or to taste

THE SECRETS OF SUCCESS lie in using the right kind of potato, mashing them thoroughly to eliminate lumps, then reheating them with hot milk and plenty of butter. Mrs Beeton recommended 1 oz (30 g) butter to every 1 lb (500 g) mashed potatoes. This may seem extravagant, but mashed potatoes made her way taste very good.

METHOD
Boil the potatoes in their jackets in salted water (page 163). When done, drain them and let them get thoroughly dry, then peel them and put them into a clean saucepan. Beat them with a large fork, then add the hot milk, the butter and salt to taste and stir all the ingredients well over a low to moderate heat. When thoroughly hot, turn them into a hot serving dish, draw the fork backwards over the potatoes to make the surface rough and serve.

NOTES
Varieties of potato good for mashing should have a floury texture. These include King Edward, Pentland Squire and Wilja.
Beating The recipe says to do this with a large fork, but a potato masher or grubber is more effective. Alternatively, use a mechanical potato ricer or work the potatoes through a fine drum sieve.

Mrs Beeton writes

"They may be browned at the top with a salamander, or before the fire. Some cooks press the potatoes into moulds, then turn them out, and brown them in the oven; this is a pretty mode of serving, but it makes them heavy. In whatever way they are sent to table, care must be taken to have them quite free from lumps."

Purée de Pommes de Terre ❧

A FRENCH POTATO PURÉE is a great luxury, smoother and richer than ordinary mashed or creamed potatoes and well worth the little extra time it takes to make.

METHOD
Peel the potatoes and boil them in salted water (page 162). Drain them well, then pound them smoothly in a mortar or beat them with a fork. Add the stock and rub the potatoes through a sieve. Put the purée into a very clean saucepan with the butter and stir it well over a low to moderate heat for 6 to 7 minutes until thoroughly hot. It will then be ready to serve.

NOTES
Stock should be light, say chicken or vegetable, or you could use cream as Mrs Beeton suggested below. Single cream will be less rich than double, or you may prefer the tangy flavour of crème fraîche. You will get a smoother result if the stock or cream is hot when it is added to the potatoes.

Sieve A fine drum sieve is excellent for puréeing potatoes, but it is hard work pushing the potatoes through. A mechanical potato ricer is easier, but the result will not be as smooth.

VARIATION
Sweet potatoes can be substituted for all or half of the ordinary potatoes. Their raw flesh discolours quickly when exposed to the air, so boil them straight after peeling, or put them into a bowl of acidulated water while you are peeling them. Serve them sprinkled with a little grated nutmeg or ginger, two spices that suit them well.

Mrs Beeton writes

"A purée should be rather thinner than mashed potatoes, and is a delicious accompaniment to delicately broiled mutton cutlets. Cream or milk may be substituted for the broth when the latter is not at hand".

"THE SWEET POTATO – is but rarely eaten in Britain; but in America it is often seen at table , and is there very highly esteemed."

Time ¾ hour
Sufficient for 4 to 6 persons
Seasonable at any time

INGREDIENTS
about 2 lb (1 kg) potatoes
salt
½ pint (300 ml) good stock
2 oz (60 g) butter

∞ Potatoes à la Maître d'Hôtel

Time ¾ hour

Sufficient for 3 persons

Seasonable all the year

INGREDIENTS

6 potatoes

2 oz (60 g) butter

4 tablespoons gravy

1 tablespoon finely chopped
   parsley

pepper and salt to taste

2 tablespoons lemon juice

WHEN A DISH IS GIVEN THE NAME 'à la maître d'hôtel', it means it contains parsley and butter, and sometimes lemon juice. This recipe has all three ingredients. It is an excellent way to cook potatoes, whether they are new or old.

METHOD

Wash the potatoes clean and boil them in their jackets (page 163). When they are done, drain them and let them cool, then peel them and cut the potatoes into thick slices (if they are too thin, they would break in the sauce). Put the butter into a sauté pan with the gravy and parsley, pepper and salt. Heat these ingredients and mix well together. Put in the potatoes and shake them two or three times so that they become well covered with the sauce. When quite hot through – after about 15 minutes – squeeze in the lemon juice and serve.

NOTES

Gravy Although Mrs Beeton specified gravy in the ingredients, a light stock such as chicken or vegetable would be a better choice.

Mrs Beeton writes
_____

"QUALITIES OF POTATOES – In making a choice from the many varieties of potatoes which are everywhere found, the best way is to get a sample and taste them, and then fix upon the kind which best pleases your palate."

Mrs Beeton described these as 'Fried Potatoes French Fashion' and suggested using clarified dripping as an alternative to butter. This would make a very tasty dish, but butter is healthier.

Method

Peel the potatoes and cut them into thin slices as nearly the same size as possible. Make some butter quite hot in a frying pan, put in the potatoes and fry them on both sides until a nice brown. When they are crisp and done – after 20 to 30 minutes – take them out of the pan and place them on a cloth in a warm place to drain the grease from them. Serve very hot, after sprinkling them with salt.

Notes

Butter is an excellent fat for frying potatoes because it gives them such a good colour and flavour, but it has a low smoke point and burns easily. Many French recipes for sauté potatoes combine a little oil with the butter to prevent this from happening. You can use any oil you like – 2 tablespoons would be sufficient.

Cloth Use several sheets of kitchen paper to absorb the excess butter from the potatoes.

Mrs Beeton writes

"These are delicious with rump steak, and, in France, are frequently served thus as a breakfast dish. The remains of cold potatoes may also be sliced and fried by the above recipe, but the slices must be cut a little thicker."

Time ½ to ¾ hour
Sufficient for 3 persons
Seasonable at any time

INGREDIENTS
6 potatoes
2 oz (60 g) butter
salt

✑ *To Roast Potatoes*

Time 1¼ hours
Sufficient for 4 persons
Seasonable all the year

INGREDIENTS
1½–2 lb (750g–1 kg) old
  potatoes
1 teaspoon salt
4 tablespoons oil

MRS BEETON DID NOT GIVE instructions for roasting potatoes, but this is a simple and foolproof way to do them, in keeping with her other methods for cooking potatoes. It is not essential to let them go cold after boiling and before roasting, but it does help to make them crisp. For even crisper results, you can rough up the surface of the potatoes with a fork after boiling.

METHOD

Peel the potatoes and cut them into equal-sized pieces. Put them into a saucepan of water, add the salt and bring to the boil. Drain and leave until cold. Heat the oil in a roasting tin in the oven until very hot – about 5 minutes. Put the potatoes in the oil and turn them so they are coated, then roast them for 15 minutes. Remove the tin from the oven and carefully shake the potatoes around in the oil, then return to the oven for a further ¾ hour or until the potatoes are golden brown and crisp. Turn them several more times during roasting so that they cook evenly.

The oven should be preheated to 425°F (220°C) Gas 7.

NOTES

Varieties of main crop potato suitable for roasting are King Edward, Maris Piper, Fianna and Pentland Squire. When new potatoes are in season, they can be roasted without first being brought to the boil in water.

Oil Olive oil is a good type to use for flavour, especially if you are roasting new potatoes, otherwise use groundnut oil, which can be heated until very hot without burning.

THIS IS A VERY SIMPLE, German-style method of making a good potato salad. It is less rich than the more usual mayonnaise-based potato salads.

METHOD

Cut the potatoes into slices about ½ inch (1 cm) in thickness. Put these into a salad bowl with oil and vinegar and season with pepper, salt and parsley. Stir the salad well, that all the ingredients may be thoroughly incorporated, and it is ready to serve.

NOTES

Cold boiled potatoes Use a firm, waxy variety of potato such as Charlotte, Jersey, Maris Bard or Rocket, and boil them either in or out of their jackets (pages 162-163).

Oil and vinegar You can use a fruity olive oil or a light sunflower oil, whichever flavour you prefer. Vinegar is a popular ingredient in Germany and you may find it too strong in this recipe. Add 2 tablespoons to start with, then taste and add more if you like.

Mrs Beeton writes

"This should be made two or three hours before it is wanted. Anchovies, olives, or pickles may be added to this salad, as also slices of cold beef, chicken or turkey."

Time ½ hour plus cooling
Sufficient for 4 or 6 persons
Seasonable at any time

INGREDIENTS
10 or 12 cold boiled
  potatoes
6 tablespoons salad oil
4 tablespoons tarragon
  vinegar
pepper and salt to taste
1 teaspoon finely chopped
  parsley

✎ Spinach with Cream

Time ½ hour
Sufficient for 5 or 6 persons
Seasonable from March to
   July for spring spinach;
   winter spinach from
   November to March

INGREDIENTS
about 2 lb (1 kg) spinach
salt and pepper to taste
2 oz (60 g) butter
8 tablespoons cream
1 small teaspoon caster
   sugar
a very little grated nutmeg

DESCRIBED BY MRS BEETON as '*à la française*', to distinguish it from plain, English-style boiled spinach, this recipe is rich with butter, cream and seasonings. The detailed instructions given for cleaning the spinach before cooking are valid today for organic spinach. If you buy the ready trimmed and washed spinach available in bags from the supermarket, further cleaning will not be necessary.

METHOD

Pick over the spinach carefully and trim the stalks. Have ready two large bowls filled with water. Put the spinach into one of these and thoroughly wash it, then take it out and put it into the other bowl of water (by this means all the grit will be left at the bottom). Wash it again and repeat the process if the spinach is not perfectly free from dirt. Put the spinach into a very large saucepan with about ½ pint (300 ml) water, just sufficient to keep it from burning, and add 1 teaspoon salt or to taste. Place the pan over a moderate to high heat and boil for 10 minutes, pressing the spinach down and turning it frequently with a wooden spoon so that it cooks evenly. When it has boiled for 10 minutes or until it is perfectly tender, drain it into a colander and squeeze it quite dry. Chop it finely and put it into a saucepan with the butter. Stir over a low heat until the butter has dried away, then add the remaining ingredients and toss until hot. Serve on a hot dish.

NOTES

Cream This can be single or double cream or crème fraîche. If using single cream, take care that it does not boil or it will curdle.

Mrs Beeton writes

"SPINACH – This is a Persian plant. It has been cultivated in our gardens about two hundred years, and is the most wholesome of vegetables. It is not very nutritious, but is very easily digested. It is very light and laxative. Wonderful properties have been ascribed to spinach. It is an excellent vegetable, and very beneficial to health. Plainly dressed, it is a resource for the poor; prepared luxuriantly, it is a choice dish for the rich."

MRS BEETON'S CALLED THIS RECIPE 'Baked Tomatoes' and described it as 'excellent'. It is simplicity itself to make, but relies on ripe, flavoursome tomatoes if it is to match up to her description. Make it in late summer or early autumn when you can be confident of getting tomatoes with flavour. Vine-ripened tomatoes are often the best, or you could use plum tomatoes, which are also good at that time of year.

METHOD

Take off the stalks from the tomatoes, cut them into thick slices and put them into a deep baking dish. Add a plentiful seasoning of pepper and salt, cover with bread crumbs and drizzle with melted clarified butter. Bake for 20 to 30 minutes and serve very hot.

The oven should be preheated to 400°F (200°C) Gas 6.

NOTES

Clarified butter (page 344) is the purest form of butter, but ordinary melted butter can be used. A fruity olive oil would also go well with the tomatoes and you will need about 4 tablespoons.

Bread crumbs Use fresh or dried. If you choose dried, they will make a crisp topping.

Mrs Beeton writes

"This vegetable, dressed as above, is an exceedingly nice accompaniment to all kinds of roast meat. The tomatoes, instead of being cut in slices, may be baked whole; but they will take rather longer time to cook."

"TOMATOES – The tomato is a native of tropical countries, but is now cultivated considerably both in France and England. Its skin is of a brilliant red, and its flavour, which is somewhat sour, has become of immense importance in the culinary art. It is used both fresh and preserved. When eaten fresh, it is served as an *entremets*; but its principle use is in sauce and gravy; its flavour stimulates the appetite, and is almost universally approved."

Time 30 to 40 minutes
Sufficient for 5 or 6 persons
Seasonable in August, September and October; but forced tomatoes may be had that much earlier

INGREDIENTS
8 or 10 tomatoes
pepper and salt to taste
about 2 oz (60 g) bread crumbs
2 oz (60 g) melted clarified butter

Tomatoes au Vinaigre

Time 20 to 25 minutes

Sufficient for 4 or 5 persons

Seasonable from August to
    October

INGREDIENTS

8 tomatoes

pepper and salt to taste

2 oz (60 g) butter

2 tablespoons vinegar

ORIGINALLY CALLED 'STEWED TOMATOES', this recipe is extremely versatile – it can be served as a vegetable dish or a tomato sauce. For the best flavour, be sure to use sun-ripened tomatoes.

METHOD

Slice the tomatoes and put them in a saucepan. Season them with pepper and salt and place small pieces of butter on them. Cover tightly with the lid and simmer for 20 to 25 minutes or until the tomatoes are perfectly tender. Add the vinegar, stir two or three times, and serve with any kind of roast meat, with which they will be found a delicious accompaniment.

NOTES

Tomatoes Plum tomatoes are ideal, or any sweet flavoursome variety of round tomato, such as Ailsa Craig or Alicante.

Vinegar Use red or white wine vinegar. Alternatively, use balsamic vinegar, which has a special affinity with tomatoes.

VARIATION

Tomato sauce Rub through a sieve to remove the tomato skins, then thin down with vegetable stock, dry white wine or water. Shredded fresh basil can be added just before serving.

Mrs Beeton writes

"THE TOMATO, OR LOVE APPLE – This vegetable is a native
of Mexico and South America, but also found in the East Indies,
where it is supposed to have been introduced by the Spaniards.
In this country it is much more cultivated than it formerly was;
and the more the community becomes acquainted with the many
agreeable forms in which the fruit can be prepared,
the more widely will its cultivation be extended."

Mashed Turnips ☙

Mrs Beeton used turnips here, but the Scots would use swedes and call the dish 'bashed neeps', which always causes confusion. You can use either, whichever you prefer.

Method

Peel the turnips, quarter them and put them into salted boiling water. Boil them until tender – about 30 minutes – then drain them in a colander and squeeze them as dry as possible by pressing them with the back of a large plate. When quite free from water, rub the turnips with a wooden spoon through the colander into a very clean saucepan. Add the butter, cream or milk, cayenne or white pepper and, if necessary, a little salt. Keep stirring over a moderate heat until the butter is well mixed with them and the turnips are hot.

Notes

Cream or milk For a smooth result, this should be hot. Double cream will make the turnips good and rich, but you may prefer to use a lighter single cream or milk.

Variation

Bashed Neeps Use about 1½ lb (750 g) swedes instead of turnips and follow the above recipe.

Mrs Beeton writes

"VEGETABLES REDUCED TO PUREE – persons in the flower of youth, having healthy stomachs, and leading active lives, may eat all sorts of vegetables, without inconvenience. An old proverb says, 'At twenty one can digest iron.' But for aged persons, the sedentary, or the delicate, it is quite otherwise. Then the gastric power has considerably diminished, the digestive organs have lost their energy, the process of digestion is consequently slower, and the least excess at table is followed by derangement of the stomach for several days.
Those who generally digest vegetables with difficulty, should eat them reduced to a pulp or purée, that is to say, with their skins and tough fibres removed. Subjected to this process vegetables which, when entire, would create flatulence and wind, are then comparatively harmless."

Time ½ to ¾ hour
Sufficient for 4 or 5 persons
Seasonable all the year, but turnips are not so good in spring

INGREDIENTS
10 or 12 large turnips
salt
2 oz (60 g) butter
a few tablespoons cream or milk to taste
cayenne or white pepper to taste

CHAPTER 6

Milk, Cheese & Eggs

In her 'General Observations' at the beginning of this chapter in the original book Mrs Beeton claimed, with justification, that milk, as a nourishing food, was 'of such importance in domestic economy as to render all the improvements in its production extremely valuable'.

She then elaborated on this in the recipe section.

'Milk is one of the most complete articles of food. That is to say, it contains a very large number of the elements which enter into the composition of the human body. It "disagrees" with fat, heavy, languid people of slow circulation and, at first, with many people of sedentary habits and stomachs weakened by stimulants of different kind. But if exercise can be taken and a little patience shown, this bland and soothing article of diet is excellent for the majority of thin, nervous people, especially for those who have suffered much from emotional disturbances, or have relaxed their stomachs by too much tea or coffee taken too hot.'

Butter had been made in Britain 'since time immemorial'. In Victorian times, certain kinds had a better reputation than others.

'*Epping butter* is the kind most esteemed in London. *Fresh butter* comes to London from Buckinghamshire, Suffolk, Oxfordshire, Yorkshire, Devonshire &c. Cambridge butter is esteemed next to fresh. *Devonshire butter* is nearly similar in quality to the latter. Irish butter sold in London is all salted, but is generally good. *Dutch butter* is in good repute all over Europe, America and even India.

The different varieties of English cheese were given brief descriptions, but there was also mention of Parmesan, which she described as 'the most celebrated of all cheese'; Dutch cheese with its 'peculiar pungent taste'; and Swiss cheeses, which she said were 'remarkable for their fine flavour'.

Fresh new-laid hen's eggs were 'most esteemed as delicate food', and she gave lengthy instructions on how to choose them and ascertain their freshness. As so often throughout her book, Mrs Beeton was always keen to discourse upon effect of food on the digestion.

'Eggs contain for their volume a greater quantity of nutriment than any other article of food. But it does not follow that they are always good for weak stomachs. Quite the contrary; for it is often a great object to give the stomach a large surface to work upon, a considerable volume of *ingesta*, over which the nutritive matter is diffused, and so exposed to the action of the gastric juice at many points.'

To Make an Omelet

Time 4 to 6 minutes
Sufficient for 1 person
Seasonable at any time

INGREDIENTS
2 eggs
salt and pepper
2 pieces of butter, each the
    size of a walnut

MRS BEETON GAVE INSTRUCTIONS for a 6-egg omelet, but this quantity is rather impractical. It is better to make a 2-egg omelet for each person. Mrs Beeton went on to suggest that the cook serve the omelet 'very expeditiously on a hot dish, and never cook it until it is just wanted,' which was sound advice. Cook and serve each omelet quickly and only deal with one at a time. If an omelet is left to stand, it will lose its fluffiness and go rubbery.

METHOD

Break the eggs into a bowl and beat them with a pinch each of salt and pepper until extremely light. Add one of the pieces of butter, cut into small pieces, and stir this into the mixture. Put the other piece of butter into a frying pan and make it quite hot over a gentle heat. As soon as it begins to bubble, whisk the eggs very briskly and pour them into the pan. Stir the omelet with a spoon one way until the mixture thickens and becomes firm. When it is set underneath – after 1 to 1½ minutes – fold half of it over so that it assumes an oval shape and slide it out of the pan on to a hot plate.

NOTES

Frying Mrs Beeton gave her readers this very useful tip: 'In making an omelet, be particularly careful that it is not too thin, and to avoid this do not make it in too large a frying pan as the mixture would then spread too much and taste of the outside'. For a perfect 2-egg omelet, the correct size of pan is 7 inches (18 cm). A non-stick omelet pan with sloping sides is best, especially if you are new to omelet making.

VARIATIONS

Mrs Beeton said, 'The flavour of this omelet may be very much enhanced by adding minced parsley, minced onion or eschalot, or grated cheese, allowing 1 tablespoonful of the former, and half the quantity of the latter, to the above proportion of eggs. Shrimps or oysters may also be added; the latter should be scalded in their liquor, and then bearded and cut into small pieces.' She also gave additional recipes for an omelet using 2 tablespoons minced ham, and a kidney omelet using 2 lamb's kidneys, skinned and finely diced.

Mrs Beeton used 1 dessertspoonful (2 teaspoons) of rice-flour in her batter to stabilize and thicken it, but this is not necessary and has been omitted from this recipe. She also used 6 eggs to make 1 very large omelet to serve 3 or 4 persons, but you will get more successful results with individual omelets.

METHOD

Separate the yolks from the whites of the eggs. Add the sugar to the egg yolks with any of the flavourings that may be preferred and stir these ingredients well together. Whip the whites of the eggs and fold them lightly into the egg yolk batter. Put the butter into a small frying pan. As soon as the butter begins to bubble, pour the batter into it and cook the omelet over a low heat until it is set underneath – 1 to 1½ minutes. Put it in the oven and bake until browned on the top – about 5 minutes. Sprinkle icing sugar over the omelet and serve it immediately.

The oven should be preheated to 350°F (180°C) Gas 4.

NOTES

Frying pan Use a 7 inch (18 cm) omelet pan, preferably one with a non-stick finish. For this recipe it needs to be ovenproof, so check the handle and, if necessary, wrap this in a double thickness of heavy-duty foil to protect it from the oven's heat. An alternative is to pop the pan under a hot grill, keeping the handle away from the element or flame.

Time 12 to 15 minutes
Sufficient for 1 person
Seasonable at any time

INGREDIENTS
2 eggs
1 tablespoon caster sugar
a few drops of vanilla
    essence or orange-flower
    water or 1 teaspoon finely
    grated lemon rind
a piece of butter the size of
    a walnut
icing sugar to serve

❧ Bachelor's Omelet

Time ¼ hour
Sufficient for 1 person
Seasonable at any time

INGREDIENTS
1 teaspoon flour
½ teacup milk
2 eggs
salt and cayenne pepper
1 oz (30 g) butter
chopped fresh herbs to taste
a few thin slices of onion to
    taste

MRS BEETON NO DOUBT thought that an omelet was an easy dish for an inexperienced cook like a bachelor to make, suitable for a quick and nutritious supper on cook's night off.

METHOD
Make a thin cream of the flour and milk. Beat the eggs, mix with the flour and milk and add a pinch of salt and a few grains of cayenne. Melt the butter in a small frying pan and, when very hot, pour in the batter. Let the pan remain for a few minutes over a moderate heat until the omelet is set to your liking, then sprinkle over some chopped herbs and a few onion slices. Double the omelet over and shake it out of the pan on to a hot dish.

NOTES
Frying pan Mrs Beeton specified a small pan. An 8 inch (20 cm) pan is the ideal size.

Mrs Beeton writes

"A simple sweet omelet
can be made by the same process,
substituting sugar or preserve
for the chopped herbs."

To Make Pancakes &

THIS RECIPE HAS BEEN CHANGED from Mrs Beeton's original, which simply said, 'to every egg allow 1 oz flour and about 1 gill of milk' to make a batter "the consistency of thick cream'. With these ingredients, the batter would have been very thin. The quantities given in this recipe make pancakes that resemble French crêpes. To get the batter really smooth and lump-free, beat it with an electric mixer, then leave it to stand at room temperature before using. This allows time for the starch grains in the flour to burst and the pancakes will be less likely to stick to the pan. Whisk the batter after standing and add a little more milk if it seems too thick.

METHOD

Whisk the egg well in a bowl, then add the flour, salt and a few drops of milk. Beat until a perfectly smooth batter is formed, then gradually add the remainder of the milk. The amount of milk must be regulated by the size of the egg, but when ready for frying the batter should have the consistency of thick cream. Heat a small frying pan until hot. Put into it a small piece of butter, allowing about ½ oz (15 g) to each pancake, and heat until the butter is melted. Pour in about ½ teacupful batter and swirl it around so that it covers the entire base of the pan. Fry it over a moderate heat for about 1 minute or until it is nicely brown on the underside. Turn the pancake over and fry for 30 seconds on the other side. When the pancake is done, slide it out. Keep hot. Proceed in this manner until sufficient pancakes are cooked, then serve them quickly and continue to make a further quantity, as pancakes are never good unless eaten almost immediately they come from the pan.

NOTES

Frying pan A non-stick pan about 5 inches (13 cm) in diameter is ideal for French-style crêpes, and you should be able to make 12 of this size quite easily. Practice makes perfect with pancakes, so do not be surprised if the first few are not as good as the rest.
Butter gives the pancakes a good colour and flavour, but it can burn. For the inexperienced cook, groundnut oil is better for frying. Dip a wad of kitchen paper in oil and wipe it over the inside of the pan before heating it. Repeat after every 2 or 3 pancakes.

Time ¼ to ½ hour
Sufficient to make 8 to 12
    pancakes
Seasonable at any time but
    specially served on Shrove
    Tuesday

INGREDIENTS
1 egg
4 oz (125 g) flour
a pinch of salt
about ½ pint (300 ml) milk
butter, for frying

Mrs Beeton writes

"To render the pancakes very light, the yolks and whites of the eggs should be beaten separately, and the whites added the last thing to the batter before frying. The batter may be flavoured with a little grated lemon rind, or the pancakes may have preserve rolled in them instead of sugar. Send sifted sugar and a cut lemon to table with them."

✑ *Rich Pancakes*

Time ¼ to ½ hour
Sufficient to make 12
 pancakes
Seasonable at any time but
 specially served on Shrove
 Tuesday

INGREDIENTS
3 eggs
½ pint (300 ml) cream
2 oz (60 g) caster sugar
½ glass of sherry
¼ teaspoon grated nutmeg
about 4 oz (125 g) flour
extra caster sugar to serve

THE ORIGINAL RECIPE FOR these sweet dessert pancakes specified double the quantity of ingredients used here, but this would have made them exceedingly rich, so the quantities have been halved. The batter still makes the same number of pancakes, but they are thinner. Rich pancakes are sufficiently different from ordinary pancakes to be perfect for a special occasion, such as Pancake Day, as Mrs Beeton stated when suggesting when they might be seasonable.

METHOD

Beat the eggs well in a bowl, mix with them the cream, sugar, sherry and nutmeg, then add as much flour as will make the batter nearly as thick as that for ordinary pancakes. Heat a frying pan until hot, wipe it with a clean cloth, then pour in sufficient batter to make a thin pancake and fry it for about 3 minutes. Serve the pancakes piled one above the other, sprinkling sifted caster sugar between each one.

NOTES

Cream Single, whipping or double cream may be used, depending on the richness you require. For less rich pancakes, use milk or half cream and half milk.

Frying pan Use a non-stick pan about 7 inches (18 cm) in diameter.

THESE DELIGHTFUL LITTLE savoury pastries are like hot cheese straws. They are quick and easy, and make ideal canapés to serve with cocktails or pre-dinner drinks.

METHOD

Rub the butter into the flour, add the grated cheese, cayenne and salt and mix these ingredients well together. If necessary, moisten with sufficient water to make into a pastry-like dough. Roll the dough out on a lightly floured surface and cut it into fingers about 4 inches (10 cm) in length. Bake until a very light golden colour and serve very hot.

The oven should be preheated to 350°F (180°C) Gas 4.

NOTES

Cheese For a good flavour, use a hard cheese such as a mature farmhouse or vintage Cheddar. You could also use Parmesan, or a mixture of the two.

Mrs Beeton writes

"CHEESE – One of the most important products of coagulated milk is cheese. Unfermented, or cream-cheese, when quite fresh, is good for subjects with whom milk does not disagree; but cheese, in its commonest shape, is only fit for sedentary people, as an after-dinner stimulant, and in very small quantity. Bread and cheese, as a meal, is only fit for soldiers on march or labourers in the open air, who like it because it 'holds the stomach a long time'."

Time 15 to 20 minutes
Sufficient for 6 or 7 persons
Seasonable at any time

INGREDIENTS
½ lb (250 g) butter
½ lb (250 g) flour
½ lb (250 g) grated cheese
⅓ teaspoon cayenne pepper
⅓ teaspoon salt

✑ *Macaroni Cheese*

Time ½ hour
Sufficient for 4 or 6 persons
Seasonable at any time

INGREDIENTS
1 pint (600 ml) milk
2 pints (1.2 litres) water
salt and pepper to taste
½ lb (250 g) macaroni
6 oz (175 g) grated
   Parmesan or Cheshire
   cheese
¼ lb (125 g) butter
about 2 oz (60 g) bread
   crumbs

Mrs Beeton writes
───────────

"CHEESE – It is well
known that some persons
like cheese in a state of
decay, and even 'alive'.
There is no accounting
for tastes, and it may be
hard to show why
mould, which is
vegetation, should not be
eaten as well as salad, or
maggots as well as eels.
But, generally speaking,
decomposing bodies are
not wholesome eating,
and the line must be
drawn somewhere."

MRS BEETON COOKED PASTA in a mixture of milk and water. 'In boiling the macaroni,' she said, 'let it be perfectly tender but firm, no part beginning to melt, and the form entirely preserved. It may be boiled in plain water, with a little salt instead of using milk, but should then have a small piece of butter mixed with it'. The usual method of making macaroni cheese is to boil the pasta in water, drain it and mix it with a cheese sauce, then bake it in the oven. If you prefer to do this, see the Variation below.

METHOD

Put the milk and water into a saucepan with sufficient salt to flavour it. Bring it quickly to the boil, drop in the macaroni and boil until it is quite tender but still firm and holding its shape – about 10 minutes. Drain the macaroni, reserving the cooking liquid, and put it into a deep baking dish. Have ready the grated cheese, and sprinkle it amongst the macaroni with about two-thirds of the butter cut into small pieces, reserving some of the cheese for the top layer. Season with a little pepper, then pour in about ½ pint (300 ml) of the cooking liquid. Cover with a top layer of cheese, then some very fine bread crumbs. Gently melt the remainder of the butter and pour it gently over the bread crumbs. Place the dish under a hot grill to brown the crumbs, turning it once or twice so that it may be equally coloured. Serve very hot.

NOTES

Seasoning A pinch or two of cayenne pepper or English mustard powder greatly improves the flavour of macaroni cheese; sprinkle it over the macaroni at the same time as the pepper.
Bread crumbs For a crisp finish, use dried bread crumbs.

VARIATION

Cook the macaroni as Mrs Beeton instructed, then drain and reserve ¾ pint (450 ml) of the cooking liquid. Make Simple White Sauce (page 230) using 1½ oz (40g) each of butter and plain flour and the measured cooking liquid. Stir in two-thirds of the grated cheese and seasoning to taste, then mix with the macaroni in the baking dish. Top with the remaining cheese and bake in the oven preheated to 375°F (190°C) Gas 5 for 10 to 15 minutes.

THESE ARE LIKE INDIVIDUAL cheese soufflés, but rather than being light and fluffy, they have a slightly firm texture. They make a good dinner party first course as long as you plan ahead – like all soufflés, they have to be served immediately they come out of the oven. If not, they will sink down beneath the rims of the dishes and look rather unattractive.

METHOD

Boil the crumb of the roll in the milk for 5 minutes. Drain off the milk and put the bread in a bowl with the cheeses, melted butter, the yolks of the eggs and seasoning. Beat these ingredients well together. Whisk the whites of the eggs until stiff and fold them in until evenly incorporated. Divide the mixture between 4 small ramekin dishes, which should not be more than half filled. Bake them for 10 to 12 minutes, and serve them very hot and very quickly.

The oven should be preheated to 375°F (190°C) Gas 5.

NOTES

Crumb of a small roll You will need 2 oz (60 g) fresh white bread crumbs.

Ramekin dishes These were described by Mrs Beeton as 'small pans or saucers'. Use individual soufflé dishes or ramekins with a capacity of ¼ pint (150 ml) each. Brush them with melted butter before starting to make the recipe.

Mrs Beeton writes

"A celebrated gourmand remarked
that a dinner without cheese
is like a woman with one eye."

Time ½ hour
Sufficient for 4 persons
Seasonable at any time

INGREDIENTS
the crumb of a small roll
4 tablespoons milk
¼ lb (125 g) finely grated
  Cheshire cheese
¼ lb (125 g) finely grated
  Parmesan cheese
3 oz (90 g) butter, melted
4 eggs
pepper, salt, and pounded
  mace to taste

⁓ *Cheese Pastries*

Time ½ hour
Sufficient for 6 or 7 persons
Seasonable at any time

INGREDIENTS
a puff pastry sheet
6 oz (175 g) grated
    Parmesan, Cheshire or
    Stilton cheese
beaten egg or egg yolk to
    glaze

ORIGINALLY CALLED 'Pastry Ramakins' by Mrs Beeton, these were recommended for serving with the cheese course, but they also make good canapés to serve with drinks at the beginning of a meal. She said they could be made with 'the remains or odd pieces of paste left from large tarts, &c.', but here they are made with a sheet of puff pastry. She also said, 'where expense is not objected to, Parmesan is the best kind of cheese to use for making this dish'. Mrs Beeton was right – Parmesan gives the best flavour.

METHOD
Sprinkle the middle of the pastry sheet with half of the grated cheese. Fold the paste in three, roll it out to the same size as before and sprinkle the middle with the remaining cheese. Fold and roll out the pastry again, then with a pastry cutter, stamp out shapes in any way that may be desired. Put the shapes on a wet baking sheet, brush with egg or egg yolk and bake for 10 minutes. Serve quickly.

The oven should be preheated to 400°F (200°C) Gas 6.

NOTES
Puff pastry sheet You can buy frozen ready rolled puff pastry sheets measuring 11 x 9 inches (280 x 229 mm). One sheet should make about 24 pastries.

Mrs Beeton writes

"Stilton cheese, or British Parmesan as it is sometimes called, is generally preferred to all other cheeses by those whose authority few will dispute. In serving a Stilton cheese, the top of it should be cut off to form a lid, and a napkin or piece of white paper with a frill at the top pinned round. When the cheese goes from table, the lid should be replaced."

ORIGINALLY CALLED 'Toasted Cheese' or 'Welsh Rare-Bit', this recipe is really just a variation of cheese on toast. Opinions vary about how Welsh rarebit ought to be made, but most versions melt the cheese with beer or ale, mustard and seasonings before putting it on the toast and grilling it. At the end of her recipe, Mrs Beeton did allude to the advisability of melting the cheese but she did not include these instructions in the original method.

METHOD

Cut the bread into slices about ½ inch (1 cm) in thickness. Take off the crusts, toast the bread slightly without hardening or burning it, then spread it with butter. Cut some slices, not quite so large as the bread, from a good rich fat cheese. Lay them on the toasted bread and melt them under high heat. Be careful that the cheese does not burn and let it be equally melted. Spread over the top a little made mustard and a seasoning of pepper and salt. Serve very hot, on very hot plates.

VARIATIONS

Spiced Welsh Rarebit Melt the butter in a small saucepan with 1 teaspoon each of made mustard and Worcestershire sauce, salt and pepper. Add 4 tablespoons beer or light ale, then remove from the heat and grate in the cheese. Stir well to mix, spoon on to hot buttered toast and grill as above. Sometimes an egg yolk or two is added with the cheese for extra richness.

Scotch Rarebit Omit the Worcestershire sauce. Instead of the beer, use 2 tablespoons port.

Golden Buck Top each Welsh rarebit with a poached egg.

Mrs Beeton writes

"To facilitate the melting of the cheese, it may be cut into thin flakes or toasted on one side before it is laid on the bread. As it is so essential to send this dish hot to table, it is a good plan to melt the cheese in small round silver or metal pans, and to send these pans to table, allowing one for each guest."

Time ¼ hour
Sufficient for 4 persons
Seasonable at any time

INGREDIENTS
4 slices of bread
about 2 oz (60 g) butter
4–6 oz (125–175 g) Cheshire
   or Gloucester cheese
made mustard to taste
pepper and salt to taste

✑ Scotch Woodcock

Time 10 to 15 minutes
Sufficient for 4 persons
Seasonable at any time

INGREDIENTS

3 eggs
¼ pint (150 ml) cream
4 slices of hot buttered toast
4 anchovies

THIS DISH WAS VERY POPULAR in Victorian times, when it was the custom to serve it as a savoury course at the end of meal. Now it is more likely to be appreciated as a nutritious and tasty snack, lunch or supper. The mixture is like rich, lightly scrambled eggs, and would benefit from a seasoning of freshly ground black pepper or cayenne pepper. Don't add salt because the anchovies are salty enough.

METHOD

Separate the yolks from the whites of the eggs. Beat the yolks in a heavy saucepan and stir the cream into them. Bring to just below boiling point, stirring all the time. Do not allow it to boil or the mixture will curdle. Have ready some hot buttered toast, spread with anchovies pounded to a paste, then pour the hot sauce on top. Serve very hot and very quickly.

NOTES

Cream Use double cream, to help to prevent the egg mixture from curdling.

Anchovies Mrs Beeton said to allow 1 anchovy to each slice of bread. This would have been the salted variety of anchovy which came from a barrel. Similar ones are still sold loose from large cans in Italian and Spanish delicatessens. These need to be rinsed, dried and filleted before being used. Alternatively, use canned anchovies and mash them to a paste with some unsalted butter before spreading the mixture on hot unbuttered toast.

MRS BEETON WAS MOST explicit with her instructions and timings for boiling eggs. Nothing has changed, and her method still holds good today. If you follow her advice, you will have a perfectly boiled egg every time.

Have ready a saucepan of boiling water. Put the eggs into it gently with a spoon, letting the spoon touch the bottom of the saucepan before it is withdrawn so that the egg may not fall and consequently crack. For those who like eggs lightly boiled, 3 minutes will be found sufficient; 3¾ to 4 minutes will be ample time to set the white nicely. If liked hard, 6 or 7 minutes will not be found too long. Should the eggs be unusually large, allow an extra ½ minute for them. Eggs for salads should be boiled from 10 minutes to ¼ hour, and should be placed in a basin of cold water for a few minutes. They should then be rolled on the table with the hand and the shell will peel off easily.

NOTES

Eggs should be kept in the refrigerator. If you are going to boil them, leave them at room temperature for 30 minutes before you do so. If they are very cold when lowered into hot water the shells will crack.

Mrs Beeton writes

"Eggs for boiling cannot be too fresh, or boiled too soon after they are laid, but rather a longer time should be allowed for boiling a new-laid egg than for one that is three or four days old."

"EGGS – When fresh eggs are dropped into a vessel full of boiling water, they crack, because the eggs being well filled, the shells give way to the efforts of the interior fluids, dilated by heat. If the volume of hot water be small, the shells do not crack, because its temperature is reduced by the eggs before the interior dilation can take place. Stale eggs, again, do not crack, because the air inside is easily compressed."

Ꙩ *To Scramble Eggs*

Time ¼ hour
Sufficient for 4 persons
Seasonable at any time

INGREDIENTS
4 new-laid eggs
2 oz (60 g) butter
4 slices of hot buttered toast

Mrs Beeton writes

"EGGS – There are
many persons who
cannot digest eggs,
however cooked. It is
said, however, that their
digestibility decreases in
proportion to the degree
in which they are
hardened by boiling."

MRS BEETON CALLED these 'Buttered Eggs', but we know them as scrambled eggs. Her method is unusual, but the result is very successful – the eggs are beautifully creamy and light. As she said in her instructions, it is all too easy to spoil scrambled eggs and make them rubbery.

METHOD

Procure the eggs new laid if possible. Break them into a bowl and beat them well. Put the butter into another bowl, place this in boiling water and stir until the butter is melted. Pour the melted butter and the eggs into a saucepan and place over a gentle heat. When the mixture begins to warm, pour it into the bowl, then back again into the saucepan. Repeat this procedure two or three times so that the ingredients may be well incorporated. Keep stirring the eggs and butter one way until they are hot, but not boiling, and serve on hot buttered toast. If the mixture is allowed to boil, it will curdle, and so be entirely spoiled.

NOTES

Seasoning was not mentioned in the original recipe. Salt and freshly ground pepper should be added to taste, plus a pinch or two of cayenne pepper if you like.

Pouring the eggs from pan to bowl was a method of keeping the temperature of the eggs down so the result was creamy. It works well, but if you prefer not to go to this trouble, cook them in a wide-bottomed, non-stick sauté pan over the lowest possible heat and stir constantly with a wooden spoon.

VARIATIONS

Beat 1 to 2 tablespoons milk or single or double cream with the eggs in the bowl.

Add 2 to 4 tablespoons finely chopped fresh herbs, such as basil, parsley, chervil or chives, when the eggs are almost ready to serve.

Fold in up to ¼ lb (125 g) smoked salmon strips just before serving.

MRS BEETON RECOMMENDED serving fried eggs 'on slices of fried bacon or ham.' An alternative suggestion was to 'place the eggs in the middle of the dish with the bacon put round as a garnish'. Breakfast wasn't specifically mentioned, possibly because this makes a satisfying meal at any time of day.

METHOD

Place a frying pan over a gentle heat, put in the fat and allow it to become very hot. Break the eggs into cups, slip them into the fat and let them remain until the whites are delicately set – about 2 to 3 minutes. Whilst they are frying, ladle a little of the fat over them. Take them out with a slice, drain them for a minute from their greasy moisture, then trim them neatly.

NOTES

Fat for frying   Groundnut oil is a healthier alternative to the saturated animal fats that are suggested. If you use a non-stick frying pan, 2 tablespoons oil should be sufficient. A mixture of 1 tablespoon each of oil and butter gives fried eggs a very good colour and flavour. If you choose the butter only option, take care that it does not burn, or the flavour of the fried eggs will be spoiled.

Mrs Beeton writes

"VENERATION OF EGGS – Many of the most learned philosophers held eggs in a kind of respect, approaching to veneration, because they saw in them the emblem of the world and the four elements. The shell, they said, represented the earth; the white, water; the yolk, fire; and air was found under the shell at one end of the egg."

Time 5 minutes
Sufficient for 2 persons
Seasonable at any time

INGREDIENTS
4 eggs
¼ lb (125 g) lard, butter or
   clarified dripping

⁂ To Poach Eggs

Mrs Beeton writes

"To poach an egg to
perfection is rather a
difficult operation so,
for inexperienced cooks,
a tin egg-poacher may
be purchased, which
greatly facilitates this
manner of dressing eggs.
This consists of a tin plate
with a handle, with a
space for three perforated
cups. An egg should be
broken into each cup,
and the machine then
placed in a stewpan of
boiling water. When the
whites of the eggs appear
set, they are done, and
should then be carefully
slipped on to the toast or
spinach, or with whatever
they are served."

MRS BEETON HAD LOTS TO SAY about poaching eggs, all of it
perfectly sound advice. Her comments included the following: 'eggs
for poaching should be perfectly fresh, but not quite new-laid; those
that are about 36 hours old are the best for the purpose. If quite new-
laid, the white is so milky it is almost impossible to set it. On the
other hand, if the egg be at all stale, it is equally difficult to poach it
nicely'. Mrs Beeton suggested allowing 2 eggs per person, but advised
the reader never to poach more than four at a time.

METHOD

Bring some water to the boil in a deep frying pan. Break each egg
into a cup without damaging the yolk. When the water boils, remove
the pan to the side of the heat and gently slip the egg into it. Place
the pan over a gentle heat and keep the water simmering until the
white looks nicely set – 2½ to 3½ minutes according to the size of
the egg. Take the egg out gently with a slice, cut away the ragged
edges of the white and serve either on toasted bread or on slices of
ham or bacon, or on spinach, etc. A poached egg should not be
overdone, as its appearance and taste will be quite spoiled if the yolk
is allowed to harden. When the egg is slipped into the water, the
white should be gathered together, to keep it a little in form, or the
cup should be turned over it for ½ minute.

NOTES

Well-shaped eggs If you swirl the water in one direction with a
small whisk before adding the eggs this helps prevent the whites from
going ragged at the edges and gives the poached eggs a neat shape.

Poached Eggs with Cream ☙

SERVED OVER A SLICE OF COOKED HAM OR BACON on hot buttered toast or muffins, this is like the American brunch dish, 'Eggs Benedict'. The sauce isn't quite the same as the classic Hollandaise, but it is very good nevertheless.

METHOD

Put the water, vinegar and 1 teaspoon salt into a frying pan and break each egg into a separate cup. Bring the water to the boil and slip the eggs gently into it without breaking the yolks. Simmer for 3 to 4 minutes, but not longer. With a slice, lift them out on to a hot dish and trim the edges. Empty the pan of its contents, put in the cream and add a seasoning to taste of pepper, salt and sugar. Bring to boiling point, then add the butter, broken into small pieces, and toss the pan round and round until the butter is melted. Pour the sauce over the eggs and serve immediately.

NOTES

Cream It is important to use double cream with a minimum butterfat content of 40 percent, because it is boiled. Creams with a lower butterfat content will curdle.

Mrs Beeton writes

"To ensure the eggs not being spoiled whilst the cream, &c.
is preparing, it is a good plan to warm the cream with the butter, &c.
before the eggs are poached, so that it may be poured over them
immediately after they are dished."

"PRIMITIVE METHOD OF COOKING EGGS – The shepherds
of Egypt had a singular manner of cooking eggs without the aid of
fire. They placed them in a sling which they turned so rapidly that the
friction of the air heated them to the exact point required for use."

Time ¼ hour
Sufficient for 2 persons
Seasonable at any time

INGREDIENTS
1 pint (600 ml) water
4 teaspoons vinegar
salt, pepper and caster
  sugar to taste
4 fresh eggs
2½ fl oz (75 ml) cream
1 oz (30 g) butter

❧ Scotch Eggs

Time ½ hour
Sufficient to make 6 Scotch
  eggs
Seasonable at any time

INGREDIENTS
6 eggs
12 tablespoons Forcemeat
  (page 340)
hot lard

HOMEMADE SCOTCH EGGS are far superior to any that you can buy, and they are very quick and easy to make. Mrs Beeton suggested serving them with good brown gravy, but they will make a lighter meal if served with a salad.

METHOD

Boil the eggs for 10 minutes. Strip off the shells and cover the eggs with forcemeat. Fry the eggs in very hot lard for 5 to 7 minutes until they are a nice brown, drain them well and serve.

NOTES

Forcemeat is made from ham, breadcrumbs, suet, lemon and herbs. Pounded anchovies were suggested as an alternative to the ham in the original recipe and Mrs Beeton said that 'the flavour of the ham or anchovy in the forcemeat must be preponderate, as it should be very relishing'. If you don't want to make your own forcemeat, use ready made sausagemeat or one of the many fresh stuffings available in the chiller cabinets at supermarkets.

Lard Use groundnut oil for a healthier alternative.

Hard-boiled eggs Turn to page 187 for instructions.

Mrs Beeton writes

"To enhance the appearance of the eggs, they may be rolled
in beaten egg and sprinkled with bread crumbs; but this is scarcely
necessary if they are carefully fried."

Yorkshire Pudding ❧

THERE IS NO MYSTIQUE about making a good Yorkshire pudding – in the old days cooks used to make it without even measuring or weighing the ingredients. Mrs Beeton cooked her Yorkshire pudding slowly under the joint for 1½ hours, but nowadays this is not practical and we prefer to cook it quickly at a high temperature. This recipe has been adapted accordingly.

METHOD

Put the flour into a basin with the salt and gradually stir into this enough milk to make it into a stiff batter. When this is perfectly smooth and there are no lumps, add the remainder of the milk and the eggs, which should be well beaten. Beat the mixture for a few minutes. Put a knob of dripping into a shallow tin and heat in the oven until very hot. Pour in the batter, put the pudding into the oven and bake it for 30 minutes. Cut the pudding into small square pieces, put them on a hot dish and serve.

The oven should be preheated to 425°F (220°C) Gas 7.

NOTES

Flour Use plain flour.

Standing Time Leave the batter to stand at room temperature for at least 30 minutes before using, to allow time for the starch grains in the flour to burst, then whisk the batter well before pouring it into the tin. The consistency of the batter should be like thick pouring cream, so you may need to add a little more milk after the batter has been standing.

Beef dripping can be used if you have some from roasting a joint of beef, but groundnut oil or white vegetable fat is a healthier alternative. For the pudding to rise well, the fat or oil should be very hot before the batter is poured in. Heat it in the tin in the oven for 10 minutes.

VARIATION

Individual Yorkshire puddings can be made in a 12-hole bun tin. Follow the recipe above and bake for 15 minutes only.

Time ¾ hour
Sufficient for 5 or 6 persons
Seasonable at any time

INGREDIENTS
¼ lb (125 g) flour
¼ teaspoon salt
8 fl oz (250 ml) milk
3 eggs
beef dripping

CHAPTER 7

Savoury Butters, Gravies & Sauces

Mrs Beeton originally included pickles and forcemeats with butters, gravies and sauces. These appeared together in a huge chapter towards the front of the book, between the fish and the meat. It was an important chapter, and Mrs Beeton's opening remarks explain why.

'The preparation and appearance of sauces and gravies are of the highest consequence, and in nothing does the talent and taste of the cook more display itself.'

Strict rules applied regarding which sauces to serve with what, and there were many recipes for classic French sauces, each with a recommendation in the title for the type of food it should accompany. Although some of these seemed to come straight from a French chef's kitchen and took a fair amount of time and skill to make, Mrs Beeton was at pains to point out that they need not be costly items.

'The general basis of most gravies and some sauces is the same stock as that used for soups, and by the employment of these, with perhaps an additional slice of ham, a little spice, a few herbs and a slight flavouring from some cold sauce or ketchup, very nice gravies may be made for very small expenditure.'

Economy and frugality in the kitchen were constantly on her mind.

'It may be established as a rule that there exists no necessity for good gravies to be expensive, and that there is no occasion, as many would have the world believe, to buy ever so many pounds of fresh meat in order to furnish an ever so little quantity of gravy.'

Both savoury and sweet sauces were included in the same chapter. Food was often plainer then than now, and sauces were essential to the overall flavour of many dishes. Mrs Beeton had some stern words to say on the subject of flavour: 'Sauces should possess a decided character, and whether sharp or sweet, savoury or plain, they should carry out their names in a distinct manner, although of course not so much flavoured as to make them too piquant on the one hand, or too mawkish on the other.'

Sensible and practical advice was also on hand.

'Gravies and sauces should be sent to the table very hot, and there is all the more necessity for the cook to see to this point, as, from their being usually served in small quantities, they are more liable to cool quickly than if they were in a larger body.'

✍ Anchovy Butter

Time 20 minutes
Sufficient for 4 to 6 persons

INGREDIENTS
2 anchovies
a few parsley sprigs
¼ lb (125 g) unsalted butter

FRESH ANCHOVIES are used here, but canned anchovies will do just as well, and you can use them straight from the can. To save even more time, you can use chopped fresh parsley and not bother with the scalding and sieving. A little grated lemon rind and juice and a few grindings of black pepper can be added for extra flavour. Serve pats of this butter on hot fish.

METHOD
Wash, bone and dry the anchovies and pound them to a paste in a mortar. Scald the parsley, chop it and rub it through a sieve. Mix all the ingredients together well and make the butter into pats immediately.

Mrs Beeton writes

"This makes a pretty dish, if fancifully moulded, for breakfast or supper, and should be garnished with parsley."

✍ Maître d'Hôtel Butter

Time ¼ hour
Sufficient for 4 persons

INGREDIENTS
¼ lb (125 g) butter
3 tablespoons finely
   chopped parsley
salt and pepper to taste
the juice of 1 large lemon

MRS BEETON SAID: 'If this is used as a sauce, it may be poured either under or over the meat or fish it is intended to be served with'. We tend to prefer it chilled and served as a butter, cut into small rounds. When these are placed on top of hot meat, poultry or fish, the butter melts and flavours the food.

METHOD
Work the ingredients well together with a wooden spoon until they are thoroughly mixed.

NOTES
Chilling Put the maître d'hôtel butter between 2 sheets of cling film and pat it flat with a rolling pin. Chill it for 1 to 2 hours, then stamp out rounds with a cutter in any shape you fancy.

SAVOURY BUTTERS, GRAVIES & SAUCES

THE STOCK FOR THIS GRAVY is made from the leftovers of a joint of meat or a cooked chicken or turkey, plus celery, herbs and spices. It is very tasty, and makes good use of ingredients that might otherwise be thrown away.

METHOD

Slice the onion and fry in the butter in a large saucepan until it is pale brown. Chop the bones in small pieces and put them in the pan with the trimmings, salt, peppercorns, spice, herbs and celery. Cover with boiling water and simmer gently for 1½ or 2 hours. Strain into a basin, then put it back into the saucepan and flavour with walnut pickle or ketchup, pickled-onion liquor, or any store sauce that may be preferred. Thicken with a little butter and flour, kneaded together on a plate, and the gravy will be ready for use. After the thickening is added, the gravy should just boil, to take off the rawness of the flour.

NOTES

Savoury herbs Use whatever you have. A bouquet garni would be suitable, or rosemary, thyme, oregano or marjoram.

Flavouring Mrs Beeton recommended ingredients that are not used much today. We would probably add a dash of red wine, sherry or port, Worcestershire sauce, brown sauce, tomato ketchup or Tabasco.

Thickening Make a paste (*beurre manié*) of 1 teaspoon each of butter and flour. Add it little by little to the stock, whisking it vigorously after each addition until the liquid boils and thickens slightly. If you prefer a thicker gravy, make and add more *beurre manié*.

Mrs Beeton writes

"CELERY – The roots of celery are principally used in England for flavouring soups, sauces, and gravies, and for serving with cheese at the termination of a dinner, and as an ingredient for salad.
In Italy, however, the green leaves and stems are also employed for stews and soups, and the seeds are also more frequently made use of on the continent than in our own islands. We ourselves think that this mild aromatic plant might oftener be cooked than it is: for there are very few nicer vegetable preparations brought to table than a well-dressed plate of stewed celery."

Time 2 hours or rather more
Sufficient for 4 to 6 persons

INGREDIENTS
1 onion
1 oz (30 g) butter
bones and trimmings of a
    cooked joint or poultry
¼ teaspoon salt
¼ teaspoon peppercorns
¼ teaspoon allspice berries
a small bunch of savoury
    herbs
½ head of celery
flavouring
thickening

෴ *Orange Gravy*

Time ½ hour
Sufficient for a small tureen

INGREDIENTS
1 small onion
½ pint (300 ml) White Stock
  (page 335)
3 or 4 strips of lemon or
  orange peel
a few leaves of basil if
  at hand
the juice of a Seville orange
  or lemon
salt and pepper to taste
1 glass of port

MRS BEETON RECOMMENDED this sauce for wild fowl, widgeon and teal. Made with Seville orange juice, it is sharp and tangy, delicious with any game bird, and also with duck, chicken and turkey.

METHOD
Put the onion, cut in slices, into a saucepan. Add the stock, lemon or orange peel and basil and let them simmer very gently for ¼ hour or rather longer, should the stock not taste sufficiently of the peel. Strain the liquid into a clean saucepan, add the remaining ingredients and heat through until on the point of boiling. Serve very hot in a small tureen or bowl, which should have a cover to it.

NOTES
White stock is made from veal and poultry trimmings. You can equally well use chicken or vegetable stock.
Seville orange January and February are the months when Seville oranges are in season. Their bittersweet juice is good with the rich meat of game birds and duck, but if they are out of season, use lemon juice as the recipe suggests. A combination of half sweet orange juice and half lemon juice also gives an excellent flavour.

Mrs Beeton writes

"SEVILLE ORANGE (*Citrus vulgaris*) – This variety, called also bitter orange, is of the same species as the sweet orange, and grows in great abundance on the banks of the Gudalquiver, in Andalusia, whence this fruit is chiefly obtained. In that part of Spain there are very extensive orchards of these oranges, which form the chief wealth of the monastries. The best marmalade and the richest wine are made from this orange; and from its flowers the best orange-flower water is distilled. Seville oranges are also preserved whole as a sweetmeat."

THIS GRAVY IS BASED on a meatless stock, which is useful for serving with vegetarian dishes. Make sure to use plenty of herbs to give the stock a good flavour. If you prefer, use dry white wine or cider instead of the beer, or omit the alcohol altogether. Without the thickening and colouring, the vegetable stock can be kept in the refrigerator or freezer.

METHOD

Slice the onions and carrot, coat them in flour and fry in the butter until a nice light-brown colour. Stir in the boiling water and the remaining ingredients and simmer gently for about an hour. Strain and leave until cold, then skim off any fat. Thicken it, and, if necessary, add a few drops of colour.

NOTES

Savoury herbs Use a large fresh bouquet garni made up of parsley, bay leaf, thyme and celery or leek.

Thickening Mrs Beeton would have used a paste (*beurre manié*) of butter and flour, but the gravy will taste better if it is boiled until it reduces and thickens naturally. After cooling and skimming, boil it in a saucepan for half an hour or more until it acquires the consistency and flavour you like. Taste for seasoning before using.

Colouring Mrs Beeton directed her readers to use a homemade burnt sugar or caramel colouring. This can be bought in bottles as 'browning', but it is hardly necessary.

Time 1¼ to 1½ hours plus
   cooling
Sufficient for about 2½ pints
   (1.4 litres)

INGREDIENTS
2 large onions
1 large carrot
a little flour
2 oz (60 g) butter
3 pints (1.8 litres) boiling
   water
a bunch of savoury herbs
a wineglassful of good beer
salt and pepper to taste
thickening
colouring

৶ Anchovy Sauce

Time 5 minutes
Sufficient for 4 to 6 persons

INGREDIENTS
4 anchovies
1 oz (30 g) butter
½ pint (300 ml) melted
  butter
cayenne pepper to taste
lemon juice when liked

YOU CAN USE canned anchovies instead of the fresh ones suggested here. Serve the sauce with fish, especially brill, turbot and sole, and with boiled potatoes.

METHOD
Wash and bone the anchovies and pound them in a mortar to a paste with 1 oz (30 g) butter. Make the melted butter hot, stir in the pounded anchovies and cayenne and simmer for 3 or 4 minutes. If liked, add a squeeze of lemon juice.

Mrs Beeton writes

"A more general and expeditious way of making this sauce is
to stir in 1½ tablespoonfuls of anchovy essence to ½ pint
of melted butter, and to add seasoning to taste.
Boil the whole up for 1 minute,
and serve hot."

৶ Apple Sauce

Time ½ hour
Sufficient to serve with
  1 goose or 2 ducks

INGREDIENTS
3 large cooking apples
2–3 oz (60–90 g) sugar
a small piece of butter

THE ORIGINAL RECIPE gave no quantities for the ingredients. They have been included here, and will make enough sauce to accompany a good-sized roast goose or joint of pork.

METHOD
Pare, core and quarter the apples and throw them into cold water to preserve their whiteness. Put them in a saucepan with sufficient water to moisten them and boil until soft enough to pulp. Beat them with a wooden spoon, adding sugar to taste and a small piece of butter.

Mrs Beeton called this recipe Béchamel or French White Sauce. It is not the standard béchamel made with a butter and flour roux and infused milk, but it is a very good recipe nevertheless, and can be used whenever a béchamel or white sauce is required. For a simple white sauce, see page 230.

METHOD

Put the stock into a saucepan with the parsley, cloves, bay leaf, herbs and mushrooms. Add a seasoning of salt, but no pepper, as this would give the sauce a dusty appearance. When it has boiled long enough to extract the flavour of the herbs and seasonings – about 1 hour – strain it and boil it quickly again, until it is nearly half reduced. Now mix the arrowroot smoothly with the cream and let it simmer very gently for 5 minutes over a low heat. Pour into it the reduced stock and continue to simmer over a low heat for 10 minutes, if the sauce is thick. If, on the contrary, it is too thin, it must be stirred over a high heat until it thickens.

NOTES

White stock is made from veal and poultry trimmings. You can equally well use chicken stock, either homemade or one of the fresh stocks sold in cartons at supermarkets.
Savoury herbs Use parsley, thyme or rosemary.
Cream Use double cream. To make the sauce less rich, use milk, or half milk and half cream.

Mrs Beeton writes

"This is the foundation of many kinds of sauces, especially white sauces. Always make it thick, as you can easily thin it with cream, milk, or white stock."

"THE CLOVE – The clove-tree is a native of the Molucca islands, particularly Amboyna, and attains the height of a laurel-tree, and no verdure is ever seen under it. As an aromatic, the clove is highly stimulating, and yields an abundance of oil. There are several varieties of the clove; the best is called the royal clove, which is scarce, and which is blacker and smaller than the other kinds. It is a curious fact, that the flowers, when fully developed, are quite inodorous, and that the real fruit is not in the least aromatic."

Time 1½ hours
Sufficient for 4 to 6 persons

INGREDIENTS
2 pints (1.2 litres) White
  Stock (page 335)
1 small bunch of parsley
2 cloves
½ bay leaf
a small bunch of savoury
  herbs
3 or 4 mushrooms, when
  obtainable
salt to taste
1 tablespoon arrowroot
1 pint (600 ml) cream

✒ Bread Sauce

Time 1¾ hours
Sufficient to serve with
  1 large or 2 to 4 smaller
  birds

INGREDIENTS
1 onion
1 pint (600 ml) milk
¾ lb (375 g) bread from a
  stale loaf
1 oz (30 g) butter
pounded mace, cayenne
  pepper and salt to taste

THICK AND RICH, especially if Mrs Beeton's advice to add cream is followed, bread sauce is traditionally served with roast turkey, chicken and game.

METHOD
Peel and quarter the onion and simmer it in the milk until it is perfectly tender – about ½ hour. Break the bread into small pieces, carefully picking out any crust and hard outside pieces. Put the bread in a saucepan and strain the milk over it. Cover and leave to soak for an hour. Now beat it with a fork until very smooth and add the butter with a seasoning of pounded mace, cayenne and salt. Bring it to the boil and serve.

Mrs Beeton writes

"To enrich this sauce, a small quantity of cream
may be added just before serving."

"MACE – This is the membrane which surrounds the shell of the
nutmeg. Its general qualities are the same as those of the nutmeg,
producing an agreeable aromatic odour, with a hot and acrid taste.
It is of an oleaginous nature, is yellowish in its hue, and is used
largely as a condiment. In 'Beeton's Dictionary' we find that the
four largest of the Banda Islands produce 150,000 lbs of it annually,
which, with nutmegs, are their principal articles of export."

THIS IS TRADITIONALLY served with lamb. For serving with fish, especially skate and salmon, Mrs Beeton gave another recipe for a caper sauce. It is the same as this one except that it is seasoned at the end with pepper and 1 teaspoon anchovy essence.

METHOD
Chop the capers two or three times. Cut the butter up into small pieces, put it in a saucepan, melt it, then dredge it with flour. Add the water and a seasoning of salt. Stir it one way constantly until all the ingredients are thoroughly blended and very smooth. Bring it to the boil and add the capers, with their liquid. Keep stirring well over the heat, let the sauce just simmer, then serve in a sauce boat.

NOTES
Salt Take care when adding salt because capers are often very salty. It is best to make the sauce without salt and taste it before serving.
Caper liquid By this Mrs Beeton meant the liquid from the jar in which the capers are packed.

Mrs Beeton writes

"Pickled nasturtium-pods are fine flavoured, and by many are eaten in preference to capers. They make an excellent sauce."

"CAPERS – These are the unopened buds of a low trailing shrub, which grows wild among the crevices of the rocks of Greece, as well as in northern Africa; the plant, however, has come to be cultivated in the south of Europe. After being pickled in vinegar and salt, they are imported from Sicily, Italy, and the south of France."

Time ¼ hour
Sufficient to serve with a leg of lamb

INGREDIENTS
3 tablespoons capers
¼ lb (125 g) butter
2 teaspoons flour
1 wineglassful of water
salt to taste
1 tablespoon caper liquid

ᴄᴀ Celery Sauce

Time 1 hour
Sufficient for 1 turkey

INGREDIENTS
1 head of celery
salt and white pepper
½ pint (300 ml) White Stock
2 blades of mace
a small bunch of savoury
   herbs
1 tablespoon arrowroot
¼ pint (150 ml) cream
lemon juice

RICH, CREAMY AND FLAVOURED with fresh herbs, this is a good sauce for turkey and other poultry.

METHOD
Bring the celery to the boil in salted water, drain and slice. Put the stock into a saucepan with the mace and herbs and let it simmer for ½ hour to extract their flavour. Strain the liquid into a clean pan, add the celery and reheat, then add a thickening of arrowroot mixed to a paste with a little cold water. Just before serving, put in the cream and bring to the boil, then squeeze in a little lemon juice. If necessary, add a seasoning of salt and white pepper.

NOTES
White stock is made from veal and poultry trimmings. You can use chicken or vegetable stock instead.
Savoury herbs Thyme, sage, rosemary or tarragon can be used.
Arrowroot This thickening agent gives sauces a translucent appearance. After adding the paste to the sauce, bring it to the boil, stirring. Add the cream and reheat, but do not cook the sauce for long, or it will start to thin down.
Cream Use double cream.

Mrs Beeton writes

ARROWROOT – This nutritious fecula is obtained from the roots of a plant which is cultivated in both the East and West Indies.
The best is obtained from the West Indies, but a large quantity of what is sold in London is adulterated with potato-starch. As a means of knowing arrowroot when it is good, it may be as well to state, that the genuine article, when formed into a jelly, will remain firm for three or four days, whilst the adulterated will become as thin as milk in the course of twelve hours.

THIS IS A TRADITIONAL SAUCE to serve with the Christmas turkey, although it also goes well with chicken.

METHOD

Make a small slit in the outer shell of each chestnut, then immerse them in boiling water for 10 minutes. Drain and immerse in cold water, then take off the outer shell from the chestnuts and put them into a large saucepan of warm water over a high heat. As soon as this becomes too hot for the fingers to remain in it, take out the chestnuts and peel off the skins. Put the chestnuts into a saucepan with the stock and lemon peel and let them simmer for 1½ hours or until the chestnuts are quite tender. Rub the chestnuts and stock through a sieve with a wooden spoon into a clean pan. Add seasoning and the cream or milk and let it just simmer but not boil, stirring all the time. Serve very hot and quickly.

NOTES

White stock is made from veal and poultry trimmings. You can use chicken or vegetable stock instead.

Cream Use single or whipping cream.

Time 2 to 2¼ hours
Sufficient for 1 turkey

INGREDIENTS
½ lb (250 g) chestnuts
½ pint (300 ml) White Stock
  (page 335)
2 strips of lemon peel
salt, pepper and cayenne
  pepper to taste
¼ pint (150 ml) cream or
  milk

Mrs Beeton writes

"If milk is used instead of cream, a very small quantity of thickening may be required: that, of course, the cook will determine."

ॐ *Cream Sauce*

Time 10 minutes
Sufficient for 2 persons

INGREDIENTS

2 oz (60 g) butter

1 teaspoon flour

salt and cayenne pepper
   to taste

⅓ pint (200 ml) cream

a small quantity of pounded
   mace or lemon juice when
   liked

THIS IS A ROUX-BASED white sauce enriched with cream. Mrs Beeton recommended it for fish or white dishes such as chicken and other poultry.

METHOD

Put the butter into a saucepan, dredge in the flour and keep shaking the pan around until the butter is melted. Add the seasoning and cream and stir until it boils. Let it just simmer for 5 minutes, then add either pounded mace or lemon juice to taste, to give it more flavour.

NOTES

Cream Use double cream.

THIS RICH EGG-BASED SAUCE is very good with fish, especially salmon, and with chicken. It will be lighter if only one or two eggs are used, and it is very good with chopped fresh herbs added to it – dill for fish, tarragon for chicken. If you prefer, you can use cream instead of the eggs.

METHOD

Cut the cucumbers into small pieces, after peeling them and taking out the seeds. Put them in a saucepan with the stock and seasoning. Simmer gently until the cucumbers are tender, which will be in about ¼ hour. Then add the yolks of the eggs, well beaten, and stir them into the sauce, but do not allow it to boil. Serve very hot.

NOTES

Cucumbers Small homegrown cucumbers would have been used in Mrs Beeton's day. These have the best flavour, but if you can't get them at the greengrocer, use 1 medium-sized cucumber.
White stock is made from veal and poultry trimmings. You can use chicken or vegetable stock instead.

Mrs Beeton writes

"THE CUCUMBER – Though the melon is far superior in point of flavour to this fruit, yet it is allied to the cucumber, which is known to naturalists as *Cucumis sativus*. The modern Egyptians, as did their forefathers, still eat it, and others of its class."

Time ½ hour
Sufficient for 4 to 6 persons

INGREDIENTS
3 or 4 cucumbers
½ pint (300 ml) White Stock
 (page 335)
cayenne pepper and salt
 to taste
the yolks of 3 eggs

ஒ Dutch Sauce

Time ¼ hour

Sufficent for 4 to 6 persons

INGREDIENTS

½ teaspoon flour

2 oz (60 g) butter

4 tablespoons vinegar

the yolks of 2 eggs

salt to taste

the juice of ½ lemon

SERVE THIS TANGY SAUCE with fish. The lemon and vinegar flavourings are especially good with oily fish like mackerel and herring.

METHOD

Put all the ingredients, except the lemon juice, into a saucepan. Set it over the heat and keep continually stirring. When the sauce is sufficiently thick, take it off, as it should not boil. If it happens to curdle, strain the sauce through a sieve. Add the lemon juice and serve immediately.

Mrs Beeton writes

"Tarragon vinegar may be used instead of plain,
and, by many, is considered far preferable."

"THE LEMON – This fruit is a native of Asia, and is mentioned
by Virgil as an antidote to poison. It is hardier than the orange, and,
as one of the citron tribe, was brought into Europe by the Arabians.
The lemon was first cultivated in England in the beginning of the
17th century, and is now often to be found in our green-houses.
The kind commonly sold, however, is imported from Portugal, Spain,
and the Azores. Some also come from St. Helena; but those
from Spain are esteemed the best."

THIS IS MRS BEETON'S version of the classic French *sauce espagnole*, so called because it was originally made with Spanish ham. It is a brown sauce which is used as the foundation of many other sauces and gravies. French chefs can take days to make a perfect *sauce espagnole* – boiling, skimming and reducing it until it takes on a brilliant shiny glaze. This recipe, also called 'Brown Spanish Sauce', is more simple and a lot less time-consuming.

METHOD
Cut up the ham and veal into small square pieces, put them into a saucepan and moisten with ½ pint (300 ml) of the stock. Simmer until the bottom of the pan is covered with a nicely coloured glaze, then put in a few more spoonfuls of stock to detach it. Add the remainder of the stock with the herbs, spices, onions and shallots and simmer very gently for 1 hour. Strain and skim off every particle of fat. When required for use, thicken with butter and flour. Add the sherry or Madeira and, if necessary, a seasoning of cayenne.

NOTES
Veal Ask your butcher for the cheapest cut available and make sure he includes some bones with the meat.
White stock is made from veal and poultry trimmings. Brown veal stock is used in a classic *sauce espagnole*, but you can use white stock instead, or even chicken stock.
Savoury herbs Use thyme.
Thickening A paste (*beurre manié*) of 1 teaspoon each of butter and flour can be added by degrees and boiled until the sauce thickens, although this is often omitted these days and the sauce thickened by simple reduction.

Mrs Beeton writes

"SHALLOT OR ESCHALOT – This plant is supposed to have been introduced to England by the Crusaders, who found it growing wild in the vicinity of Ascalon. It is a bulbous root, and when full grown, its leaves wither in July. They ought to be taken up in the autumn, and when dried in the house, will keep till spring. It is called by old authors the 'barren onion,' and is used in sauces and pickles, soups and made dishes, and as an accompaniment to chops and steaks.

Time 1½ hours
Sufficient for about 1 pint
(600 ml) sauce

INGREDIENTS
2 slices of lean ham
1 lb (500 g) veal
1½ pints (900 ml) White
Stock (page 335)
2 or 3 sprigs of parsley
½ bay leaf
2 or 3 sprigs of savoury
herbs
2 cloves
1 blade of mace
6 spring onions, chopped
3 shallots, chopped
thickening of butter and
flour
2 glasses of sherry or
Madeira
cayenne pepper to taste

ࣰ Fennel Sauce

Time ¼ hour
Sufficient for 4 persons

INGREDIENTS
¼-½ fennel bulb
¼ lb (125 g) butter
2 teaspoons flour
1 wineglassful of water
salt to taste

MRS BEETON RECOMMENDED this sauce for mackerel, but the aniseed flavour of fennel goes well with most fish, especially the oily varieties. Try it with herring or even salmon.

METHOD
Chop the fennel rather small, carefully cleansing it from any grit or dirt. You will need rather more than 1 tablespoon chopped fennel. Cut the butter up into small pieces, put it into a saucepan, melt it and dredge it with flour. Stir in the water and a seasoning of salt. Stir it one way constantly until all the ingredients are thoroughly blended and very smooth. Bring it to the boil and add the fennel. Simmer for a minute or two and serve in a sauce boat.

Mrs Beeton writes

"FENNEL – This elegantly-growing plant, of which the Latin name is *Anthum foeniculum*, grows best in chalky soils, where, indeed, it is often found wild. It is very generally cultivated in gardens, and has much improved on its original form. Various dishes are frequently ornamented and garnished with its graceful leaves, and these are sometimes boiled in soups, although it is more usually confined, in English cookery, to the mackerel sauce as here given."

Roast beef is traditionally served with horseradish sauce in England. You can buy it ready made in jars, but this homemade version is infinitely better, especially if you mix it with cream as Mrs Beeton suggested at the end of the recipe. Horseradish sauce can be served hot or cold.

METHOD

Mix the grated horseradish well with the sugar, salt, pepper and mustard. Moisten it with sufficient vinegar to give it the consistency of cream and serve in a bowl. To serve with hot roast beef, heat it in a *bain marie* in a saucepan of boiling water. Make it hot, but do not allow it to boil or it will curdle.

NOTES

Horseradish You can buy fresh roots of horseradish at greengrocers and supermarkets.

Vinegar Malt vinegar can be used, but it has a harsh flavour. It is better to use a cider or wine vinegar. About 4 tablespoons will be sufficient.

Bain marie Stand the bowl of sauce in a saucepan of boiling water. This way it will heat gently. If it gets too hot, the vinegar will separate from the sauce.

Mrs Beeton writes

"To very much improve the appearance and flavour of this sauce, add 3 or 4 tablespoons cream."

"THE HORSERADISH – This has been, for many years, a favourite accompaniment of roast beef, and is a native of England. It grows wild in wet ground, but has long been cultivated in the garden, and is, occasionally, used in winter salads and in sauces. On account of the great volatility of its oil, it should never be preserved by drying, but should be kept moist by being buried in sand. So rapidly does its volatile oil evaporate, that even when scraped for the table, it almost immediately spoils by exposure to the air."

Time ¼ hour or rather longer
Sufficient for about ¼ pint (150 ml)

INGREDIENTS
4 tablespoons grated horseradish
1 teaspoon caster sugar
1 teaspoon salt
½ teaspoon pepper
2 teaspoons made mustard
vinegar

✎ Italian Sauce

Time ½ hour

Sufficient for a small dish

INGREDIENTS

½ pint (300 ml) Medium
   Stock (page 334)

a few chopped mushrooms
   and shallots

½ glass of Madeira or
   sherry

the juice of ½ lemon

½ teaspoon caster sugar

1 teaspoon chopped parsley

THIS SAUCE IS DELICIOUS with meat, poultry and game, and is
especially good with steak.

METHOD

Put the stock into a saucepan with the mushrooms, shallots and
Madeira or sherry. Simmer gently for ¼ hour, then add the remaining
ingredients and let them just boil. When the sauce is done enough,
keep it hot in a *bain marie*.

NOTES

Medium stock is a meaty stock made with beef and veal. If you
don't want to make it yourself, use the fresh beef stock that is sold in
cartons in supermarkets.

Bain marie Pour the sauce into a bowl, then stand the bowl in a
saucepan of boiling water. This is only necessary if you are not serving
the sauce immediately.

Mrs Beeton writes

"The mushrooms
should not be chopped
long before they are wanted,
as they will then become black."

THIS IS A CREAMY SAUCE infused with the flavours of lemon and lemon thyme. It is very good with all kinds of poultry, particularly chicken. If you can't get lemon thyme, use ordinary thyme instead and double the quantity of lemon rind.

METHOD

Peel the lemon rather thin, taking care to have none of the white pith. Squeeze the juice. Put the cream into a saucepan with the lemon rind, peppercorns and thyme. Let these infuse for ½ hour, then simmer gently for a few minutes or until there is a nice flavour of lemon. Strain into a clean pan and reheat. Add a thickening of butter and flour in the given proportion. Stir this well in. Mix in the stock and add a little salt. This sauce should not boil after the cream and stock are mixed together. Put in the lemon juice at the moment of serving and stir well.

NOTES

Cream Double cream is best, both for richness and to help prevent the sauce curdling.

Infuse The cream should be heated with the flavourings until hot, then the pan covered tightly and the mixture left to cool. After ½ hour or so, the cream will be infused with the flavours of lemon, pepper and thyme.

Thickening Make a paste (*beurre manié*) with the butter and flour and add it to the sauce a little at a time, whisking it vigorously after each addition until the liquid boils and thickens.

White stock is made from veal and poultry trimmings. You can use chicken stock. A teacupful is about 7 fl oz (200 ml) and the stock should be heated before being mixed with the cream mixture.

Mrs Beeton writes

"LEMON THYME – Two or three tufts of this species of thyme, *Thymus citriodorus*, usually find a place in the herb compartment of the kitchen-garden. It is a trailing evergreen, is of smaller growth than the common kind, and is remarkable for its smell, which closely resembles that of the rind of a lemon."

Time ¾ hour
Sufficient for 2 large
  chickens

INGREDIENTS
1 lemon
¾ pint (450 ml) cream
½ teaspoon white
  peppercorns
1 sprig of lemon thyme
3 oz (90 g) butter
2 teaspoons flour
1 teacupful of White Stock
  (page 335)
salt to taste

❧ Maître d'Hôtel Sauce

Time ¼ hour

Sufficient for 4 to 6 persons

INGREDIENTS

¼ lb (125 g) butter

2 teaspoons flour

1 wineglassful of water

salt and pepper to taste

1 heaped tablespoon
  chopped parsley

the juice of ½ large lemon

2 finely chopped shallots
  when liked

THE SAME FLAVOURINGS are used here as in Maître d'Hôtel Butter, but the addition of water makes the butter less rich (Mrs Beeton described this as *maîgre*). It also goes further and serves more people. It is like a thin parsley sauce, made with melted butter rather than béchamel, and it goes well with grilled, fried or poached fish, and also with chicken.

METHOD

Cut the butter up into small pieces, put it in a saucepan and melt it. Dredge it with flour. Add the water and a seasoning of salt and pepper. Stir it one way constantly until blended smooth, then bring it to the boil and stir in the remaining ingredients. Let the sauce just simmer for 1 minute, then it is ready to serve.

Mrs Beeton writes

"PARSLEY – If there be nothing new under the sun, there are, at any rate, different uses found for the same thing; for this pretty aromatic herb was used in ancient times, as we learn from mythological narrative, to adorn the head of a hero, no less than Hercules; and now – was ever fall so great? – we moderns use it in connection with the head of – a calf. According to Homer's *Iliad*, warriors fed their chariot-steeds on parsley; and Pliny acquaints us with the fact that, as a symbol of mourning, it was admitted to furnish the funeral tables of the Romans."

NOTHING COMPARES WITH THE FLAVOUR of homemade mint sauce, the traditional accompaniment for roast lamb in England. Mrs Beeton's original quantities of mint and sugar were on the frugal side, so they have been increased.

METHOD

Wash the mint, which should be young and fresh-gathered, free from grit. Pick the leaves from the stalks, chop them very finely and put them into a sauce boat. Add the sugar and vinegar and stir until the former is dissolved. This sauce is better by being made 2 or 3 hours before required, as the vinegar then becomes impregnated with the flavour of the mint.

NOTES

Vinegar Malt vinegar would have been used in Victorian days, but it is very strong. Cider vinegar is good in mint sauce, or you could use a red or white wine vinegar.

Mrs Beeton writes

"By many persons,
the above proportion of sugar would not
be considered sufficient; but as tastes vary,
we have given the quantity, which we
have found to suit a general palate."

Time ¼ hour
Sufficient to serve with a
  middling-sized joint
  of lamb

INGREDIENTS
4 tablespoons chopped mint
2 tablespoons caster sugar
¼ pint (150 ml) vinegar

LIFE WAS REGIMENTED
AND HARD FOR
SERVANTS IN VICTORIAN
DAYS, AND IT WAS THE
COOK WHO RULED THE
ROOST IN THE KITCHEN,
ESPECIALLY IN SMALLER
HOMES WHERE THERE
WAS NO BUTLER OR
OTHER MALE STAFF.
THESE QUOTATIONS,
FROM MRS BEETON'S
'INTRODUCTION TO
COOKERY' MAKE
FASCINATING READING.

IF THE QUALITY OF EARLY RISING be of the first importance to the mistress, what must it be to the servant! In a cook, this quality is most essential; for an hour lost in the morning, will keep her toiling, absolutely toiling, all day, to overtake that which might otherwise have been achieved with ease. In large establishments, six is a good hour to rise in the summer, and seven in the winter.

HER FIRST DUTY, in large establishments and where it is requisite, should be to set her dough for the breakfast rolls, provided this has not been done on the previous night, and then to engage herself with those numerous little preliminary occupations which may not inappropriately be termed laying out her duties for the day. This will bring in the breakfast hour of eight, after which, directions must be given, and preparations made, for the different dinners of the household and family.

IN THOSE NUMEROUS HOUSEHOLDS where a cook and housemaid are only kept, the general custom is, that the cook should have the charge of the dining room. In establishments of this kind, the cook will, after having lighted her kitchen fire, carefully brushed the range and cleaned the hearth, proceed to prepare for breakfast. She will thoroughly rinse the kettle, and, filling it with fresh water, will put it on the fire to boil. She will then go to the breakfast-room, or parlour, and there make all things ready for the breakfast of the family.

THE CLEANING of the kitchen, pantry, passages, and kitchen stairs must always be over before breakfast, so that it may not interfere with the other business of the day. Everything should be ready, and the whole house should wear a comfortable aspect when the heads of the house and members of the family make their appearance.

BY THE TIME THAT THE COOK has performed the duties mentioned above, and well swept, brushed, and dusted her kitchen, the breakfast-bell will most likely summon her to the parlour, to 'bring in' the breakfast. It is the cook's department, generally, in the smaller establishments, to wait at breakfast, as the housemaid by this time has gone up-stairs into the bedrooms, and has there applied herself to her various duties.

IT IS IN HER PREPARATION of the dinner that the cook begins to feel the weight and responsibility of her situation, as she must take upon herself all the dressing [cooking] and the serving of the principal dishes, which her skill and ingenuity have mostly prepared. 'A place for everything, and everything in its place', must be her rule, in order that time may not be wasted in looking for things when they are wanted, and in order that the whole apparatus of cooking may move with the regularity and precision of a well-adjusted machine – all must go on simultaneously. The vegetables and sauces must be ready with the dishes they are to accompany, and in order that they may be suitable, the smallest oversight must not be made in their preparation.

WHEN THE DINNER-HOUR has arrived, it is the duty of the cook to dish-up such dishes as may, without injury, stand, for some time, covered on the hot plate or in the hot closet; but such as are of a more important or *recherché* kind, must be delayed until the order 'to serve' is given from the drawing-room. Then comes haste; but there must be no hurry – all must work with order. The cook takes charge of the fish, soups, and poultry; and the kitchen-maid of the vegetables, sauces and gravies. These she puts into their appropriate dishes, whilst the scullery-maid waits on and assists the cook. Everything must be timed as to prevent its getting cold, whilst great care should be taken, that, between the first and second courses, no more time is allowed to elapse than is necessary, for fear that the company in the dining-room lose all relish for what has yet to come of the dinner.

WHEN THE DINNER has been served, the most important feature in the daily life of the cook is at the end. She must, however, now begin to look to the contents of her larder, taking care to keep everything sweet and clean, so that no disagreeable smells may arise from the gravies, milk or meat that may be there. These are the principal duties of a cook in a first-rate establishment.

৯ A Very Rich and Good Mushroom Sauce

Time 15 to 20 minutes
Sufficient for 8 people or to
   serve with 2 chickens

INGREDIENTS
1 lb (500 g) button
   mushrooms
2 oz (60 g) butter
½ oz (15 g) flour
1 pint (600 ml) cream
salt and pepper to taste
a little grated nutmeg
1 blade of mace, pounded

QUICK AND EASY TO MAKE, this sauce is very good poured over plain grilled chicken or served in a sauce boat alongside roast chicken. It can also be tossed with pasta.

METHOD
Rub the mushrooms with a cloth dipped in salt, to take off the skins, and cut off the stalks. Put the mushroom caps in a saucepan with the butter and stir over a low heat for a few minutes. Add the flour and stir for 1 minute, then add the remaining ingredients. Simmer for about 10 minutes, stirring all the time. Taste the sauce for seasoning before serving.

NOTES
Cream Use double cream or crème fraîche.

৯ To Mix Mustard

INGREDIENTS
mustard powder
salt
water

ENGLISH MUSTARD IS HOT AND FIERY. Mrs Beeton had plenty to say about the proper way to make it.

METHOD
Mustard should be mixed with water that has been boiled and allowed to cool. Hot water destroys its essential properties, and raw cold water might cause it to ferment. Put the mustard in a cup with a small pinch of salt and mix with it gradually sufficient boiled water to make it drop from the spoon without being watery. Stir and mix well and rub the lumps well down with the back of a spoon, as well-mixed mustard should be perfectly free from these. The mustard-pot should not be more than half full, or rather less if it will not be used in a day or two, as it is so much better when freshly mixed.

SAVOURY BUTTERS, GRAVIES & SAUCES

Brown Mushroom Sauce &

THIS SAUCE IS VERY GOOD with steak. If you like, you can add a splash or two of red wine, sherry, port or Madeira to it, plus a sprinkling of finely chopped fresh parsley just before serving.

METHOD

Prepare the mushrooms by cutting off the stalks and wiping the caps free from grit and dirt. Heat the stock or gravy in a saucepan, thicken it with the butter and flour and stir it over the heat until it boils. Put the mushrooms into the stock or gravy and let them simmer very gently for about 10 minutes. Add the ketchup, taste and add salt and pepper if necessary, then serve.

NOTES

Good beef stock or gravy Use either of the recipes on pages 197 and 199, or you can use a carton of fresh beef stock from the supermarket.

Thickening Use 1 teaspoon each of butter and flour to make a paste (*beurre manié*) and add it to the stock or gravy a little at a time, whisking vigorously until the liquid boils and thickens.

Mushroom ketchup is a spicy bottled condiment that will intensify the mushroom flavour of this sauce. You can get it in some delicatessens. An alternative is to use a few dried mushrooms (porcini or shiitake). Soak them in warm water for 20 to 30 minutes, then drain and finely chop them. Add them to the gravy at the beginning.

Mrs Beeton writes

"The large flap mushrooms cut into small pieces will answer for a brown sauce, when the buttons are not obtainable."

"THE MUSHROOM – The cultivated or garden mushroom is a species of fungus, which, in England, is considered the best, and is there usually eaten. The tribe, however, is numerous, and a large proportion of them are poisonous; hence it is always dangerous to make use of mushrooms gathered in their wild state. In some parts of Europe, as in Germany, Russia, and Poland, many species grow wild, and are used as food; but in Britain, two only are generally eaten."

Time rather more than
  10 minutes
Sufficient for 4 to 6 persons

INGREDIENTS
½ lb (250 g) button
  mushrooms
½ pint (300 ml) good beef
  stock or gravy
thickening of butter and
  flour
1 tablespoon mushroom
  ketchup
salt and pepper to taste

✑ *White Mushroom Sauce*

Time ¼ hour
Sufficient for 4 persons

INGREDIENTS
rather more than ½ lb
  (250 g) button mushrooms
lemon juice and water
1 oz (30 g) butter
½ pint (300 ml) Béchamel
  Sauce (page 201)
¼ teaspoon caster sugar
salt and pepper to taste

THIS SAUCE IS GOOD served with grilled or pan-fried chicken or turkey; it is also good tossed with pasta. For a special occasion, stir in a few spoonfuls of cream just before serving.

METHOD
Turn the mushrooms white by putting them into lemon juice and water, having previously cut off the stalks and wiped the caps perfectly free from grit. Chop them, and put them in a saucepan with the butter. Heat very gently. When the mushrooms are softened, add the béchamel, sugar and seasoning and simmer for about 5 minutes. If the mushrooms are not done enough, allow rather more time, but they should not boil longer than necessary or they will then lose their colour and flavour. Rub the mushrooms and liquid through a sieve and serve very hot. After this, the mushroom sauce should be warmed in a *bain marie*.

NOTES
Sieving This can be hard work. Instead, purée the sauce in a food processor or blender. For a really smooth consistency, work it through a sieve after puréeing. Alternatively, leave it textured. After puréeing, you may need to adjust the concistency of the sauce by thinning it down with a little milk or cream.

Mrs Beeton writes

"GROWTH OF THE MUSHROOM AND OTHER FUNGI –
The quick growth of the mushroom and other fungi is no less
wonderful than the length of time they live, and the numerous
dangers they resist while they continue in the dormant state.
To spring up 'like a mushroom in a night' is a scriptural mode
of expressing celerity."

MRS BEETON GAVE THIS SAUCE an English name, but it is her version of the classic French *sauce genevoise*, which was originally called *sauce génoise* by the great French chef Carême. Classic recipes use red wine, but sherry is used here. It is a sauce to serve with fish, especially salmon and trout.

METHOD

Cut up the onion and carrot into small rings and put them into a saucepan with the parsley, mushrooms, bay leaf, cloves and mace. Add the butter and simmer very gently over a low heat until the onion is quite tender. Pour in the stock and sherry and cook slowly for 1 hour, then strain into a clean saucepan and reheat it. Now make a thickening of butter and flour, add it to the sauce and stir it over the heat until perfectly smooth and mellow. Add the lemon juice, bring it to the boil and it will be ready to serve.

NOTES

White stock is made from veal and poultry trimmings. You can use fish, chicken or vegetable stock instead.

Thickening Use 1 teaspoon each of butter and flour to make a paste *(beurre manié)*. Add it little by little to the sauce, whisking vigorously after each addition until the sauce boils and thickens.

Time 2 hours
Sufficient for 4 slices of
  salmon

INGREDIENTS
1 onion
1 small carrot
a small bunch of parsley
5 or 6 mushrooms when
  obtainable
1 bay leaf
6 cloves
1 blade of mace
2 oz (60 g) butter
1½ pints (900 ml) White
  Stock (page 335)
1 glass of sherry
thickening of butter and
  flour paste
the juice of half a lemon

✺ Brown Onion Sauce

Time 1 hour
Sufficient for 4 persons

INGREDIENTS
6 large onions
2 oz (60 g) butter
rather more than ½ pint
    (300 ml) good stock or
    gravy
salt and pepper to taste

NOWADAYS WE CALL THIS onion gravy, the perfect partner for grilled or fried sausages and mashed potatoes. Mrs Beeton sieved the onions out of the sauce, but you can leave them in if you prefer a sauce with a chunky texture.

METHOD
Slice the onions and fry them until pale brown in a saucepan with the given quantity of butter, keeping them well stirred so that they do not get black. When a nice colour, pour the stock or gravy over them and let them simmer gently until tender. Now skim off every particle of fat, add the seasoning, and rub them through a sieve. Put the sauce back in the pan and heat until boiling, then serve.

NOTES
Good stock or gravy Gravy left over from a roast would be ideal. A Cheap Gravy (page 197) is another option.

✺ Sweet Sauce For Venison

Time 5 minutes
Sufficient for 6 to 8 persons

INGREDIENTS
a small jar of redcurrant
    jelly
1 glass of port

INSTRUCTIONS FOR THIS RECIPE ARE short and sweet. It is the traditional accompaniment for venison and is also good with other rich meats, poultry or game. If you find it too sweet, sharpen it by adding lemon juice to taste.

METHOD
Put all the ingredients into a small saucepan and set them over the heat. When melted, pour into a sauce boat and serve. It should not be allowed to boil.

THIS IS THE CLASSIC *sauce soubise*, which takes it name from Charles de Rohan, Prince of Soubise, an 18th century French aristocrat with a keen interest in the culinary arts. Serve it with eggs, veal and vegetables. It also goes well with chicken, turkey and lamb.

Time 1 to 1¼ hours
Sufficient for a moderate-
sized dish

INGREDIENTS
6 onions
1 bay leaf
a small piece of ham
seasoning to taste of
cayenne pepper and
pounded mace
½ pint (300 ml) hot
Béchamel Sauce
(page 201)

METHOD
Peel the onions and cut them in halves. Put them in a saucepan with just sufficient water to cover them and add the bay leaf, ham, cayenne and mace. Be careful to keep the lid closely shut and simmer the onions until tender – about ¾ hour. Take them out and drain thoroughly, then rub them through a sieve (an old one does for the purpose) with a wooden spoon. Put them in the béchamel and keep stirring over the heat until it boils, then serve. If the sauce should require any more seasoning, add it to taste.

NOTES
Ham This can be omitted. No salt is added in Mrs Beeton's recipe, possibly because of the natural saltiness of the ham, so if you do not include ham, you may need to add a little salt.
Sieving To make this easier, you can purée the onions in a blender or food processor first.
Béchamel sauce Use Mrs Beeton's recipe, as this is made with stock and cream, the ideal combination for a classic French *sauce soubise*.

Mrs Beeton writes

"HISTORY OF THE ONION – It is not supposed that any variety of the onion is indigenous to Britain, as when the large and mild roots imported from warmer climates have been cultivated in these islands a few years, they deteriorate both in size and sweetness. It is therefore most likely that this plant was first introduced into England from continental Europe, and that it originally was produced in a southern climate, and has gradually become acclimatized to a colder atmosphere."

✑ *Oyster Sauce*

Time ½ hour
Sufficient for 4 or 5 persons

INGREDIENTS
2 dozen oysters
3 cloves
1 blade of mace
2 oz (60 g) butter
½ teaspoon flour
cayenne pepper and salt
   to taste

IN VICTORIAN DAYS when oysters were plentiful and cheap, oyster sauce was often served with grilled steaks. Mrs Beeton gave a graphic description of how the dish should be served. 'Have ready in the centre of a dish walls of mashed potatoes, browned; into the middle pour the oyster sauce, quite hot, and round the potatoes place, in layers, slices of the beef, which should be previously broiled over a nice clear fire.' Nowadays, we simply spoon the sauce over the steak.

METHOD
Put the oysters in a saucepan, with their liquor strained. Add the cloves, mace, butter, flour and seasoning and let them simmer gently for 5 minutes.

NOTES
Oysters are in season from September to April, when there is an 'r' in the month. For this recipe they need to be shelled or 'shucked'. Hold each oyster in a cloth with the rounded side of the shell down and the hinge facing you. Insert an oyster knife just below the hinge and twist it to prise the two shells apart. Work the knife between the two shells, severing the muscle, then lift off the top shell. Run the knife blade under the oyster to detach it from the bottom shell. Make sure not to spill any of the liquor, which is needed for the sauce. The beard is the dark frilly edge on the oyster. It can easily be cut off with kitchen scissors.

Mrs Beeton writes

"EXCELLENCE OF THE ENGLISH OYSTER – The French assert that the English oysters, which are esteemed the best in Europe, were originally procured from Cancalle Bay, near St Malo; but they assign no proof for this. It is a fact, however, that the oysters eaten in ancient Rome were nourished in the channel which then parted the Isle of Thanet from England, and which has since been filled up, and converted to meadows."

Shrimp Sauce ↶

THIS IS A PRETTY SAUCE to serve with fish, especially white fish fillets such as fried plaice. It also goes well with salmon. At the end of the recipe Mrs Beeton suggested adding anchovy sauce. This is an excellent idea – if you add a drop or two of anchovy essence, it will accentuate the flavour of the shrimps.

METHOD

Cut the butter up into small pieces, put it in a saucepan, melt it, then dredge it with flour. Stir in the water and a seasoning of salt. Stir it one way constantly until all the ingredients are thoroughly blended and very smooth. Put in the shrimps, season with cayenne, and let the sauce just simmer. Do not allow it to boil.

NOTES

Shrimps are fiddly to peel, but they are very good in sauces, whereas prawns, which are larger and easier to prepare, tend to be bland. Brown shrimps have more flavour than the pretty pink ones. They are sold cooked, usually by weight rather than volume. For this recipe you will need 2–3 oz (60–90 g).

Mrs Beeton writes

"When liked, a teaspoonful
of anchovy sauce may be added."

Time ¼ hour
Sufficient for 3 or 4 persons

INGREDIENTS
¼ lb (125 g) butter
2 teaspoons flour
1 wineglassful of water
salt to taste
⅓–½ pint (200–300 ml)
    peeled shrimps
cayenne to taste

✎ Sauce Allemande

Time ½ hour

Sufficient for 4 to 6 persons

INGREDIENTS

1 pint (600 ml) White Stock
   (page 335)

a bunch of savoury herbs
   including parsley

6 spring onions

6 chopped mushrooms

thickening of flour and
   butter

the yolks of 2 eggs

THIS EGG-ENRICHED SAUCE was given its literal translation of German Sauce by Mrs Beeton and described as 'a general favourite – used for many made dishes'. In classic French cuisine, with the addition of a little cream, it is known as *sauce velouté* or *sauce Parisienne*, and it forms the basis of many other sauces. It is good with fish and poultry.

METHOD

Put the stock into a saucepan with the herbs, onions and mushrooms and let it simmer very gently for about ½ hour. Strain it into a clean saucepan, then stir in sufficient thickening to make it of a proper consistency. Let it boil for a few minutes, then skim off all the fat. Stir into it the beaten yolks of the eggs, which have been previously strained. Let it just simmer and stir it without ceasing. Do not let it boil or the eggs will curdle.

NOTES

White stock is made from veal and poultry trimmings. You can equally well use chicken or vegetable stock.

Savoury herbs Use a fresh bouquet garni of parsley, thyme, bay leaf and a piece of celery.

Thickening Use a very small amount of butter and flour (1 teaspoon each) to make a paste *(beurre manié)*. Add it to the sauce and whisk vigorously until it boils.

Sauce Robert ❧

THIS CLASSIC FRENCH SAUCE dates back to the 16th century. It is a brown onion sauce made piquant with mustard and vinegar, originally created to serve with pork but often served with steak and other meats and poultry. As Mrs Beeton said: 'This sauce will be found an excellent accompaniment to roast goose, pork, mutton cutlets, and various other dishes'.

METHOD

Put the butter into a saucepan and set it over the heat. When browning, throw in the onions, which must be cut into small slices. Fry them until brown, but do not burn them. Add the flour, shake the onions in it and fry everything together for a minute or two. Put in the gravy or stock and seasoning and boil it gently for 10 minutes. Skim off the fat, add the mustard, vinegar and lemon juice and bring it to just to the boil. Pour round the steaks, or whatever dish the sauce has been prepared for.

NOTES

Gravy or stock Use Medium Stock (page 334) or a well-flavoured beef stock.

Time ½ hour
Sufficient for about 2 lb
 (1 kg) steak

INGREDIENTS
2 oz (60 g) butter
3 onions
1 teaspoon flour
4 tablespoons gravy or stock
salt and pepper to taste
1 teaspoon made mustard
1 teaspoon vinegar
the juice of ½ lemon

Time ½ hour

Sufficient for a medium-sized dish of cutlets

INGREDIENTS

2 oz (60 g) butter

1 small carrot

6 shallots

1 small bunch of savoury
herbs, including parsley

½ bay leaf

2 cloves

6 peppercorns

1 blade of mace

3 allspice berries

2 slices of lean ham

4 tablespoons vinegar

½ pint (300 ml) Medium
Stock (page 334)

1 small lump of sugar

pinch of cayenne pepper

salt to taste

VINEGAR, HERBS AND SPICES give this rich meaty sauce its piquant flavour. It is recommended for cutlets and roast meat.

METHOD

Put the butter into a saucepan with the carrot and shallots, both of which must be cut into small slices. Add the herbs, bay leaf, spices and ham (which must be chopped rather finely), and let these ingredients simmer over a low heat until the bottom of the pan is covered with a brown glaze. Keep stirring with a wooden spoon, then stir in the remaining ingredients and simmer very gently for ¼ hour. Skim off every particle of fat, strain the sauce through a sieve into a clean pan and serve very hot.

NOTES

Savoury herbs Use rosemary if the sauce is to be served with lamb; thyme with beef and sage with pork.

Medium stock is rich and meaty. If you don't use this, you can use any good beef or chicken stock.

Mrs Beeton writes
_____

"Care must be taken that this sauce be not made too acid, although it should possess a sharpness indicated by its name. Of course the above quantity of vinegar may be increased or diminished at pleasure, according to taste."

QUITE RIGHTLY, MRS BEETON recommended making this sauce 'in September and October'. There is little point in making a fresh tomato sauce at any other time of year because the tomatoes will not be sufficiently ripe and therefore will not have a good flavour. She said the shallots and spices could be omitted 'when their flavour is objected to'. Instead, you could add some chopped fresh basil just before serving.

METHOD

Cut the tomatoes in two and squeeze the seeds out. Put them in a saucepan with all the other ingredients and let them simmer gently until the tomatoes are tender enough to pulp – about 1 hour. Rub everything through a sieve into a clean pan, boil it for a few minutes and serve.

NOTES

Gravy The original recipe made reference to two recipes for rich beef gravy. Adding gravy is not uncommon in some traditional Italian recipes for tomato sauce, the reasoning being that the gravy gave an inexpensive vegetable sauce a meaty taste without the need for meat – which was costly. If the tomatoes you are using are flavoursome and you prefer to keep the sauce strictly vegetarian, you can use water instead of gravy. For extra flavour, use red or white wine or vegetable stock, or a mixture of these.

Mrs Beeton writes

"TOMATO OR LOVE APPLE – The plant which bears this fruit is a native of South America, and takes its name from a Portuguese word. The tomato fruit is about the size of a small potato, and is chiefly used in soups, sauces, and gravies. It is sometimes served to table roasted or boiled, and when green makes a good ketchup or pickle. In its unripe state, it is esteemed as an excellent sauce for roast goose or pork, and when quite ripe, a good store sauce may be prepared from it."

Time 1¼ hours or rather more

Sufficient for 2 persons

INGREDIENTS

6 tomatoes

2 shallots

1 clove

1 blade of mace

salt and cayenne pepper to taste

¼ pint (150 ml) gravy

❧ *White Sauce*

Time ¼ hour
Sufficient to make about
 1 pint (600 ml)

INGREDIENTS
2 small onions
1 carrot
2 oz (60 g) butter
½ a small teacupful flour
1 pint (600 ml) milk
salt and cayenne pepper to
 taste

THIS WAS DESCRIBED by Mrs Beeton as 'White Sauce made without Meat', to distinguish it from Béchamel Sauce (page 201), which is made with meat stock. It is a simple sauce, but it can be made even more simple by omitting the vegetables at the beginning – see the Variation at the end of the recipe.

METHOD

Cut up the onions and carrot very small and put them into a saucepan with the butter. Simmer them until the butter is nearly dried up, then stir in the flour and then the milk. Boil gently until it thickens, strain and season with salt and cayenne, and the sauce will be ready to serve.

NOTES

Flour The usual proportions are 2 oz (60 g) each of butter and flour to 1 pint (600 ml) milk for a fairly thick or coating sauce. For a thinner, pouring sauce, use 1½ oz (40 g) each butter and flour to 1 pint (600 ml) milk.

VARIATION

Simple White Sauce Melt the butter in a saucepan, sprinkle in the flour and stir for 1 to 2 minutes to make a golden roux. Remove the pan from the heat and add the milk a little at a time, whisking vigorously after each addition. When all the milk has been added, return the pan to the heat and bring the sauce to the boil, whisking constantly. Simmer for a few minutes, season and serve.

MRS BEETON'S ORIGINAL RECIPE used a small amount of oil and a large amount of vinegar, then finished the mayonnaise off with stock and cream. The recipe here is more traditional. It makes a rich and creamy mayonnaise, which can be flavoured as you wish. For best resuslts, use a hand-held electric mixer or a balloon whisk.

METHOD

Put the yolks of the eggs into a bowl with a seasoning of salt and pepper. Have ready the oil and vinegar or lemon juice in separate jugs. Add the oil a drop at a time to the eggs, constantly stirring and rubbing the mixture with a wooden spoon, as this is the secret of having a nice smooth sauce. It cannot be stirred too frequently and it should be made in a very cool place or, if ice is at hand, it should be mixed over it. When enough of the oil is incorporated with the eggs that the mayonnaise begins to turn pale and thick, add the remainder in a thin, steady stream. When all of the oil has been added in this way, gradually add the vinegar or lemon juice and taste the mayonnaise until it is to your liking. Add more salt and pepper if necessary.

NOTES

Salad oil Sunflower or olive oil is good in mayonnaise, or you could use a mixture of the two.

Flavourings If you like, add 1 to 2 teaspoons Dijon mustard with the egg yolks at the beginning. Or add 1 to 2 tablespoons chopped fresh herbs at the end.

Curdling If the mayonnaise does not thicken as you add the oil, or if it shows signs of curdling, start again in a clean bowl with a fresh egg yolk and work the curdled mixture into it a drop at a time.

Food processor method Put 1 whole egg and 1 egg yolk into the bowl with the seasonings. With the machine running, add the oil in a slow steady stream through the funnel. Add the vinegar or lemon juice in the same manner.

Time 20 to 30 minutes
Sufficient for about ½ pint
 (300 ml)

INGREDIENTS
the yolks of 2 eggs
salt and white pepper
 to taste
8 fl oz (250 ml) salad oil
2 tablespoons cider or wine
 vinegar or lemon juice

Mrs Beeton writes

"For a fish mayonnaise, this sauce may be coloured with lobster-spawn, pounded; and for poultry or meat, where variety is desired, a little parsley-juice may be used to add to its appearance. Cucumber, tarragon, or any other flavoured vinegar, may be substituted for plain, where they are liked."

✑ Rémoulade

Time ½ hour
Sufficient for 4 persons

INGREDIENTS
3 eggs, plus 1 egg yolk
½ teaspoon made mustard
salt and cayenne pepper
   to taste
1 tablespoon tarragon or
   malt vinegar
3 tablespoons olive oil

MRS BEETON ALSO DESCRIBED this as 'French salad dressing', maybe because it is not a classic *sauce rémoulade*, which is made with anchovies, capers, gherkins and herbs. This recipe is simpler, a kind of spicy mayonnaise. It goes well with cold meats, fish and shellfish.

METHOD

Boil 3 eggs quite hard for about ¼ hour, put them into cold water and let them remain in it for a few minutes. Strip off the shells, put the yolks in a mortar and pound them very smoothly. Add to them, very gradually, the mustard, seasoning and vinegar, keeping all well stirred and rubbed down with the back of a wooden spoon. Put in the oil drop by drop, and when this is thoroughly mixed with the other ingredients, add the yolk of a raw egg. Stir well, then it will be ready for use.

Mrs Beeton writes

"This sauce should not be curdled. To prevent this, the only way is to mix a little of everything at a time, and not to cease stirring. The quantities of oil and vinegar may be increased or diminished according to taste, as many persons would prefer a smaller proportion of the former ingredient."

"TARRAGON – The leaves of this plant, known to naturalists as *Artemisia dracunculus*, are much used in France as a flavouring ingredients for salads. From it also is made the vinegar known as tarragon vinegar, which is employed by the French in mixing their mustard. It originally comes from Tartary, and does not seed in France."

MRS BEETON DESCRIBED this recipe as excellent, then went on to say: 'If this dressing is properly made, it will have a soft creamy appearance and will be found very delicious with crab or cold fried fish (the latter cut into dice), as well as with salads'.

METHOD

Put the mustard into a salad bowl with the sugar and add the oil drop by drop, carefully stirring everything well together. Proceed in this manner with the milk and vinegar, which must be added very gradually or the sauce will curdle. Put in the seasoning, then the mixture will be ready for use. In mixing salad dressings, the ingredients cannot be added too gradually, or stirred too much.

NOTES

Salad oil Use olive oil, as mentioned in the paragraph about olives and olive oil at the end of the recipe.

Mrs Beeton writes

"This recipe can be confidently recommended by the editress, to whom it was given by an intimate friend noted for her salads."

"THE OLIVE AND OLIVE OIL – Both in Greece and Portugal the fruit is eaten in its ripe state; but its taste is not agreeable to many palates. To the Italian shepherd, bread and olives, with a little wine, form a nourishing diet, but in England, olives are usually only introduced by way of dessert, to destroy the taste of the viands which have been previously eaten, that the flavour of the wine may be the better enjoyed. There are three kinds of olives imported to London – the French, Spanish, and Italian: the first are from Provence, and are generally accounted excellent; the second are larger, but more bitter; and the last are from Lucca, and are esteemed the best. The oil extracted from olives, called olive oil, or salad oil, is, with the continentals, in continual request, more dishes being prepared with than without it, we should imagine. With us, it is principally used in mixing a salad, and when thus employed, it tends to prevent fermentation, and is an antidote against flatulency."

Time ¼ hour
Sufficient for a small salad

INGREDIENTS
1 teaspoon made mustard
1 teaspoon caster sugar
2 tablespoons salad oil
4 tablespoons milk
2 tablespoons vinegar
cayenne pepper and salt
  to taste

℘ Sweet Cherry Sauce

Time ½ hour
Sufficient for 4 or 5 persons

INGREDIENTS
1 lb (500 g) cherries
1 oz (30 g) butter
1 tablespoon flour
½ pint (300 ml) water
1 wineglass of port
a little grated lemon rind
1 or 2 pounded cloves
   to taste
2 tablespoons lemon juice
sugar to taste

THIS WAS DESCRIBED AS a German recipe for sweet puddings, seasonable in June, July and August. In the original recipe a few of the cherry kernels were pounded to a smooth paste in a mortar, but this seems unnecessary hard work and has therefore been omitted. It also seems like hard work to sieve the sauce, and a pity not to keep the colourful pieces of cherry in it. You may prefer to ignore this instruction.

METHOD
Stone the cherries. Put the butter and flour into a saucepan, stir them over the heat until pale brown, then stir in the cherries, water and port. Simmer these gently for ¼ hour or until the cherries are quite cooked. Rub everything through a sieve into a clean pan and add the remaining ingredients. Let the sauce boil for another 5 minutes and serve in a bowl.

℘ Sweet Lemon Sauce

Time ¼ hour
Sufficient for 7 or 8 persons

INGREDIENTS
the rind and juice of 1 lemon
a few lumps of sugar
1 oz (30 g) butter
1 tablespoon flour
1 large wineglass of sherry
1 wineglass of water
the yolks of 4 eggs

THIS SMOOTH TANGY SAUCE tastes good with hot sweet puddings, especially steamed puddings. The egg yolks make it quite rich; if you prefer a lighter sauce, use half the quantity of egg yolks.

METHOD
Rub the rind of the lemon on some lumps of sugar. Squeeze out the lemon juice and strain it. Put the butter and flour into a saucepan and stir them over the heat. When pale brown, stir in the sherry, water and strained lemon juice. Crush the lumps of sugar that were rubbed on the lemon and stir these into the sauce, which should be very sweet. When these ingredients are well mixed and the sugar is melted, put in the beaten egg yolks. Keep stirring the sauce until it thickens, then serve. Do not, on any account, allow it to boil, or it will curdle and be entirely spoiled.

SAVOURY BUTTERS, GRAVIES & SAUCES

THIS IS REAL CUSTARD, made with eggs. The brandy can be omitted and other flavourings used instead, as Mrs Beeton suggested at the end of the recipe.

METHOD

Put the milk into a saucepan and let it boil. Beat the eggs in a bowl, stir into them the sugar, then the milk. Place the bowl in a saucepan of boiling water and keep stirring well until the custard thickens. Do not allow it to boil, or it will curdle. Pour the sauce into a jug, stir in the brandy and grate a little nutmeg over the top.

NOTES

Eggs You can use more of these to make a richer custard. In some of her recipes Mrs Beeton used as many as 8 eggs, but 3 or 4 would be ample. Another way of enriching custard is to add an extra 1 to 2 egg yolks rather than whole eggs.

Cooking the custard in a bowl set in a pan of boiling water protects the eggs from direct heat and so helps to prevent them from curdling. If you mix 2 teaspoons cornflour with the eggs and sugar, you can dispense with the bowl and make the custard in the saucepan.

Mrs Beeton writes

"This sauce may be made very much nicer by using cream instead of milk; but the above recipe will be found quite good enough for ordinary purposes. When liked, a few drops of vanilla or almond essence, or the grated rind of a lemon, can be used instead of the brandy and nutmeg."

VANILLE or VANILLA – is the fruit of the *vanillier*, a parasitical herbaceous plant, which flourishes in Brazil, Mexico, and Peru. The fruit is a long capsule, thick and fleshy. Certain species of this fruit contain a pulp with a delicious perfume and flavour. Vanilla is principally imported from Mexico. The capsules for export are always picked at perfect maturity. The essence is the form in which it is used generally and most conveniently. Its properties are stimulating and exciting. It is in daily use for ices, chocolates, and flavouring confections generally.

Time 20 minutes
Sufficient for 2 fruit tarts or
  1 pudding

INGREDIENTS
1 pint (600 ml) milk
2 eggs
3 oz (90 g) sugar
1 tablespoon brandy
nutmeg

A Good Sweet Sauce
for Various Boiled Puddings

Time 10 to 15 minutes
Sufficient for a pudding

INGREDIENTS
¼ lb (125 g) butter
¼ lb (125 g) icing sugar
a wineglassful of brandy
  or rum

WE WOULD CALL THIS a brandy or rum butter rather than a sauce, and serve it chilled with Christmas pudding.

METHOD
Beat the butter to a cream until no lumps remain. Add the sugar and brandy or rum, stir once or twice until everything is thoroughly mixed, then serve.

NOTES
Butter Use unsalted butter.
Chilling Pack the flavoured butter into a bowl, cover and chill in the refrigerator until firm. It can be made up to 1 to 2 weeks before it is needed, as long as the butter used is fresh. This sauce can also be frozen.

An Excellent Wine Sauce for Puddings

Time ¼ hour
Sufficient for 7 or 8 persons

INGREDIENTS
2 oz (60 g) butter
1 teaspoon flour
2 oz (60 g) caster sugar
pinch of salt
½ pint (300 ml) sherry
  or Madeira
the yolks of 4 eggs

RICH WITH EGG YOLKS and heady with alcohol, this is one of many wine sauces included by Mrs Beeton in her original book. It is a very special recipe, which she said was delicious with plum and bread puddings. It should be served separately in a jug, and not poured over the pudding.

METHOD
Put the butter and flour into a saucepan and stir them over the heat until thickened, then add the sugar, salt and sherry or Madeira and mix these ingredients well together. Beat the egg yolks, stir them briskly into the sauce and heat gently until it is on the point of simmering. Keep stirring the sauce and do not allow it to boil or it will instantly curdle.

THIS WAS OFTEN REFERRED TO as brandy sauce by Mrs Beeton, and she described it as 'very rich and excellent'. It is the classic sauce to serve with Christmas pudding, although brandy butter is more popular these days – see A Good Sweet Sauce for Various Boiled Puddings (opposite).

METHOD

Put the sugar in a bowl with part of the brandy and the butter. Heat it very gently over simmering water until it is warm and the sugar and butter are dissolved, then add the rest of the brandy with the Madeira. Either pour it over the pudding, or serve in a jug.

NOTES

Icing sugar to taste Start by using 2 tablespoons, then add more if necessary.

Madeira is a fortified wine from the island of the same name. There are many different types, ranging from pale and golden to tawny and dark, and it can be either dry or sweet. If don't have any, you can use port or sherry instead.

Time 10 minutes
Sufficient for a pudding
  made for 6 persons

INGREDIENTS
icing sugar to taste
1 wineglass of brandy
2 oz (60 g) very fresh butter
1 glass of Madeira

CHAPTER 8

Sweet Pastries
& Hot Puddings

M rs Beeton learnt pastry making in Germany when she attended finishing school in Heidelberg. She loved it, and her enthusiasm shows in this chapter. After a few opening paragraphs on the history of pudding making and the various cereals used, she made the amusing observation that in Britain we preferred quantity to quality.

'Here from the simple suet dumpling up to the most complicated Christmas production, the grand feature of substantiality is primarily attended to. Variety in the ingredients is held only of secondary consideration with the great body of people, provided that the whole is agreeable and of sufficient abundance.'

Her introduction to pastry making had an authoritative tone.

'Although from puddings to pastry is but a step, it requires a higher degree of art to make the one than the other. Pastry is one of the most important branches of the culinary science. It unceasingly occupies itself with ministering pleasure to the sight as well as to the taste.'

Ingredients were discussed in detail, and there was plenty of information on equipment, illustrated by black and white line drawings. Mrs Beeton's basic rules were sound, and they still hold good today.

'The freshness of all pudding ingredients is of much importance, as one bad article will taint the whole mixture.'

'Strict cleanliness must be observed in pastry-making; all the utensils used should be perfectly free from dust and dirt, and the things required for pastry kept entirely for that purpose.'

'The art of making pastry requires much practice, dexterity and skill. It should be touched as lightly as possible, made with cool hands and in a cool place (a marble slab is better than a board for this purpose). The coolest part of the house should be selected for the process during warm weather."

Recipes were given for many different types of pastry, from a Common Paste for Family Pies to French Puff-Paste or *Feuilletage*. Sweet pastries were followed by baked, boiled and steamed puddings, fruit tarts, batter puddings, dumplings, charlottes, turnovers, rice puddings and several different Christmas plum puddings. In Victorian times, no family dinner was complete without a hot pudding or pastry, and according to the menus in the 'Bills of Fare' at the end of the book, a choice of hot pastries and puddings was served at formal dinners. These came as part of the third course, together with the cold jellies and creams, before the final course of dessert and ices.

Basic pastry recipes are given on pages 337 to 339.

Rich Baked Apple Pudding

Time 1 to 1¼ hour
Sufficient for 6 persons
Seasonable from August
  to March

INGREDIENTS
6 large apples
6 oz (175 g) moist sugar
¼ lb (125 g) butter
4 eggs
1 pint (600 ml) bread
  crumbs
a piece of butter the size of
  a walnut

MRS BEETON GAVE two versions of this pudding. This one she described as 'more economical' because it has fewer eggs and less butter than the other, but it is still plenty rich enough. It is similar to an apple charlotte, but is made with bread crumbs rather than slices of bread. With its hot buttery, juicy fruit, it is absolutely delicious topped with scoops of vanilla ice cream.

METHOD
Peel, core and cut the apples into slices. Cook them with the sugar until reduced to a pulp – about 20 minutes – then add the butter, melted, and the eggs, which should be well whisked. Beat the pudding for 2 or 3 minutes. Butter a pie dish, put in a layer of bread crumbs, then apple, then another layer of bread crumbs. Continue until all the apple and bread crumbs are used. Flake over these a few tiny pieces of butter and bake for about 40 minutes.

The oven should be preheated to 375°F (190°C) Gas 5.

NOTES
Apples Use a good cooking apple such as Bramley.
Moist sugar Light soft brown sugar or demerara sugar can be used. Dark brown and molasses sugars would make the pudding too dark and their strong flavours would mask the delicate flavour of the cooked apples.
Bread crumbs Use freshly made bread crumbs from a loaf that is 1 to 2 days old. You will need 7 oz (200 g).

Mrs Beeton writes

"THE APPLE – The most useful of all the British fruits is the apple, which is a native of Britain, and may be found in woods and hedges, in the form of the common wild crab, of which all our best apples are merely seminal varieties, produced by culture or particular circumstances. In most temperate climates it is very extensively cultivated, and in England, both as regards variety and quantity, it is excellent and abundant. Immense supplies are also imported from the United States and from France. The apples grown in the vicinity of New York are universally admitted to be the finest of any; but unless selected and packed with great care, they are apt to spoil before reaching England."

SWEET PASTRIES & HOT PUDDINGS

Apple Pie ☙

THIS WAS DESCRIBED AS either a tart or a pie by Mrs Beeton, but since it has a pastry lid, we would call it a pie today. Mrs Beeton was rather vague about the quantities of pastry and apples, the size of the dish and the baking time. This recipe provides the essential details. Serve the pie hot or cold, with custard or cream.

METHOD

Make a border around the edge of a pie dish with some of the puff pastry. Fill the dish with apples, peeled, cored and cut into slices, sweeten with sugar, then add the lemon peel and juice and 2 or 3 tablespoons water. Cover with the remaining pastry, cut it evenly round close to the edge of the pie dish and bake from ½ to ¾ hour, or rather longer should the pie be very large. When it is three-parts done, take it out of the oven. Put the white of an egg on a plate and whisk it to a froth with the blade of a knife. Brush the pie over with this, then sprinkle on it some caster sugar and then a few drops of water. Put the pie back into the oven and finish baking, being particularly careful that it does not catch or burn, which it is very liable to do after the crust is iced.

The oven should be preheated to 375°F (190°C) Gas 5.

NOTES

Pie dish For this amount of pastry and filling, use a 9 inch (23 cm) round ceramic or metal pie dish with a rim .

Puff pastry may be homemade (page 337), or you can use bought puff pastry. A speedy solution is to use an 11 x 9 inch (280 x 229 mm) sheet of ready rolled pastry, available in the freezer cabinets at most supermarkets. Brush the rim of the pie dish with water before sticking on the pastry border, then brush this with more water and press the lid into place. Any pastry trimmings can be used to make leaves or other decorations for the top of the pie. Stick them on with a little water before baking.

Apples A dessert apple such as Granny Smiths or McIntosh is good because it is sweet and it holds its shape well during baking.

VARIATION

Short Crust Pastry (page 338) can be used instead of puff. The method and baking instructions will be the same.

Time ¾ to 1 hour
Sufficient for 6 persons
Seasonable from August to March, but the apples become flavourless after February

INGREDIENTS
½ lb (250 g) puff pastry
2 lb (1 kg) apples
¼ lb (125 g) caster sugar
½ teaspoon finely grated lemon peel
1 tablespoon lemon juice
egg white and a little caster sugar to glaze

Mrs Beeton writes

"Many things are suggested for the flavouring of apple pie; some say 2 or 3 tablespoonfuls of beer, others the same quantity of sherry, which very much improves the taste; whilst the old-fashioned addition of a few cloves is, by many persons, preferred to anything else, as also a few slices of quince."

❧ *Bakewell Pudding*

Time ¾ hour
Sufficient for 4 or 5 persons
Seasonable at any time

INGREDIENTS
¼ lb (125 g) puff pastry
5 egg yolks
1 egg white
3–4 oz (90–125 g) caster
  sugar to taste
¼ lb (125 g) butter
1 oz (30 g) flaked almonds
jam

THIS IS THE REAL, traditional Bakewell pudding, not to be confused with the modern-day Bakewell tart, which has a sponge cake filling. The original version of this rich and creamy egg-based pudding was invented in 1859 by the cook at The Rutland Arms in Bakewell, Derbyshire, the inn where Jane Austen wrote *Pride and Prejudice*. It is still made in the town today, following a 'secret' recipe. Mrs Beeton's recipe is one of the many versions that was popular in the nineteenth century. It is an easy pudding to make, and truly delicious. Serve it warm, with pouring cream or custard.

METHOD

Roll out the pastry thinly on a lightly floured surface and use to line a pie dish. Put over this a layer of any kind of jam, ½ inch (1 cm) thick. Put the yolks of 5 eggs into a basin with the white of 1 egg and beat these well. Add the sugar, the butter, which should be melted, and the almonds, which should be well pounded. Beat all together until well mixed, then pour into the dish over the jam. Bake the pudding for ½ hour.

The oven should be preheated to 350°F (180°C) Gas 4.

NOTES

Puff pastry may be homemade (page 337) or you can use bought puff pastry and roll it out to fit the dish. A quicker alternative is to use a 11 x 9 inch (280 x 229 mm) sheet of ready rolled pastry, available in the freezer cabinets at supermarkets. You may need slightly more than the weight specified by Mrs Beeton, depending on how thinly the pastry is rolled.

Pie dish Use a 1½ pint (900 ml) oval pie dish or tin or a 9 inch (23 cm) flan dish or sandwich tin.

Jam Raspberry jam is traditional, but any other red fruit jam may be used instead.

Almonds It is best to use flaked almonds and pound them firmly in a mortar, but ground almonds can be used instead. Buy organic ground almonds if possible: they tend to be more moist and also have more flavour. You can add up to a total of ¼ lb (125 g).

Mrs Beeton writes
—————

"Butter is indispensable in almost all culinary preparations. Good fresh butter, used in moderation, is easily digested; it is softening, nutritious, and fattening, and is far more easily digested than any other of the oleaginous substances sometimes used in its place."

Bread-and-Butter Pudding ∽

BREAD-AND-BUTTER PUDDING was originally made as a means of using up leftover bread and butter from the previous day's tea-time, and in frugal times it made a filling and satisfying end to a meal. Today we need no such excuses. We make it because we love it so much, and rich creamy versions like the ones Mrs Beeton suggested as an alternative to her basic recipe are the most popular. You can use any bread you like, either fresh or a few days old, white or brown.

METHOD

Cut 9 slices of bread and butter not very thick and put them into a pie dish with currants between each layer and on the top. Sweeten and flavour the milk by adding a few drops of essence of vanilla or a little grated nutmeg, or by infusing a little lemon peel in it. Well whisk the eggs and stir these into the milk. Strain this over the bread and butter. Bake for 1 hour or rather longer.

The oven should be preheated to 350°F (180°C) Gas 4.

NOTES

Vanilla Natural vanilla essence is extracted from vanilla pods, which are the pods of a climbing orchid. Check the label and only buy this natural essence, which is often labelled 'vanilla extract'. It is more expensive than synthetic essence made from chemicals, but its flavour is subtle and refined rather than strong and coarse. The very best vanilla extract is said to come from Veracruz in Mexico, and you may find this in delicatessens and gourmet food shops.

Mrs Beeton writes

"This pudding may be very much enriched
by replacing some of the milk with cream,
by adding candied peel, or using more eggs
than stated above. It should not be turned out,
but served from the pie dish, and is better
for being made about 2 hours
before it is baked."

Time 1¼ hours
Sufficient for 6 or 7 persons
Seasonable at any time

INGREDIENTS
9 thin slices of bread and
   butter
¼ lb (125 g) currants
caster sugar to taste
1½ pints (900 ml) milk
flavouring of vanilla, grated
   nutmeg or lemon peel
4 eggs

✎ Cherry Pie

Time 1 hour
Sufficient for 5 or 6 persons
Seasonable in June, July
  and August

INGREDIENTS
1½ lb (750 g) cherries
2 small tablespoons caster
  sugar
½ lb (250 g) short crust
  pastry (page 338)
extra caster sugar to serve

MRS BEETON CALLED THIS a cherry tart, but it has a pastry lid, so we would call it a pie. Fresh homegrown cherries are in season for a very short time, and making them into a pie is one of the best ways to use them. Red or black cherries can be used and their stones should be removed first, although Mrs Beeton didn't say so. The quickest way to do this is with a cherry pitter, a neat little gadget that pushes the stone out of the centre and leaves the fruit whole.

METHOD

Pick the stalks from the cherries and put them with the sugar into a deep pie dish just capable of holding them, with a small cup placed upside down in the midst of them. Make a border around the edge of the dish with some of the pastry, put on the cover and ornament the edges. Bake for 30 to 40 minutes. Strew finely sifted sugar over and serve hot or cold, although the latter is the more usual.

The oven should be preheated to 375°F (190°C) Gas 5.

NOTES

Short Crust pastry may be homemade or you can use bought short crust. The speediest solution is to use an 11 x 9 inch (280 x 229 mm) sheet of ready rolled pastry, available from the freezer cabinet of the supermarket. Brush the rim of the pie dish with water before sticking on the pastry border, then brush this with more water and press the lid into place.

Deep pie dish An 8 to 9 inch (20 to 23 cm) metal or glass pie plate is good for a cherry pie. The fruit makes an attractive dome shape in the centre.

Ornament the edges Pressing the rim of the pastry with your fingers, tap all round the edge with the back of a knife held horizontally. Turn the knife so that the blade is vertical and make indentations about ¼ inch (5 mm) apart to make a fluted edge. Any pastry trimmings can be used to make leaves or other decorations for the top of the pie. Stick them on with a little water before baking.

Mrs Beeton writes

" It is more economical to make two or three tarts at one time, as the trimmings from one tart answer for lining the edges of the dish for another, and so much paste is not required as when they are made singly. Unless for family use, never make fruit pies in very large dishes; select them, however, as deep as possible."

"CHERRIES – According to Lucullus, the cherry-tree was known in Asia in the year of Rome 680. Seventy different species of cherries, wild and cultivated, exist, which are distinguishable from each other by the difference of their form, size, and colour. The most wholesome cherries have a tender and delicate skin; those with a hard skin should be very carefully masticated."

✂ *Custard Tart*

Time 1¾ hours

Sufficient for 5 or 6 persons

Seasonable at any time

INGREDIENTS

1 pint (600 ml) milk

¼ lb (125 g) caster sugar

the rind of ¼ lemon

4 eggs

½ lb (250 g) Short Crust
    Pastry (see page 338)

nutmeg

Mrs Beeton writes

"The flavour of this
pudding may be varied
by substituting almonds
for the lemon rind;
and it may be very much
enriched by using half
cream and half milk,
and doubling the
quantity of eggs."

ALTHOUGH MRS BEETON called this 'Baked Custard Pudding', we know it as custard tart, an old-fashioned English dessert that is usually served completely plain. The pastry case needs to be baked before the custard is added or it will be soggy. Instructions were not given in the original recipe for this technique, which is called 'baking blind', but they are given in the notes below the recipe.

METHOD

Put the milk into a saucepan with the sugar and lemon rind. Bring to the boil, cover and remove from the heat. Let this infuse for about ½ hour or until the milk is well flavoured. Whisk the eggs and strain the milk into them, stirring all the while. Have ready a pie dish lined with the pastry ready baked. Strain the custard into the dish and grate a little nutmeg over the top. Bake for about 1 hour.

The oven should be preheated to 325°F (170°C) Gas 3.

NOTES

Infusing This culinary term means to flavour a liquid by steeping it with an aromatic ingredient. In this recipe Mrs Beeton suggested infusing milk with a little lemon rind. By this she meant to put the milk and a few strips of lemon rind in a pan, heat it until hot, then cover the pan tightly and leave the milk to cool with the lemon still in it. The milk is then strained to remove the rind but leave the flavour behind. Take care when paring a lemon to remove the outer coloured part of the rind only. This is called the zest and it contains the flavoursome oil of the fruit. The white pith underneath the zest is bitter and should not be used.

Baking blind Roll out bought or homemade short crust pastry to fit a 9 inch (23 cm) loose-bottomed flan tin. Chill for 30 minutes, then prick the base all over with a fork, line with foil and fill with baking beans. Bake on a hot baking sheet in a preheated oven at 375°F (190°C) Gas 5 for 15 minutes, then remove the foil and beans and bake for another 5 minutes.

SWEET PASTRIES & HOT PUDDINGS

MRS BEETON SAID THESE were suitable for picnics and her original recipe made 12 turnovers. The quantities given here are for half this number to serve for a hot dessert with pouring custard or cream. Mrs Beeton left the choice of fruit to the reader, but suitable fruits are suggested in the notes below. She was also rather vague about whether the fruit was better raw or cooked, but cooked fruit is definitely more successful. Raw fruit exudes too much juice and tends to make the pastry soggy.

METHOD

Roll out the pastry on a lightly floured surface to a thickness of about ¼ inch (5 mm) and cut out 6 circles, each measuring about 8 inches (20 cm). Pile the fruit on one half of each circle, wet the pastry edges and fold the pastry over the fruit. Press the edges together and ornament them. Brush the turnovers with the white of an egg and sift over a little sugar. Place on hot baking sheets and bake for about 20 minutes.

The oven should be preheated to 425°F (220°C) Gas 7.

NOTES

Puff pastry can be homemade or bought. Ornament the edges by pressing with your fingers and tapping with the back of a knife held horizontally. Turn the knife so that the blade is vertical and make indentations about ¼ inch (5 mm) apart to make fluted shapes.

Fruit Use 2 lb (1 kg) fruit and stew it with ¼ lb (125 g) sugar until soft. Apples, blackberries, rhubarb, gooseberries and stoned apricots or plums are all suitable. Let the fruit get cold before spooning it on to the pastry or it will make the pastry soggy.

Time ½ hour or rather longer
Sufficient for 6 turnovers
Seasonable at any time

INGREDIENTS

¾ lb (375 g) Puff Pastry (page 337)
any kind of fruit
egg white and caster sugar

Mrs Beeton writes

"Instead of putting the fruit in raw, it may be boiled down with a little sugar first, and then enclosed in the crust; or jam, of any kind, may be substituted for fresh fruit."

Golden Pudding

Time 2¾ hours
Sufficient for 5 or 6 persons
Seasonable at any time

INGREDIENTS
¼ lb (125 g) bread crumbs
¼ lb (125 g) suet
¼ lb (125 g) marmalade
¼ lb (125 g) caster sugar
4 eggs
extra caster sugar to serve

Mrs Beeton writes

"The mould may be ornamented with stoned raisins, arranged in a fanciful pattern, before the mixture is poured in, which would add very much to the appearance of the pudding. For a plainer pudding, double the quantities of the bread crumbs, and if the eggs do not moisten it sufficiently, use a little milk."

WHEN YOU HAVE SOME SPARE or leftover bread, this is an easy steamed pudding to make from storecupboard ingredients. It is a good, old-fashioned nursery pudding which no-one can refuse, especially on cold winter days. Serve it with a large jug of custard.

METHOD
Put the bread crumbs into a bowl. Mix them with the suet, which should be finely grated, the marmalade and sugar. Stir all these ingredients well together. Beat the eggs to a froth, stir into the pudding and mix well. Put the pudding into a buttered mould or basin, tie down with a floured cloth and boil for 2½ hours. When turned out, sift a little sugar over the top and serve.

NOTES
Bread crumbs These should be fresh rather than dried, but they can be made from a loaf that is a few days old. White bread crumbs are traditional in steamed puddings, but you can experiment with different types.
Suet Buy this ready shredded in a packet. It is sold in the baking section of the supermarket.
Floured cloth Instead of this old-fashioned method, cover the top of the pudding with a circle of buttered greaseproof paper, butter side down, then cover the basin with a double thickness of foil, making a pleat in the centre to allow for the pudding to expand. Tie the foil under the rim with string and make a handle for lifting the pudding. Put the pudding on a trivet or upturned saucer in a large saucepan and pour in hot water to come about halfway up the side of the basin. Bring to the boil, then keep the water at a gentle simmer, topping it up with more water if the level becomes low.

DID MRS BEETON NAME THIS steamed pudding after the Father of History because it was made with Greek figs? She gave no other clue, so this seems quite likely. In fact, it is like a modern day figgy pudding, sticky and rich. An Excellent Wine Sauce for Puddings (page 236) was recommended for serving with it, but this is made with egg yolks and sherry and is very rich. Chilled crème fraîche or vanilla ice cream would be a more suitable accompaniment.

METHOD

Chop the figs very finely and mix with the suet. Add the remaining ingredients, taking care that the eggs are well whisked. Beat the mixture for a few minutes, put it into a buttered mould and tie it down with a floured cloth. Boil the pudding for 2½ hours.

NOTES

Figs Use dried or semi-dried figs that are plump and moist.
Suet Buy this ready shredded in a packet. It is sold in the baking section of the supermarket.
Moist sugar Use dark soft brown sugar.
Floured cloth Follow the instructions opposite for covering the pudding with greaseproof paper and foil.

Mrs Beeton writes

"For baked or boiled puddings, the moulds, cups,
or basins, should be always buttered before the mixture
is put in them, and they should be put into the saucepan
directly they are filled."

Time 2¾ hours
Sufficient for 6 persons
Seasonable at any time

INGREDIENTS
½ lb (250 g) good figs
6 oz (175 g) suet
½ lb (250 g) bread crumbs
6 oz (175 g) moist sugar
pinch of salt
nutmeg to taste
3 eggs

✑ Roly-Poly Jam Pudding

Time 2½ hours
Sufficient for 5 or 6 persons
Seasonable in winter, when
   fresh fruit is not
   obtainable

INGREDIENTS
¾ lb (375 g) Suet Crust
   Pastry (page 339)
4 tablespoons of any kind
   of jam
melted jam to serve

Mrs Beeton writes

"Mincemeat or
marmalade may be
substituted for the jam,
and makes excellent
puddings."

THIS IS NURSERY FOOD *par excellence*, steaming hot suet pastry oozing sweet jam and served with a runny jam sauce – plus lashings of custard. Mrs Beeton used ¾ lb (375 g) jam for the filling, but this is far too much. You will find the amount suggested here is ample. For a custard recipe, turn to page 235.

METHOD
Roll out the pastry on a lightly floured surface to a thickness of about ½ inch (1 cm). Spread the jam equally over it, leaving a small margin of pastry without any. Roll it up, fasten the ends securely and tie it in a floured cloth. Put the pudding into boiling water and boil for 2 hours. Serve with melted jam.

NOTES
Suet crust pastry is quick and easy to make. Roll it out on a floured surface to a 12 x 8 inch (30 x 20 cm) rectangle and spread it with the jam, leaving a ¼ inch (5 mm) margin. Brush this margin with milk, then roll up the pastry like a Swiss roll, starting from one of the short sides. Seal the join and the ends.
Floured cloth Instead of this old-fashioned method, put the roly-poly join side down on a large sheet of greased greaseproof paper or foil and make a loose parcel.
Boiling is not the best cooking method because the water tends to seep into the roly-poly. It is better to place the foil package in the top of a steamer over boiling water and steam it for 2 hours.

Lemon Tart ⌒

THIS WAS CALLED 'Baked Lemon Pudding', but it really is a lemon tart, which is equally good served warm or cold. Mrs Beeton suggested it be turned out of the dish for serving, but it is easier to leave it in. An alternative is to make the case with short crust pastry and bake it in a loose-bottomed metal flan tin so that it can be lifted out for serving. If you decide on this option, the pastry case should be baked blind before the filling is poured in. For instructions on baking blind, see the recipe for Custard Tart (page 246).

METHOD

Beat the egg yolks to a froth. Mix with them the sugar and warmed, melted butter. Stir these ingredients well together, putting in the grated rind and strained juice of the lemon. Line a shallow dish with the pastry, put in the mixture and bake for ½ hour. Sift icing sugar over the tart and serve.

The oven should be preheated to 375°F (190°C) Gas 5.

NOTES

Puff pastry may be homemade or you can use bought puff pastry and roll it out to fit the dish. A quicker alternative is to use an 11 x 9 inch (280 x 229 mm) sheet of ready rolled pastry, available in the freezer cabinet of the supermarket. Prick the pastry base all over with a fork before pouring in the filling.
Shallow dish Use an 8 inch (20 cm) flan dish.

VARIATION

Very Rich Lemon Tart In a large bowl, mix ½ lb (250 g) sugar with ¼ pint (150 ml) double cream and add the yolks of 8 eggs and ½ lb (250 g) butter, which should be previously warmed and melted. Stir in 2 oz (60 g) ground almonds and the grated rind and strained juice of 2 large lemons; mix everything well together. Pour this filling into a 9 inch (23 cm) dish lined with ½ lb (250 g) puff pastry. Bake for 50 minutes to 1 hour.

Time ¾ hour
Sufficient for 5 or 6 persons
Seasonable at any time

INGREDIENTS
the yolks of 4 eggs
¼ lb (125 g) caster sugar
¼ lb (125 g) butter
1 lemon
6 oz (175 g) Puff Pastry
 (page 337)
icing sugar to serve

Mrs Beeton writes

"LEMON – The lemon is a variety of the citron. The juice of this fruit makes one of our most popular and refreshing beverages – lemonade, which is gently stimulating and cooling, and soon quenches the thirst. It may be freely partaken by bilious and sanguine temperaments; but persons with irritable stomachs should avoid it, on account of its acid qualities. The fresh rind of the lemon is a gentle tonic, and, when dried and grated, is used in flavouring a variety of culinary preparations."

✎ *Manchester Pudding*

Time 1¾ hours plus cooling
Sufficient for 5 or 6 persons
Seasonable at any time

INGREDIENTS

½ pint (300 ml) milk

a strip of lemon peel

3 oz (90 g) grated bread
   (bread crumbs)

4 egg yolks

2 egg whites

2 oz (60 g) butter

3 tablespoons caster sugar
   or to taste

3 tablespoons brandy

6 oz (175 g) Puff Pastry
   (page 337)

4 tablespoons jam

icing sugar to serve

A LOT OF GOOD FOOD comes from Lancashire, and this pudding is no exception. In fact it is a tart rather than a pudding: a puff pastry case filled with jam and topped with a rich custardy mixture flavoured with lemon and brandy. Some versions have a meringue topping, but Mrs Beeton knew when to stop. It is perfectly delicious as it is and needs no accompaniment. Serve it whole for dessert or cut into slices as a tea-time pastry.

METHOD

Put the milk into a saucepan with the lemon peel. Bring to the boil, cover and remove from the heat. Let this infuse for about ½ hour or until the milk is well flavoured. Strain it on to the bread crumbs and boil it for 2 or 3 minutes. Add the egg yolks and whites, the butter, sugar and brandy. Stir all these ingredients well together, then leave until cold. Line a pie dish with puff pastry and at the bottom put a thick layer of any kind of jam. Pour the above mixture, cold, on the jam. Bake the pudding for ¼ hour, then lower the oven temperature and bake for a further ¾ hour. Serve cold, with a little icing sugar sifted over.

The oven should be preheated to 400°F (200°C) Gas 6, then decreased to 350°F (180°C) Gas 4.

NOTES

Puff pastry may be homemade or you can use bought puff pastry. A speedy solution is to use an 11 x 9 inch (280 x 229 mm) sheet of ready rolled pastry, available in the freezer cabinet of the supermarket. Prick the pastry base all over with a fork before pouring in the filling.

Pie dish Use an 8 inch (20 cm) flan dish.

THERE IS NOTHING QUITE LIKE homemade mince pies at Christmas, and they are very quick and easy to make if you use bought pastry. Buy a good-quality mincemeat and if it doesn't already have brandy, whisky or liqueur in it, boost its flavour by adding a splash or two of your own.

METHOD

Roll out the pastry on a lightly floured surface to a thickness of about ¼ inch (5 mm) and line some good-sized patty pans with it. Fill them with mincemeat, cover with more pastry and cut off all round close to the edge of the pans. Bake for 25 minutes, or longer, if the pies are very large. Brush them over with the white of an egg beaten with the blade of a knife to a froth, then sprinkle over a little sugar. Put them back into the oven for a minute or two to dry the egg. Serve the pies hot, on a white doily. They may be merely sprinkled with sugar instead of being glazed, if preferred.

The oven should be preheated to 400°F (200°C) Gas 6.

NOTES

Puff pastry may be homemade or bought. After rolling it out, stamp out 12 discs with a pastry cutter or the rim of a glass and use to line a 12-hole bun tin. Fill with the mincemeat, then brush the pastry edges with water. Stamp out 12 more discs, press on to the pies as lids, then cut a small slit in the centre of each.

VARIATION

Nowadays, short crust pastry is more often used for mince pies than puff pastry. It can be used in this recipe if you prefer; the method and baking time will be the same.

Time ¾ to 1 hour
Sufficient for 12 pies
Seasonable at Christmas
   time

INGREDIENTS
¾ lb (375 g) good Puff
   Pastry (page 337)
¾ lb (375 g) mincemeat
egg white and caster sugar
   to glaze

Mrs Beeton writes

"To re-warm the pies, put them on the patty pans, and let them remain in the oven for 10 minutes or ¼ hour, and they will be almost as good as if freshly made."

✺ An Unrivalled Plum Pudding

Time 9 to 11 hours

Sufficient for 2 puddings

Seasonable in winter

INGREDIENTS

½ lb (250 g) muscatel
raisins

10 oz (300 g) currants

2 oz (60 g) mixed candied
peel

6 oz (175 g) sultanas

10 oz (300 g) moist sugar

¾ lb (375 g) fresh bread
crumbs

2 lb (1 kg) finely chopped
suet

the grated rind of 2 lemons

2 teaspoons freshly grated
nutmeg

1 tablespoon ground
cinnamon

6 eggs

½ teaspoon almond essence

6 tablespoons brandy, with
extra for flaming

Plum-Pudding Sauce (page
237) to serve

THE ORIGINAL RECIPE for this mature, dark Christmas pudding made five 2 lb (1 kg) puddings. In Victorian times they were made in large quantities and allowed to mature, then distributed among the family in time for Christmas. In the interests of reviving this charming custom, this recipe makes two puddings, one for yourself and one to give away. They should be made towards the end of October to allow time for them to mature. In Mrs Beeton's recipe she gave instructions for wrapping and boiling the mixture in pudding cloths to make round puddings. The instructions here are for cooking the puddings in moulds or basins, which is more practical.

METHOD

Stone and cut up the raisins, but do not chop them. Wash and dry the currants. Cut the candied peel into thin slices. Mix all the fruit and the dry ingredients well together and moisten with the eggs, which should be well beaten and strained. Stir in the almond essence and brandy until everything is thoroughly mixed. Press the pudding into two buttered 2 pint (1.2 litre) moulds or basins, tie them down tightly with floured cloths and boil for 6 to 8 hours. The day it is to be eaten, plunge the pudding into boiling water and keep it boiling for at least 2 hours, then turn it out of the mould and serve with brandy sauce. On Christmas Day a sprig of holly is usually placed in the middle of the pudding and about a wineglassful of brandy poured round it. At the moment of serving, the brandy is lighted and the pudding brought to the table encircled in flame.

NOTES

Dried fruit is sold washed and dried these days and needs no preparation, unless you buy it loose from a health food store.

Candied peel Buy large pieces from a delicatessen rather than chopped candied peel in a tub. Sold loose, these large pieces are moist, with a fresh flavour. Candied peel in tubs tends to taste synthetic and can be rather dry.

Moist sugar Use dark soft brown sugar.

Floured cloth Instead of this old-fashioned method, cover the top of each pudding with a circle of buttered greaseproof paper, then cover the moulds or basin with a double thickness of foil, making a pleat in the centre to allow for the pudding to expand. Tie the foil under the rim with string and make a handle for lifting the pudding. Put each pudding on a trivet or upturned saucer in a large saucepan and pour in hot water to come about halfway up the side of the pudding. Bring to the boil, then keep the water at a gentle simmer, topping it up with more water if the level becomes low.

Storage and reheating Let each cooked pudding go cold, then remove the foil. Cover tightly with a clean, dry cloth, then foil. Store in a cool, dry place for 2 to 12 months. If storing for a long time, unwrap the pudding occasionally, then prick it with a skewer and feed it with a few tablespoons of brandy. This will help to keep it moist and well preserved. Reheat it in the mould or basin for 2 hours, following the instructions opposite.

Plum-Pudding sauce is more familiar to us as brandy sauce. Mrs Beeton's recipe is heady, with a mixture of both brandy and Madeira.

Mrs Beeton writes

"A few sweet almonds, blanched and cut in strips, and stuck on the pudding, ornament it prettily."

"SULTANA GRAPE – The small black grape grown in Corinth and the Ionian Isles is, when dried, the common currant of the grocers' shops; the white or yellow grape, grown in the same places, is somewhat larger than the black variety, and is that which produces the Sultana raisin. It has been called Sultana from its delicate qualities and unique growth: the finest are those of Smyrna."

✍ *Baked Rice Pudding*

Time 1¾ to 2¼ hours
Sufficient for 5 or 6 children
Seasonable at any time

INGREDIENTS
1 teacupful of rice
2 tablespoons sugar
2 pints (1.2 litres) milk
a good knob of butter
½ teaspoon grated nutmeg
   or to taste

Mrs Beeton gave several recipes for rice pudding. She described this one as 'plain and economical; a nice pudding for children'. With its golden brown crust and soft, creamy pudding underneath, it is the traditional rice pudding our mothers and grandmothers used to make. It is good on its own, or with baked or stewed fruit.

METHOD
Wash the rice and put it into a pie dish with the sugar. Pour in the milk and stir these ingredients well together. Add the butter cut up into very small pieces and grate a little nutmeg over the top. Bake the pudding for 2 to 2½ hours.

The oven should be preheated to 325°F (170°C) Gas 3.

NOTES
Rice Pudding or short-grain rice is the type you need; 1 teacupful weighs ¼ lb (125 g).
Butter 2 small tablespoonfuls of chopped suet were given as an alternative in the original recipe, but this would be unlikely to appeal to modern palates.
Crust To get a crust on top of the pudding, remove it from the oven and give it a good stir after the first ½ hour, then bake it undisturbed for the remainder of the time.

Mrs Beeton writes
_____

"As the rice is not previously cooked, care must be taken that the pudding be very slowly baked, to give plenty of time for the rice to swell, and for it to be very thoroughly done."

_____

"RICE – with proper management in cooking it, forms a very valuable and cheap addition to our farinaceous food, and, in years of scarcity, has been found eminently useful in lessening the consumption of flour. When boiled, the water in which it is dressed should only simmer, and not boil hard. Very little water should be used, as the grains absorb a great deal, and, consequently, swell much; and if they take up too much at first, it is difficult to get rid of it. Baking it in puddings is the best mode of preparing it."

SWEET PASTRIES & HOT PUDDINGS

Jam Tart ❧

MRS BEETON CALLED THIS 'Open Tart of Strawberry or Any Other Kind of Preserve'. She baked the pastry case empty, then spooned the jam in afterwards. This a most unusual method, which she explained in the following way: 'By making it in this manner, both the flavour and colour of the jam are preserved, which would otherwise be lost, were it baked in the oven on the pastry and, besides, so much jam is not required'. The recipe here bakes the jam and the pastry together, which gives a more pleasing result.

METHOD

Butter a tart pan. Roll out the pastry on a lightly floured surface to a thickness of ½ inch (1 cm) and line the pan with it. Prick a few holes at the bottom with a fork, then fill it with preserve or jam. Place a few stars or leaves on it, which have been previously cut out of the pastry, then bake for 15 to 20 minutes. Let the the tart cool a little before serving, or serve cold.

The oven should be preheated to 400°F (200°C) Gas 6.

NOTES

Preserve or jam You will need ¼ pint (150 ml).

Tart pan Use a 9 inch (23 cm) loose-bottomed flan tin.

Puff pastry may be homemade, or you can use bought puff pastry. A speedier solution is to use an 11 x 9 inch (280 x 229 mm) sheet of ready rolled pastry, available in the freezer cabinet of the supermarket. Short crust pastry can also be used, following the same instructions. It gives equally good results.

Time ½ hour
Sufficient 1 tart for
  3 persons
Seasonable at any time

INGREDIENTS
½ lb (250 g) Puff Pastry
  (page 337)
any kind of preserve or jam

✆ Quickly Made Puddings

Time ¾ hour plus cooling
Sufficient for 8 puddings
Seasonable at any time

INGREDIENTS
1 pint (600 ml) milk
¼ lb (125 g) butter
¼ lb (125 g) caster sugar
¼ lb (125 g) flour
5 eggs, plus 2 extra yolks
a little grated lemon rind
fruit or wine sauce to serve

THESE LITTLE LEMON-FLAVOURED CUSTARDS are bubbling hot when they first come out of the oven, so let them settle a little before serving them warm. Fresh red berries or a red berry compôte are good with them, so too is fresh pouring cream or crème fraîche.

METHOD
Make the milk hot and stir in the butter. Let it melt and cool before the other ingredients are added to it, then stir in the sugar, flour and all the eggs, which should be well whisked. Flavour with a little grated lemon rind and beat the mixture well. Butter some small cups and rather more than half fill them. Bake for 20 minutes to ½ hour. Serve with fruit or with wine sauce, a little of which may be poured over them.

The oven should be preheated to 325°F (160°C) Gas 3.

NOTES
Cups Use ramekins or individual soufflé dishes, each with a capacity of ¼ pint (150 ml).
Wine sauce An Excellent Wine Sauce for Puddings (page 236) was Mrs Beeton's suggested accompaniments for these little egg custards, but is very rich; Fresh or stewed fruit might be a better choice.

Vol-Au-Vent of Fresh Strawberries ⁊ with Whipped Cream

THIS IS QUICK AND EASY if you use ready made pastry, and yet it looks impressive. It is the perfect dessert for a party in summer, when fresh strawberries are at their sweetest and best. If you can get tiny *fraises des bois*, then so much the better. For a pretty presentation, put the whipped cream in the bottom of the vol-au-vent and pile the strawberries on top, leaving some with their green hulls intact. Or arrange some of the strawberries close together in the cream with their points facing uppermost and serve the rest in a separate bowl. Dust the finished dessert with icing sugar just before serving.

METHOD

Roll out the pastry very evenly on a lightly floured surface to a thickness of about 1½ inches (4 cm). With a large fluted pastry cutter, stamp out the desired shape, either round or oval. With the point of a small knife, make a slight incision in the pastry all round the top, about 1 inch (2.5 cm) in from the edge, which will form the lid when baked. Bake for ½ hour to 40 minutes. When nearly done, brush the pastry over with the white of an egg, then sprinkle on it some sugar and put it back in the oven to set the glaze. Withdraw it from the oven, instantly remove the cover where it is marked and remove the interior, or soft crumb, from the centre. In doing this, be careful not to break the edges of the vol-au-vent, but should they look thin in places, cover them with small flakes of the inside pastry stuck on with the white of an egg. At the moment of serving, fill the cold vol-au-vent with the strawberries, which should be broken up with sufficient sugar to sweeten them nicely. Place a few spoonfuls of whipped cream on top and serve.

The oven should be preheated to 400°F (200°C) Gas 6.

NOTES

Strawberries You will need 2 punnets of strawberries with a total weight of about ¾ lb (375 g).

Plateful of whipped cream Use ½ pint (300 ml) double or whipping cream. For a less rich dessert, use half this amount of fresh cream mixed with half crème fraîche or plain yogurt.

Fluted pastry cutter For this you can use a flan ring or the top edge of a flan tin. It will need to be about 9 inches (23 cm) in diameter and it doesn't need to be fluted. Alternatively, you can use a cake tin or plate as a guide, cutting around it with a knife.

Time 1 hour
Sufficient for 4 to 6 persons
Seasonable in June and
July

INGREDIENTS
¾ lb (375 g) Puff Pastry
(page 337)
the white of an egg and
caster sugar to glaze
1 pint (600 ml) freshly
gathered strawberries
caster sugar to taste
a plateful of whipped cream
to serve

Mrs Beeton writes

"STRAWBERRY – The name of this favourite fruit is said to be derived from an ancient custom of putting straw beneath the fruit when it begins to ripen, which is very useful to keep it moist and clean."

✑ A Very Simple Apple Charlotte

Time 1 hour or rather longer
Sufficient for 8 persons
Seasonable from July to
    March

INGREDIENTS
9 slices of bread and butter
about 6 good-sized apples
1 tablespoon grated lemon
    peel
2 tablespoons lemon juice
sugar to taste

Mrs Beeton gave a recipe for a classic French *Charlotte aux Pommes* made in a mould lined with bread and turned out. This is a simple version, in which the ingredients are layered in a pie dish. Although the instructions suggest that the charlotte is turned out on to a plate, this is really not necessary. It tastes equally good either way.

Method

Butter a large flan dish. Place a layer of bread and butter, without the crusts, at the bottom, then a layer of apples, peeled, cored and cut into thin slices. Sprinkle over these a portion of the lemon peel and juice, then sweeten with sugar. Place another layer of bread and butter and then one of apples, proceeding in this manner until the dish is full. Cover it up with the peel of the apples, to preserve the top from browning or burning. Bake for rather more than ¾ hour. Remove the apple peel, then turn the charlotte out on to a dish. Sift sugar over and serve at once.

The oven should be preheated to 375°F (190°C) Gas 5.

Notes

Apples Use a good cooking apple such as Bramley, or a dessert apple such as Golden Delicious. Discard the peelings after baking.
Sugar Use caster or demerara sugar. If using cooking apples you will need about 5 oz (150 g); for dessert apples, use 3–4 oz (90–125 g).
Flan dish Use a deep dish that holds 4 pints (2.4 litres).

Chocolate Soufflé ∞

MRS BEETON'S SERVING SUGGESTION was utterly charming – wrapping the soufflé dish in a white napkin was the correct way to serve a hot soufflé. This custom is still observed today in high class restaurants, especially in France, and we would do well to observe it. If you are worried about the soufflé sinking before it gets to the table, the best way round this is to make individual soufflés. They have a smaller surface area and are less likely to fall. This amount of mixture is enough to fill four ¼ pint (150 ml) dishes.

METHOD

Break the eggs, separating the whites from the yolks, and put them into different bowls. Add to the yolks the sugar and flour, then the chocolate, which should be very finely grated. Stir these ingredients for 2 to 3 minutes. Well whisk the whites of the eggs in the other bowl until they are stiff, then mix them lightly with the yolks until the mixture forms a smooth and light substance. Butter a round cake tin, put in the mixture and bake for ½ hour. Pin a white napkin round the tin, sift icing sugar over the top of the soufflé and serve it immediately.

The oven should be preheated to 350°F (180°C) Gas 4.

NOTES

Best chocolate   Plain or dark chocolate with at least 70 percent cocoa solids is considered the best. This will have the most intense chocolate flavour. For a chocolate to melt well in cooking it needs to have a high percentage of cocoa butter, but the precise amount is not always listed on the label. As long as the cocoa butter content is listed above that of any oil the chocolate contains, you can be sure you will be getting a good amount of cocoa butter.

Cake tin   Use a 1¾ pint (1 litre) soufflé dish.

Mrs Beeton writes

"The proper appearance of this dish depends entirely on the expedition with which it is served, and some cooks, to preserve its lightness, hold a salamander over the soufflé until it is placed on the table. If allowed to stand after it comes from the oven, it will be entirely spoiled, as it falls almost immediately."

Time ¾ hour or rather more
Sufficient for 4 to 6 persons
Seasonable at any time

INGREDIENTS
4 eggs
3 teaspoons caster sugar
1 teaspoon flour
3 oz (90 g) of the best
 chocolate
icing sugar to serve

CHAPTER 9

Chilled
& Iced Desserts

The recipes in this chapter come from two different chapters in Mrs Beeton's original book. Cold jellies and creams were served as a third course at formal dinners in Victorian days, together with hot puddings and pastries, while desserts and ices were served afterwards as a final course, so they were treated separately. Nowadays there is no such formality, except at the very grandest of banquets, so the two types of recipe have been grouped together.

This amusing anecdote about dinner-party etiquette appeared in 'The Mistress', the very first chapter of the original book.

'When dinner is finished, the dessert is placed on the table, accompanied with finger-glasses. It is the custom of some gentlemen to wet a corner of the napkin; but the hostess, whose behaviour will set the tone to all the ladies present, will merely wet the tips of her fingers, which will serve all the purposes required. The French and other continentals have a habit of gargling the mouth; but it is a custom which no English gentlewoman should, in the slightest degree, imitate.'

Cold and iced desserts marked the end of dinner, and were often beautifully and elaborately moulded and adorned. Some of these were described as 'confectionery', a term that had a different meaning then than now, best described in Mrs Beeton's own words.

'The term confectionery embraces a very large class indeed of sweet food, many kinds of which should not be attempted in the ordinary cuisine. The thousand and one ornamental dishes that adorn the tables of the wealthy should be purchased from the confectioner; they cannot profitably be made at home.'

By today's standards, many of Mrs Beeton's dessert recipes would come in the same category as confectionery, and we would be unlikely to attempt them at home.

Ice cream was regarded with some suspicion.

'The aged, the delicate and children should abstain from ices or iced beverages; even the strong and healthy should partake of them in moderation. They should be taken immediately after the repast, or some hours after, because the taking of these substances during the process of digestion is apt to provoke indisposition.'

Finally, in a section on 'Dessert Dishes' in the Confectionery chapter, we find these delightful words.

'The dessert certainly repays, in its general effect, the expenditure upon it of much pains, and it may be said that if there be any poetry at all in meals, there is poetry in the dessert.'

⌒ Compôte of Apples

Time ½ hour
Sufficient for 4 or 5 persons
Seasonable from July to
    March

INGREDIENTS
6 ripe apples
1 lemon
½ lb (250 g) granulated
    sugar
½ pint (300 ml) water
strips of angelica or candied
    citron to decorate

A COMPÔTE SHOULD NOT be confused with stewed fruit. In a compôte the fruit retains its shape, which can be whole, halves, quarters or slices, whereas stewed fruit is usually reduced down to a purée. For this apple compôte, choose a variety of sweet dessert apple that holds its shape well, such as Granny Smith's.

METHOD

Select the apples of a moderate size. Peel them, cut them in halves and remove the cores, then rub each piece over with a little lemon. Put the sugar and water together in a saucepan and let them boil until forming a thickish syrup, carefully removing all the scum as it rises. Lay in the apples with the rind of the lemon cut thin and the juice of the same. Let the apples simmer until tender, take them out very carefully and drain them in a sieve. Reduce the syrup by boiling it quickly for a few minutes. When both apples and syrup are cold, arrange the apples neatly on a glass dish, pour over the syrup and garnish with strips of green angelica or candied citron. Smaller apples may be prepared in the same manner: they should not be divided in half, but peeled and the cores pushed out with a vegetable cutter.

VARIATIONS

Compôte of Apricots Make a syrup as above, using 1 lb (500 g) sugar and 1½ pints (900 ml) water. When it is ready, put in 12 apricots while the syrup is boiling. Simmer them very gently for 15 to 20 minutes until tender, taking care not to let them break. Take them out carefully and arrange them on a glass dish. Let the syrup cool a little, pour it over the apricots and serve when cold.

Compôte of Green Figs Make a syrup as above, using ¾ lb (375 g) sugar and 1 pint (600 ml) water and boiling with it the rind of ½ lemon. Put in 1½ pints (900 ml) green figs and simmer them very slowly until tender – 2 to 3 hours. Dish them up on a glass dish. Reduce the syrup by boiling it quickly for 5 minutes, take out the lemon peel and pour the syrup over the figs. Serve when cold. A little port or lemon juice, added just before the figs are done, will be found an improvement.

Compôte of Gooseberries   Top and tail 2 pints (1.2 litres) gooseberries, which should not be very ripe. Pour over them some boiling water, take them out and plunge them into cold water mixed with 1 tablespoon vinegar (this will assist to keep the fruit a good colour). Make a syrup as described opposite, using ¾ lb (375 g) sugar and 1 pint (600 ml) water. When it boils, drain the gooseberries and put them in. Simmer them gently until the fruit is nicely pulped and tender without being broken – about 5 minutes. Dish the gooseberries on a glass dish, boil the syrup for 2 or 3 minutes and pour over the gooseberries. Serve cold.

Compôte of Oranges   Peel 6 oranges, remove as much of the white pith as possible, and divide them into small pieces without breaking the thin skin which surrounds them. Make a syrup as described opposite, using ¾ lb (375 g) sugar and 1 pint (600 ml) water and boiling with it the rind of 1 orange cut into thin strips. When the syrup has been well skimmed and is quite clear, put in the pieces of orange and simmer them for 5 minutes. Take them out carefully with a spoon without breaking them and arrange them on a glass dish. Reduce the syrup by boiling it quickly until thick – about 5 minutes. Let it cool a little, pour it over the oranges and serve when cold.

Compôte of Peaches   Peaches that are not very large, and that would not look well for dessert, answer very nicely for a compôte. Halve 15 small peaches, take out the stones and pare the fruit. Make a syrup as described opposite, using ¾ lb (375g) sugar and 1 pint (600 ml) water. Put in the peaches and simmer them gently for about 10 minutes. Take them out without breaking them and arrange them on a glass dish. Boil the syrup for 2 or 3 minutes, let it cool, then pour it over the fruit and serve when cold.

Mrs Beeton writes

"The compôte is a confiture made at the moment of need, and with much less sugar than would be ordinarily put to preserves. They are most wholesome things, suitable to most stomachs which cannot accommodate themselves to raw fruit or a large portion of sugar; they are the happy medium, and far better than ordinary stewed fruit."

✎ Apricot Cream

Time ¾ hour plus chilling
Sufficient for 6 to 8 persons
Seasonable in August,
    September and October

INGREDIENTS
12 to 16 ripe apricots
½ lb (250 g) sugar
¼ pint (150 ml) water
1½ pints (900 ml) milk
the yolks of 8 eggs
1½ tablespoons powdered
    gelatine

THIS RICH AND CREAMY dessert is made with fresh ripe apricots, so it is perfect for a late summer dinner party. Serve it well chilled with dainty almond tuiles or amaretti biscuits. The flavours of almonds and apricots are well suited to one another.

METHOD

Halve the apricots and take out the stones. Boil the apricot halves in a syrup made with ¼ lb (125 g) of the sugar and the water until they form a thin marmalade, which should then be rubbed through a sieve. Boil the milk with the remaining sugar, let it cool a little, then mix with it the yolks of the eggs, which have been previously well beaten. Put this mixture into a bowl, place this bowl in boiling water and stir it one way over the heat until it thickens. On no account let it boil. Strain through a sieve, add the gelatine, previously dissolved in a small quantity of hot water, and keep stirring until it is nearly cold. Mix in the apricot purée, stir well and put into an oiled 2½ pint (1.2 litre) mould. Chill until set. The dessert should turn out without any difficulty.

NOTES

Syrup To make a sugar syrup, heat granulated sugar and water very gently, stirring occasionally, until the sugar has dissolved, then boil rapidly without stirring for 2 to 3 minutes until syrupy.

Gelatine To dissolve the gelatine, sprinkle the powder evenly over 5 tablespoons water in a small heatproof bowl and leave for about 5 minutes or until spongy. Stand the bowl in a pan of hot water and heat gently until dissolved.

Mrs Beeton writes

"In winter-time, when fresh apricots
are not obtainable, a little jam
may be substituted for them."

THE BLANCMANGE OF OUR CHILDHOOD was most often made from a packet mix and coloured a lurid pink. Mrs Beeton's recipe is the proper homemade white blancmange, as its name suggests it should be, and the almond flavouring is correct. She described it as a supper dish, and gave two other versions – 'Arrowroot Blancmange' and 'Cheap Blancmange'. This recipe is the best of the three.

METHOD

Put the milk into a saucepan with the gelatine, lemon rind and sugar. Stir over a low heat until the sugar has disssolved, then gently warm the mixture without stirring for ¼ hour. Leave to stand until the milk is well flavoured – about 1½ hours. Add the almonds, which should be blanched and pounded in a mortar to a paste, and bring the milk just to the boil. Strain it through a fine sieve or muslin into a jug, add the almond essence and cream and stir the mixture occasionally until nearly cold. Let it stand for a few minutes, then pour it into a 2 pint (1.2 litre) mould, which should be previously oiled or dipped in cold water. There will be a sediment at the bottom of the jug, which must not be poured into the mould as it would very much disfigure the appearance of the blancmange. Chill for several hours until set. In turning it out, just loosen the edges of the blancmange from the mould, place a dish on it and turn it quickly over. It should come out easily and the blancmange should have a smooth glossy appearance when the mould is oiled, which it frequently has not when it is only dipped in water.

NOTES

Almonds For the best flavour, use whole almonds in their skins. To blanch them, put them in a bowl and pour boiling water over them. Leave them to stand for 1 to 2 minutes until their skins loosen, then drain and peel off the skins. For speed, simply use ground almonds.

Cream Single cream can be used, but if you prefer a richer blancmange, use whipping cream or double cream.

Time ½ hour plus cooling and chilling
Sufficient for 6 persons
Seasonable at any time

INGREDIENTS
1 pint (600 ml) milk
2 tablespoons powdered gelatine
the rind of ½ lemon
¼ lb (125 g) granulated sugar
1 oz (30 g) almonds
a few drops of almond essence
1 pint (600 ml) cream

Mrs Beeton writes

"The flavour may also be very much varied by adding bay-leaves, or essence of vanilla, instead of the lemon–rind and almonds. Noyeau, Maraschino, Curaçao or any favourite liqueur, added in small proportions, very much enhances the flavour of this always favourite dish. It may be garnished as fancy dictates."

Charlotte Russe

Time 1 hour plus chilling
Sufficient for 6 persons
Seasonable at any time

INGREDIENTS
24 Savoy biscuits
4 tablespoons icing sugar
¾ pint (450 ml) cream
flavouring of vanilla,
   liqueurs or wine
1 tablespoon powdered
   gelatine dissolved in
   3 tablespoons water
1 round sponge cake
   measuring 6 inches
   (15 cm) in diameter

DESCRIBED BY MRS BEETON AS 'an elegant sweet entremets', Charlotte Russe was invented by the great French cook and pastry chef Carême, who had spent part of his career working at the Russian court of Tsar Alexander 1. Carême originally called the dessert *charlotte à la parisienne*, but its name was changed when Russian dishes became very fashionable in France during the Second Empire, and it continued to be a very popular dessert all through the Victorian era. Mrs Beeton's original recipe was quite difficult to follow; this modern adaptation works very well.

METHOD

Procure about 24 Savoy biscuits, or ladies'-fingers, as they are sometimes called. Mix 3 tablespoons of the icing sugar with a little water to make a thin glacé icing. Cut 4 biscuits in half crossways and dip the rounded ends in the icing. Line the bottom of a plain round 6 inch (15 cm) mould with these biscuits, placing them like a star or rosette with their iced ends in the middle and their sugared sides facing upwards. Trim the remaining biscuits to the height of the mould, then dip one of their ends in the icing and stand them upright all round the edge with their iced ends downwards and sugared sides outwards, carefully putting them so closely together that they connect firmly. Whisk the cream to a stiff froth with the remaining sugar, the flavouring and dissolved gelatine. Fill the charlotte with the mixture and cover with a slice of sponge cake cut in the shape of the mould. Chill until you are ready to serve, then turn the dessert out on to a dish, lift off the mould and serve.

NOTES

Savoy biscuits were also known as ladies'-fingers, as Mrs Beeton said, but today we are more likely to call them sponge fingers or boudoir biscuits. The Italian ones, *biscotti savoiardi*, are especially good. If you want to make them yourself, there is a recipe for them on page 296.

Cream This must be double or whipping cream.

Flavouring Mrs Beeton recommended only 1 tablespoon, but if you are using liqueur, you will need 3 tablespoons to get a good flavour. You can use any sweet liqueur. For an orange flavour, use Cointreau, for a cherry flavour, use Kirsch. If you like the flavour of almonds, use Amaretto liqueur.

Gelatine To dissolve the gelatine, sprinkle the powder over the water in a small heatproof bowl and leave for about 5 minutes or until spongy. Stand the bowl in a pan of hot water and heat gently until it has dissolved completely.

Mrs Beeton writes

"1 tablespoonful of liqueur of any kind, or 4 tablespoonfuls of wine, would nicely flavour the above proportion of cream. For arranging the biscuits in the mould, cut them to the shape required, so that they fit in nicely, and level them with the mould at the top, that, when turned out, there may be something firm to rest upon. Great care and attention is required in the turning out of this dish, that the cream does not burst the case."

❧ Chocolate Cream

Time ½ hour plus chilling
Sufficient for 8 persons
Seasonable at any time

INGREDIENTS
the yolks of 6 eggs
3 oz (90 g) grated chocolate
¼ lb (125 g) sugar
1½ pints (900 ml) cream
1½ tablespoons gelatine
   dissolved in 4 tablespoons
   water

THIS VELVETY SMOOTH DESSERT is like a very rich egg custard flavoured with chocolate and set with gelatine. Although Mrs Beeton didn't say so, it is at its best served well chilled, with a bittersweet chocolate sauce to accompany it.

METHOD
Beat the yolks of the eggs in a bowl. Add the grated chocolate, the sugar and 1 pint (600 ml) of the cream. Stir these ingredients well together, then set the bowl in a saucepan of boiling water and stir it one way until the mixture thickens slightly – about 20 minutes. Do not allow it to boil or it will curdle. Strain the cream through a sieve into another bowl and stir in the gelatine. Leave to cool a little, then stir in the other ½ pint (300 ml) cream, which should be well whipped. Mix everything well together and pour the mixture into a 2½ pint (1.4 litre) mould, which has been previously oiled. Chill until it is time to serve.

NOTES
Chocolate Use a good-quality, plain or dark chocolate with a minimum of 70 percent cocoa solids. Also check the label to determine the cocoa butter content. If this is be listed above any oil the chocolate contains, this is an indication that the chocolate should melt well..
Cream If you use double cream there is less chance that the custard will curdle.
Gelatine To dissolve the gelatine, sprinkle the powder over the water in a small heatproof bowl and leave for about 5 minutes or until spongy. Stand the bowl in a pan of hot water and heat gently until dissolved.

Ginger Cream ❧

Time ½ hour plus chilling
Sufficient for 4 to 6 persons
Seasonable at any time

SIMPLE AND QUICK TO MAKE, this kind of rich custard-based dessert was very popular in Victorian days. The ginger that we take for granted today was a relatively new ingredient, and much in vogue at the time. The alternative decoration of candied citron (the rind of the citron fruit candied with sugar) is a good one because its bittersweet flavour helps offset the richness of the cream, but nowadays we are more likely to use a little more preserved ginger from the jar.

INGREDIENTS
3 oz (90 g) preserved (stem) ginger
4 teaspoons syrup
the yolks of 4 eggs
1 pint (600 ml) cream
1 tablespoon powdered gelatine
slices of preserved (stem) ginger or candied citron to garnish

METHOD
Slice the ginger finely. Put it into a bowl with the syrup, the well-beaten yolks of eggs and the cream. Mix these ingredients well together and stir them over a low heat for about 10 minutes or until the mixture thickens. Take it off the heat and whisk until nearly cold, then add the gelatine, which should be dissolved. Pour into a glass serving dish and chill until set. Before serving, it may be garnished with slices of preserved ginger or candied citron.

NOTES
Syrup By this Mrs Beeton meant to use the syrup from the jar of preserved (stem) ginger. In her original method she said to sweeten to taste with sifted sugar, but the ginger syrup is sweet enough without extra sugar, so this has been omitted.

Cream Use double cream.

Gelatine To dissolve gelatine, sprinkle the powder over 3 tablespoons water in a small heatproof bowl and leave for about 5 minutes or until spongy. Stand the bowl in a pan of hot water and heat gently until dissolved.

Mrs Beeton writes

"PRESERVED GINGER – comes to us from the West Indies. It is made by scalding the roots when they are green and full of sap, then peeling them in cold water, and putting them into jars, with a rich syrup; in which state we receive them. It should be chosen of a bright-yellow colour, with a little transparency: what is dark-coloured, fibrous, and stringy, is not good. Good roots, fit for preserving, and in size equal to West Indian, have been produced in the Royal Agricultural Garden in Edinburgh."

✑ *Gooseberry Fool*

Time ¾ to 1 hour

Sufficient for 6 persons

Seasonable in May
  and June

INGREDIENTS

about 1¼ lb (625 g) green
  gooseberries to make
  1 pint (600 ml) pint pulp

about 5 oz (150 g) caster
  sugar to taste

½ pint (300 ml) cream

'THIS, ALTHOUGH A VERY OLD-FASHIONED and homely dish, is, when well made, very delicious, and, if properly sweetened, a very suitable preparation for children,' said Mrs Beeton of this quintessentially English dessert. Today it is eaten more by grown-ups than children, and is special enough for a dinner party dessert, served well chilled.

METHOD

Cut the tops and tails off the gooseberries and put them into a saucepan with 2 tablespoons water and a little sugar. Let it boil until the fruit is soft enough to mash – 10 to 15 minutes. When done enough, beat it to a pulp. Work this pulp through a colander and very gradually add the lightly whipped cream. Ascertain if the mixture is sweet enough, putting in plenty of sugar or it will not be eatable. Serve in a glass dish or in small glasses.

NOTES

Colander Instead of working the pulp through a colander, you can use an electric blender to purée the fruit, but it will still need to be pushed through a sieve to remove the skin and seeds of the gooseberries.

Cream Mrs Beeton suggested using half milk and half cream in the orginal recipe, but the dessert holds its shape better when made with all cream. You can use whipping or double cream.

CHILLED & ICED DESSERTS

Italian Cream ∽

This is similar to panna cotta or 'cooked cream', an old-fashioned Italian dessert that has become fashionable in recent years. It is very rich, and is best served chilled with a cold compôte of red fruits or berries, or a citrus fruit salad. In Italy it is often set in small moulds, as Mrs Beeton suggested at the end of the recipe, then turned out on to individual plates and surrounded by fruit. This makes a very pretty presentation for a dinner party.

Method

Put the cream and milk into a saucepan with sugar to sweeten and the lemon rind. Boil until the milk is well flavoured, then strain it into a bowl. Leave to cool a little, then stir in the beaten yolks of the eggs. Put the bowl in a saucepan of boiling water over a low heat and stir the contents until they thicken – 15 to 20 minutes. Do not allow them to boil. Take the cream off the heat, stir in the lemon juice and the gelatine, which should be dissolved, and whip well. Fill a 1½ pint (900 ml) mould and chill until set. To serve, turn it out on a dish and garnish as taste may dictate.

Notes

Cream This should be double cream.

Gelatine To dissolve the gelatine, sprinkle the powder evenly over 3 tablespoons water in a small heatproof bowl and leave for about 5 minutes or until spongy. Stand the bowl in a pan of hot water and heat gently until dissolved.

Mrs Beeton writes

"The mixture may be whipped
and drained, and then put into small glasses,
when this mode of serving is preferred."

Time ½ hour plus chilling
Sufficient for 4 or 6 persons
Seasonable at any time

INGREDIENTS
½ pint (300 ml) cream
½ pint (300 ml) milk
2 oz (60 g) caster sugar
  to taste
the pared rind and juice of 1
  lemon
the yolks of 4 eggs
1 tablespoon powdered
  gelatine

✌ Lemon Creams

Time ½ hour
Sufficient for 6 persons
Seasonable at any time

INGREDIENTS
2 dozen sweet almonds
1 pint (600 ml) cream
2 glasses of sherry
the pared rind and juice of
  2 lemons
about 2 tablespoons caster
  sugar to taste

MRS BEETON GAVE SEVERAL recipes for lemon creams, some made with egg yolks and set with isinglass, that were like a modern-day mousse. She described this one as 'very good'. With its two glasses of sherry, it is very like the Elizabethan syllabub, although she didn't describe it as such. A syllabub is a sweet and frothy drink that was taken at the end of a meal in place of a dessert. The method of pouring two mixtures from one jug to another is a charming one, but nowadays it is easier to use an electric mixer. Simply whip the cream mixture, gradually adding the sherry mixture.

METHOD
Blanch and chop the almonds and put them into a jug with the cream. In another jug, put the sherry, lemon rind, strained lemon juice and sufficient sugar to sweeten nicely. Pour rapidly from one jug to the other until the mixture is well frothed. Pour it into glasses, omitting the lemon rind.

NOTES
Sweet almonds Use whole almonds in their skins and blanch them by putting them in a bowl and pouring boiling water over them. Leave them to stand for 1 to 2 minutes until their skins loosen, then drain and peel off the skins. Chop them rather finely or pound them in a mortar. If they are too chunky, they will spoil the consistency of the dessert.
Cream Use double or whipping cream and whip it in a jug or bowl until it holds its shape.
Sherry You will need about 6 fl oz (175 ml).

Mrs Beeton writes
_____

"This is a very cool and delicious sweet for summer,
and may be made less rich by omitting the almonds
and substituting orange or raisin wine for the sherry."

_____

"LEMON – Lemons appear in company with the orange in most
orange-growing countries. They were only known to the Romans at
a very late period, and, at first were used only to keep the moths from
their garments: their acidity was unpleasant to them.
In the time of Pliny, the lemon was hardly known otherwise
than as an excellent counter-poison."

THE ORIGINAL METHOD for making meringues was quite involved because it was much more difficult to control the oven temperature in Mrs Beeton's day than it is now. This updated recipe gives more consistent results. Mrs Beeton said, 'to vary their appearance, finely-chopped almonds or currants may be strewn over them before the sugar is sprinkled over; and they may be garnished with any bright-coloured preserve'. These days we prefer meringues served plain.

METHOD

Whisk the whites of the eggs to a stiff froth. With a metal spoon, quickly fold in the sugar. Drop a tablespoonful of the mixture at a time on a baking sheet lined with paper, taking care to let all the meringues be the same size. In dropping it from the spoon, give the mixture the form of an egg, and keep the meringues about 2 inches (5 cm) apart from each other on the paper. Strew over them some caster sugar and bake for 1 hour. To serve, fill them with whipped cream, flavoured with liqueur or vanilla and sweetened with sugar. Join the meringues together in pairs and pile them high in a dish.

The oven should be preheated to 275°F (140°C) Gas 1.

NOTES

Paper Use non-stick baking parchment.

Mrs Beeton writes

"Great expedition is necessary in making this sweet dish; as, if the meringues are not put into the oven as soon as the sugar and eggs are mixed, the former melts, and the mixture would run on the paper, instead of keeping its egg-shape. The sweeter the meringues are made, the crisper will they be; but, if there is not sufficient sugar mixed with them, they will most likely be tough. They are sometimes coloured with cochineal; and, if kept well covered in a dry place, will remain good for a month or six weeks."

Time 1¼ hours
Sufficient to make 2 dozen
   individual meringues
   (not pairs)
Seasonable at any time

INGREDIENTS
the whites of 4 eggs
½ lb (250 g) caster sugar
extra caster sugar for
   sprinkling

IN A CHAPTER ENTITLED
DINNERS AND DINING,
WHICH CAME
IMMEDIATELY AFTER THE
RECIPE CHAPTERS IN
HER ORIGINAL BOOK,
MRS BEETON GAVE
INSTRUCTIONS FOR
FORMAL DINNER
PARTIES, FOLLOWING
THEM UP WITH MANY
PAGES OF SUGGESTIONS
FOR ACTUAL MENUS
APPROPRIATE FOR THE
TIME OF DAY AND YEAR
AND THE NUMBER OF
PERSONS TO BE SERVED.
ONE OF THE MOST
INTERESTING REMARKS
IN THE QUOTATIONS
HERE IS ABOUT THE
NECESSITY FOR 'THE
MODERN HOUSEWIFE' TO
FEED HER FAMILY WELL.
MRS BEETON WAS WELL
AWARE OF THE DAY-TO-
DAY MONOTONY OF
PREPARING FOOD AT
HOME, SOMETHING THAT
WE STILL STRUGGLE
WITH TODAY.

MAN IS A DINING ANIMAL. Creatures of the inferior races eat and drink; man only dines. It has also been said that he is a cooking animal; but some races eat food without cooking it. The rank which a people occupy in the grand scale may be measured by their way of taking their meals, as well as by their way of treating their women. The nation which knows how to dine has learnt the leading lesson in progress. It implies both the will and the skill to reduce to order, and surround with idealisms and graces, the more material conditions of human existence; and wherever that will and that skill exist, life cannot be wholly ignoble.

DINNER, BEING THE GRAND SOLID MEAL of the day, is a matter of considerable importance; and a well-served table is a striking index of human ingenuity and resource.

DINE WE MUST, and we may as well dine elegantly as well as wholesomely.

THERE ARE PLENTY OF ELEGANT DINNERS in modern days, and they were not wanting in ancient times. It is well known that the dinner-party, or symposium, was a not unimportant, and not unpoetical, feature in the life of the sociable, talkative, tasteful Greek. Douglas Jerrold said that such is the British humour for dining and giving of dinners, that if London were to be destroyed by an earthquake, the Londoners would meet at a public dinner to consider the subject.

THE ELEGANCE with which a dinner is served is a matter which depends, of course, partly upon the means, but still more upon the taste of the master and mistress of the house. It may be observed, in general, that there should always be flowers on the table, and as they form no item of expense, there is no reason why they should not be employed every day.

THE VARIETY IN THE DISHES which furnish forth a modern dinner-table, does not necessarily imply anything unwholesome, or anything capricious. Food that is not well relished cannot be well digested; and the appetite of the over-worked man of business, or statesman, or of any dweller in towns, whose occupations are exciting and exhausting, is jaded, and requires stimulation. Men and women who are in rude health, and who have plenty of air and exercise, eat the simplest food with relish, and consequently digest it well; but those conditions are out of the reach of many men. They must suit their mode of dining to their mode of living, if they cannot choose the latter.

IT IS IN SERVING UP FOOD that is at once appetizing and wholesome that the skill of the modern housewife is severely tasked; and she has scarcely a more important duty to fulfil. It is, in fact, her particular vocation, in virtue of which she may be said to hold the health of the family, and of the friends of the family, in her hands from day to day. It has been said that 'the destiny of nations depends on the manner in which they are fed'; and a great gastronomist exclaims, 'Tell me what kind of food you eat, and I will tell you what kind of man you are'.

THE GASTRONOMIST from whom we have already quoted, has some aphorisms and short directions in relation to dinner-parties, which are well deserving of notice: 'Let the number of your guests never exceed twelve, so that the conversation may be general. Let the temperature of the dining-room be about 68°. Let the dishes be few in number in the first course, but proportionally good. The order of food is from the most substantial to the lightest. The order of drinking wine is from the mildest to the most foamy and most perfumed. To invite a person to your house is to take charge of his happiness so long as he is beneath your roof. The mistress of the house should always be certain that the coffee be excellent; whilst the master should be answerable for the quality of his wines and liqueurs.'

✍ *Orange Salad*

Time ¼ hour plus chilling
Sufficient for 5 or 6 persons
Seasonable from November
to May

INGREDIENTS
6 oranges
¼ lb (125 g) muscatel
raisins
2 oz (60 g) caster sugar
4 tablespoons brandy

THE SIMPLEST DESSERTS are often the best, and this is no exception. Orange Salad is cool and refreshing, especially when served well chilled, and it goes down well at the end of a rich or spicy meal. Mrs Beeton specified muscatel raisins, which needed to be stoned. These days raisins come ready stoned, but it is important to buy plump, moist fruit – dry, seedy raisins will spoil the dish. Look for good-quality raisins in health food shops.

METHOD
Peel 5 of the oranges. Divide them into slices without breaking the pulp and arrange them on a glass dish. Stone the raisins, mix them with the sugar and brandy and mingle them with the oranges. Squeeze the juice of the remaining orange over the salad and the dish is ready to serve.

NOTES
Segmenting oranges After peeling each whole orange, cut carefully between the membranes so that the segments are released individually. Work round the orange and when you get to the place where you started cutting there will be a core of membranes left. Squeeze this tightly over a bowl to release all of the juice, which should not be wasted.

Chilling The salad will benefit from being tightly covered and chilled in the refrigerator overnight, especially if the oranges have been sprinkled with spice as suggested by Mrs Beeton below. Cardamom goes particularly well with oranges; so too does star anise, which can be placed whole on the fruit. Star anise looks pretty as well as adding fragrance and flavour.

Mrs Beeton writes

"A little pounded spice may be put in when the flavour is liked, but this ingredient must be added very sparingly."

"ORANGE AND CLOVES – It appears to have been the custom formerly, in England, to make new year's presents with oranges stuck full with cloves. We read in one of Ben Johnson's pieces – the Christmas Masque – 'He has an orange and rosemary, but not a clove to stick in it'."

MRS BEETON ALSO CALLED THIS RECIPE '*Oeufs à la Neige*', acknowledging its French origins. She described it as a very pretty supper dish. It is made of egg-shaped balls of meringue poached in milk and served on a sea of custard, and also goes by the charmingly descriptive name of 'Floating Islands'.

METHOD

Put the milk into a wide, shallow pan with sufficient sugar to sweeten it nicely, and the lemon rind. Bring it just to the boil, then remove from the heat, cover the pan and let it steep in a warm place for ½ hour. Separate the whites from the yolks of the eggs and whisk the former to a perfectly stiff froth, or until there is no liquid remaining. Take out the lemon rind from the milk and bring the milk to boiling point. Drop in the snow a tablespoonful at a time, then keep turning them until the egg is sufficiently cooked. Place the eggs on a glass dish. Beat the yolks of the eggs, stir them into the milk and add a little more sugar. Strain this mixture into a bowl, place the bowl in a saucepan of boiling water and stir it one way until the mixture thickens. Do not allow it to boil or it will curdle. Pour this custard over the eggs, which should rise to the surface.

NOTES

Flavouring For quantities of vanilla and orange-flower water, see *Mrs Beeton writes*.

Mrs Beeton writes

"These make an exceedingly pretty addition to a supper, and should be put in a cold place after being made. When they are flavoured with vanilla or orange-flower water, it is not necessary to steep the milk. A few drops of the essence of either may be poured in the milk just before the whites are poached. In making the custard, a little more flavouring and sugar should always be added."

Time 20 to 30 minutes
Sufficient for 4 or 5 persons
Seasonable at any time

INGREDIENTS
¾ pint (450 ml) milk
about 6 oz (175 g) caster
   sugar to taste
the rind of ½ lemon or a
   flavouring of vanilla
   essence or orange-flower
   water
4 eggs

∽ Syllabub

Time ¼ hour
Sufficient to fill 8 or 9
   glasses
Seasonable at any time

INGREDIENTS
½ pint (300 ml) cream
¼ pint (150 ml) sherry
2½ fl oz (75 ml) brandy
the juice of ½ lemon
a little grated nutmeg
3 oz (90 g) caster sugar
whipped cream

THE SYLLABUB DATES BACK to the time of Elizabeth 1, but it was very popular in Victoria's reign too. This recipe is for a thin syllabub which is served in glasses like a sweet drink. In Mrs Beeton's version it was topped with the same cream 'whip' that she used for Trifle (page 282), but here a more simple topping of whipped cream is suggested. If you prefer to make the more solid version that Mrs Beeton mentioned at the end of the recipe, whip all the ingredients together and omit the whipped cream on the top.

METHOD
Mix all the ingredients together, put the syllabub into glasses and over the top of them heap a little whipped cream.

NOTES
Cream Use double cream. Single or whipping cream would not be heavy enough to hold its own against the weight of the other ingredients.

Mrs Beeton writes

"Solid syllabub is made
by whisking the mixture
to a stiff froth and putting it
in the glasses without
the whipped cream
at the top."

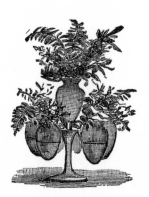

Jelly Moulded with Fresh Fruit ॐ

MRS BEETON GAVE LOTS of detail about the kind of fruit and jelly to use, but a short cut can be taken by using a commercial packet jelly and a simple layering one of one or two kinds of fruit. The simple but stunning combination of lime green jelly and red fruit is very hard to beat.

METHOD

Begin by putting a little jelly at the bottom of a 2 pint (1.2 litre) mould. Leave to harden. Arrange some fruit over the set layer of jelly recollecting that it will be reversed when turned out, then pour in some more jelly to make the fruit adhere. When that layer is set, put in another row of fruit and jelly and leave to harden as before. Continue in this way until the mould is full, then chill until required. To serve, wring a cloth in boiling water, wrap it round the mould for a minute and turn the jelly carefully out.

NOTES

Jelly Two packets of jelly will be ample. Make the jelly according to packet instructions and leave until cold but not beginning to set. Chill the first layer of jelly in the refrigerator to harden before adding a layer of fruit, then repeat this chilling with every layer. If the jelly begins to set before the mould has been filled, gently warm it through until just melted, then leave to cool again.

Mrs Beeton writes

"Peaches, apricots, plums, apples, &c., are better for being boiled in a little clear syrup before they are laid in the jelly; strawberries, raspberries, grapes, cherries, and currants are put in raw. In winter, when fresh fruits are not obtainable, a very pretty jelly may be made with preserved fruits or brandy cherries: these, in a bright and clear jelly, have a very pretty effect."

Time 10 minutes plus
   chilling
Sufficient for 6 persons
Seasonable with fresh fruit,
   from June to October; with
   dried, at any time

INGREDIENTS
rather more than 1¼ pints
   (900 ml) jelly
½ lb (250 g) nice
   strawberries or
   raspberries, or any fresh
   fruit that may be in season

✎ Trifle

Time ½ hour plus standing
Sufficient for 6 to 8 persons
Seasonable at any time

INGREDIENTS
FOR THE WHIP
3 oz (90 g) caster sugar
the whites of 2 eggs
a small glass of sherry or
    raisin wine
1 pint (600 ml) cream
FOR THE TRIFLE
6 small sponge cakes or
    6 slices of sponge cake
12 macaroons
2 dozen ratafias
½ pint (300 ml) sherry or
    sweet wine
6 tablespoons brandy
the grated rind of 1 lemon
2 oz (60 g) sweet almonds
a layer of raspberry or
    strawberry jam
1 pint (600 ml) custard

Mrs Beeton writes

"The small coloured
comfits are sometimes
used for the purpose of
garnishing a trifle, but
they are now considered
rather old fashioned."

THIS IS A TRADITIONAL TRIFLE, the kind that is usually made at Christmas, although Mrs Beeton did say that it was seasonable at any time. The instructions for 'the whip' have been retained because they are so charming, but it is not not necessary to make it the day before and leave it to drain. Use an electric mixer to whip all the ingredients together and use it to top the trifle once the custard layer is in place. At this stage the trifle will benefit from being left in the refrigerator overnight, during which time the flavours of the layers will mingle and mature.

METHOD

The whip to lay over the top of the trifle should be made the day before it is required. The flavour is better and it is much more solid than when prepared the same day. Put into a large bowl the sugar, the whites of the eggs, which should be beaten to a stiff froth, a glass of sherry or sweet wine, and the cream. Whisk these ingredients well in a cool place, taking off the froth with a skimmer as fast as it rises, then continue the whisking until there is sufficient whip, which must be put away in a cool place to drain. The next day, place the sponge cakes, macaroons and ratafias at the bottom of a trifle dish and pour over them the sherry or sweet wine mixed with the brandy. Should this amount of wine not be found quite sufficient, add a little more, as the cakes should be well soaked. Over the cakes, put the grated lemon rind, the almonds, blanched and cut into strips, and a layer of jam. Make a good custard, let this cool a little, then pour it over the cakes. The whip being made the day previously, and the trifle prepared, there remains nothing to do now but heap the whip lightly over the top. This should stand as high as possible, and it may be garnished with strips of bright currant jelly, crystallized sweetmeats or flowers.

NOTES

Almonds Use flaked almonds.
Custard Mrs Beeton suggested using 8 eggs to 1 pint (600 ml) milk. This would make the trifle extremely rich. It would be better to make the custard according to the recipe on page 235, or buy a ready made thick custard.
Garnish Use candied fruit and peel for a traditional look.

THIS UNUSUAL DESSERT takes its name from the amount of alcohol it contains. It is very simple and quick, especially as it can be made with shop bought ingredients, although the orginal purpose of the recipe was to use up cake that was a bit stale and no longer good enough for eating at teatime.

METHOD

Put the cake in a glass serving bowl or dish. Make a small hole in the centre and pour in and over the cake sufficient sweet wine or sherry mixed with the same amount of brandy to soak it nicely. When the cake is well soaked – after about 2 hours – blanch and cut the almonds into strips, stick them over the cake and pour round it a good custard.

NOTES

Cake In the original recipe Mrs Beeton said, 'Procure a cake that is three or four days old, either sponge, Savoy, or rice, answering for the purpose of a tipsy cake'. In other words, a slightly stale cake will do very nicely because the alcohol will soak into it better than it will a fresh cake. Use a round sponge cake measuring about 6 inches (15 cm) in diameter, or whatever size will fit comfortably in your chosen bowl or dish. Altenatively, use a packet of trifle sponges.

Almonds You can buy whole almonds in their skins and blanch them yourself, but for a quick and easy dessert like this it is more convenient to buy ready blanched almonds.

Rich custard Mrs Beeton said to make it with 8 eggs, but this is a good opportunity to use a carton of ready made thick custard.

Time ¼ hour plus standing
Sufficient for 4 to 6 persons
Seasonable at any time

INGREDIENTS
1 moulded sponge or Savoy
  cake
about 6 tablespoons sweet
  wine or sherry
6 tablespoons brandy·
2 oz (60 g) sweet almonds
1 pint (600 ml) rich custard

Mrs Beeton writes

"The cakes are sometimes crumbled and soaked, and a whipped cream heaped over them, the same as for trifles."

✑ Fruit Ice Cream

Time ½ hour plus freezing
Sufficient for 4 or 6 persons
Seasonable in June, July
    and August

INGREDIENTS
1 pint (600 ml) fruit purée
icing sugar to taste
1 pint (600 ml) cream

MADE WITH NATURAL INGREDIENTS, this is one of the simplest of all ice creams and yet it is still one of the best. You can use any ripe fresh fruit in season, although strawberries and raspberries are the easiest because they can be puréed raw. Today, we tend to use a blender or food processor for puréeing, although it is still necessary to sieve some mixtures to remove seeds. Mrs Beeton recommended mashing the fruit in an earthenware bowl, then using a wooden spoon to push it through a fine sieve.

METHOD

Sweeten the fruit purée nicely with sugar. Whip the cream for a few minutes, add it to the fruit purée and whisk for 5 minutes. Put the mixture into the freezing pot and freeze, taking care to stir it two or three times and to remove it from the sides of the vessel so that the mixture may be equally frozen and smooth.

NOTES

Fruit purée You will need 1¼ - 1½ lb (625 – 750 g) soft fruit to yield 1 pint (600 ml) purée.

Sugar Add enough sugar for the fruit purée to taste quite sweet. Freezing dulls the sweetness of the ice cream mixture and you need to add more sugar than usual to allow for this.

Cream Use double cream. It has a high fat content, which will give the ice cream a smooth consistency.

Freeze the mixture according to the instructions for your ice-cream maker, or freeze in a rigid container for 6 to 8 hours, stirring every 1 to 2 hours to prevent the formation of ice crystals.

Mrs Beeton writes

"Raspberry, strawberry, currant and all fruit ice-creams
are made in the same manner. A little pounded sugar sprinkled
over the fruit before it is mashed assists to extract the juice.
In winter, when fresh fruit is not obtainable, a little jam
may be substituted for it; it should be melted and worked
through a sieve before being added to the whipped cream;
and if the colour should not be good, a little prepared
cochineal or beetroot may be put in
to improve its appearance."

Iced Pudding ❧

MRS BEETON DESCRIBED this as a Parisian recipe. Looking at the illustration of the mould in which it was frozen, it was obviously intended to be a very special dessert, and yet its rather plain name gives no hint of this. The recipe directed readers to the 'method of working the freezing apparatus', which was very complicated. Today the mixture can be frozen in an ice-cream maker, then packed into a mould and re-frozen into shape.

METHOD
Pound the almonds in a mortar until reduced to a smooth paste. Put them in a saucepan and add the well-beaten eggs, the sugar, milk and almond essence. Stir these ingredients over the heat until they thicken, but do not allow them to boil. Strain the mixture, let it cool, then put it into the freezing pot and freeze. When quite frozen, fill an iced pudding mould, put on the lid and freeze the pudding until required. To serve, turn it out on a dish and garnish it with a compôte of any fruit that may be preferred, pouring a little of the fruit over the top of the pudding.

NOTES
Almonds A combination of both sweet and bitter almonds was used in the original recipe and instructions were given for blanching them. Bitter almonds were used in small quantities because of their very strong flavour, but it is quicker and easier to use ready blanched almonds and a few drops of almond essence, which is made from bitter almonds.

Freeze the mixture according to the instructions on your machine, or freeze in a rigid container for 6 to 8 hours, stirring every 1 to 2 hours to prevent the formation of ice crystals.

Time ½ hour plus freezing
Sufficient for 6 to 8 persons
Seasonable all the year
  round

INGREDIENTS
10 oz (300 g) blanched
  almonds
8 eggs
¾ lb (375 g) sugar
1½ pints (900 ml) milk
a few drops of almond
  essence
fruit compôte to serve

Mrs Beeton writes

"This pudding may be flavoured with vanilla, curaçao, or maraschine."

✑ Fruit Water Ice

Time ½ hour plus freezing
Sufficient for 4 or 6 persons
Seasonable in June, July
   and August

INGREDIENTS
12 oz (350g) sugar
1 pint (600 ml) fruit purée

MRS BEETON'S INSTRUCTIONS for making a fruit purée are as valid today as they were when she originally gave them, although nowadays we would use an electric machine to save time and effort. 'Raspberry, strawberry and other fresh-fruit-water ices are made in the same manner,' she said. 'Select nice ripe fruit and pick it off the stalks. Put it into a large earthenware bowl and strew a little caster sugar over it. Stir it with a wooden spoon until it is broken, then rub it through a hair sieve.'

METHOD
Put the sugar in a heavy saucepan and add 1 pint (600 ml) water. Heat gently, stirring occasionally, until the sugar has dissolved, then boil rapidly for ¼ hour without stirring. Pour into a bowl and leave to cool. Stir in the fruit purée, mix well together, then put the mixture into the freezing pot and freeze. When the mixture is equally frozen, put it into small glasses.

NOTES
Fruit purée Work the fruit – you will need about 1½ lb (750 g) – in a blender or food processor to make it easier to press through the sieve.
Freeze the mixture according to the instructions for your ice-cream maker, or freeze in a rigid container for 6 to 8 hours, stirring every 1 to 2 hours to prevent the formation of ice crystals.

VARIATION
Lemon Water Ice Use sugar cubes rather than granualted sugar. Rub the sugar cubes on the rinds of 4 lemons to absorb the aromatic oil; then use the sugar to make a syrup. To every 1 pint (600 ml) syrup, add ⅓ pint (200 ml) strained lemon juice and stir well. Freeze and serve as above.

Mrs Beeton writes

"Do ladies know to whom they are indebited for the introduction of ices, which all the fair sex are passionately fond of? – To Catherine de' Medici. Will not this fact cover a multitude of sins committed by the instigator of St. Bartholomew?"

THIS IS A FAIRLY LIGHT SYRUP suitable for fruit compôtes and fruit salads. You can increase the amount of sugar if you want a sweeter, thicker syrup. For a medium syrup, use 17 fl oz (500 ml) water to 1 lb (500 g) sugar; for a heavy syrup, use ¾ pint (450 ml) water.

METHOD
Put the sugar and water in a heavy saucepan and heat gently, stirring occasionally, until the sugar has dissolved. Bring to the boil and boil rapidly for ¼ hour, without stirring, carefully removing the scum as it rises. The syrup is then ready. Use hot or, more usually, cold.

NOTES
Crystallization It is important not to stir the sugar syrup while it is boiling. If you do, crystallization may occur, and the sugar syrup will be grainy.

Mrs Beeton writes

"The articles boiled in this syrup will not keep
for any length of time, it being suitable
only for dishes intended to be eaten immediately.
A larger proportion of sugar must be added
for a syrup intended to keep."

Sufficient for 1½ pints
(900 ml) sugar syrup

INGREDIENTS
1 lb (500 g) sugar
1½ pints (900 ml) water

CHAPTER 10

Baking

Mrs Beeton devoted a single chapter in her book to bread, biscuits and cakes, beginning with general observations on bread and bread-making. Scientific information about the different ingredients and their effects was followed by the do's and don'ts of the actual bread-making process, and included the following advice.

'Bread should always be at least a day old before it is eaten. Hot rolls, swimming in melted butter, and new bread, ought to be carefully shunned by everybody who has the slightest respect for that much-injured individual - the Stomach.'

Mrs Beeton gave precise and detailed instructions for the novice baker and her knowledge of breadmaking was extensive, but some of the advice she gave was not her own. The following paragraph is taken from Eliza Acton's *The English Bread-Book*, which Mrs Beeton acknowledged as 'a valuable work on bread-making that will be found very useful to our readers'.

'The first thing required for making wholesome bread is the utmost cleanliness. The next is the soundness and sweetness of all the ingredients used for it and, in addition to these, there must be attention and care through the whole process.'

A new process of bread-making was being introduced at this time. Aërated Bread, as it was called, was made commercially by impregnating the bread 'by the application of machinery with carbonic acid gas, or fixed air'. Mrs Beeton was evidently impressed with this invention.

'The whole process of bread-making is probably in course of undergoing changes which will emancipate both the housewife and the professional baker from a large amount of labour.'

Her praise was not without some reservations.

'It is a good plan to change one's baker from time to time, and so secure a change in the quality of bread that is eaten.'

Mrs Beeton provided only a few hints about the making and baking of cakes, and had even less to say about biscuits, but in an earlier chapter on 'The Housekeeper', we learn that it was that person's duty to help prepare the ingredients for baking.

'In the evening, the housekeeper will often busy herself with the necessary preparations for the next day's duties. Numberless small, but still important arrangements will have to be made, so that everything may move smoothly. At times, perhaps, attention will have to be paid to the breaking up of lump sugar, the stoning of raisins, the washing, cleansing and drying of currants &c.'

✑ Good Home-Made Bread

Time 2¾ hours

Sufficient for 2 loaves

Seasonable at any time

INGREDIENTS

1 lb 15 oz (875 g) strong
plain flour plus about
2 tablespoons for
sprinkling

2 teaspoons salt

½ oz (15 g) fresh yeast

24 fl oz (720 ml) lukewarm
milk-and-water

DON'T BE PUT OFF by the length of this recipe. These, detailed instructions are superb, exactly right for the novice baker. If you follow them to the letter, you will have perfect homemade bread every time you make it. Mrs Beeton attributed this recipe to her predecessor, Eliza Acton.

METHOD

Sift the flour and salt into a large earthenware bowl and hollow out the middle, but do not clear it entirely away from the bottom of the bowl. Put the yeast into a large basin and mix it to a smooth cream with about 8 fl oz (250 ml) of the warm milk-and-water. Pour this cream into the hole in the flour and stir in sufficient flour from around the yeast to make a thick batter, in which there must be no lumps. Sprinkle plenty of flour (about 2 tablespoons) on top, cover with a thick clean cloth and put it in a warm place. Look at it from time to time and after nearly an hour, when the yeast has risen and broken through the flour so that bubbles appear, it will be ready to be made into dough. Pour into the sponge the remainder of the warm milk-and-water and stir into it as much of the flour as you can with a spoon, then mix it with your hands and start to knead it well. When the flour is nearly all kneaded in, begin to draw the edges of the dough towards the middle, in order to mix it thoroughly. When it is free from flour and lumps and crumbs, and does not stick to the hands when touched, it will be done, and may again be covered with the cloth and left to rise a second time. After ¾ hour it should have swollen very much and begun to crack so that it is ready to bake. Turn it on to a board and, with a large sharp knife, divide it in two. Shape it quickly into loaves, then make one or two incisions across the tops of the loaves, as they will rise more easily if this is done. If baked in tins or pans, grease them with butter to prevent the dough sticking. Bake for 20 minutes, then lower the oven temperature and bake for a further 15 to 20 minutes. All bread should be turned upside down or on its side as soon as it is taken from the oven. If this is neglected, the under part of the loaves will become wet and blistered from the steam, which cannot escape from them.

The oven should be preheated to 425°F (220°C) Gas 7, then decreased to 375°F (190°C) Gas 5.

NOTES

Milk-and-water Mrs Beeton said, 'or with water only, though even a very little milk will much improve the bread'. The best compromise is to use equal quantities of both. By the time the second quantity of milk-and-water is added, it will have cooled; reheat it to lukewarm before pouring it into the 'sponge' or starter mixture.

Salt This was not used in the original recipe, but is added here for flavour.

Tins or pans This amount of dough is enough for 2 loaf tins, each measuring 8 x 4 x 2 inches (20 x 10 x 5 cm).

Glaze Before baking, you can brush the tops of the loaves with milk to give them a glazed finish, but this is not essential.

✂ Soda Bread

Time 1 hour
Sufficient for one loaf
Seasonable at any time

INGREDIENTS
1¼ lb (625 g) flour
1 teaspoon cream of tartar
1 teaspoon salt
1 teaspoon bicarbonate
 of soda
2 breakfastcupfuls of
 cold milk

SODA BREAD USES BICARBONATE OF SODA rather than yeast to make it rise. The soda needs to be combined with an acid ingredient, in this case cream of tartar, although sometimes sour milk or buttermilk is used instead, as Mrs Beeton mentioned at the end of her recipe, when the cream of tartar may be omitted. Soda Bread does not take long to make, but it is important to eat it on the day it is baked, because it soon goes stale.

METHOD

Mix the flour with the cream of tartar and salt. Dissolve the soda in the milk and pour it several times from one basin to another, before adding it to the flour. Work all the ingredients quickly into a light dough, shape it into a round loaf about 1 inch (2.5 cm) thick and place it on a greased baking sheet. Mark a large cross in the top with a floured knife and put the loaf into a well heated oven immediately. Bake for 40 minutes.

The oven should be preheated to 375°F (190°C) Gas 5.

NOTES

Flour Use plain flour.
Breakfastcupfuls A Victorian breakfast cup holds ¼ pint (150 ml), so use ½ pint (300 ml) milk here.
Testing for doneness Insert a skewer into the centre of the loaf. If the loaf is done, the skewer will come out clean. To keep the loaf soft, wrap it in a cloth immediately after baking.

Mrs Beeton writes

"Sour milk or buttermilk may be used,
but then a little less acid will be needed."

Good Plain Buns ∾

To call these 'buns' is slightly misleading because they are more like sweet, tea-time rock cakes than bread rolls, which we normally associate with buns nowadays. They are quick and easy to make with storecupboard ingredients, ideal for an impromptu or last-minute tea party – in which case you may prefer to bake them in paper cake cases so that they look more attractive. They are delicious split in half and spread with butter and jam.

METHOD
Warm the butter without oiling it, then beat it with a wooden spoon. Stir the flour in gradually with the sugar and mix these ingredients well together. Make the milk lukewarm, beat into it the yolk of the egg and the essence of lemon and stir these into the flour. Add the baking powder and beat the dough well for about 15 minutes. Divide it into 24 pieces, put them into buttered tins or cups and bake in a brisk oven for 20 minutes.

The oven should be preheated to 375°F (190°C) Gas 5.

NOTES
Warm the butter All that is necessary here is that the butter should be softened, so take it out of the refrigerator an hour or so before you bake. If you let it melt, it will become oily, which Mrs Beeton warned against in her method.
Flour Use plain flour.
Essence of lemon This has a very strong flavour and should be used sparingly, as the recipe directs. Look for it in small bottles in the baking sections of supermarkets and at health food shops.

Time ½ to ¾ hour
Sufficient to make 24 buns
Seasonable at any time

INGREDIENTS
6 oz (175 g) butter
1 lb (500 g) flour
¼ lb (125 g) caster sugar
nearly ¼ pint (150 ml) milk
1 egg yolk
a few drops of essence
  of lemon
2 teaspoons baking powder

✍ *Coconut Biscuits*

Time ¾ hour
Sufficient for 15 biscuits
Seasonable at any time

INGREDIENTS
2 egg whites
10 oz (300 g) caster sugar
6 oz (175 g) grated coconut

MRS BEETON DESCRIBED THESE AS Cocoa-Nut Biscuits or Cakes. They are indeed a cross between the two and are sometimes also called Coconut Pyramids. Children love them, not least because of their shape, and they also make pretty *petits fours* to serve with after-dinner coffee.

METHOD

Whisk the eggs whites until they are very stiff. Add the sugar gradually, then stir in the coconut. Roll a tablespoonful of the paste at a time in your hands in the form of a pyramid and place the pyramids on paper-lined baking sheets. Bake the biscuits in rather a cool oven until they are just coloured a light brown – about ½ hour.

The oven should be preheated to 275°F (140°C) Gas 1.

NOTES

Coconut Use desiccated coconut.
Paper Non-stick baking paper is best.

Dessert Biscuits ✑

THIS IS A RECIPE FOR a basic sweet biscuit dough, which can be left perfectly plain or flavoured with different ingredients, as suggested in the notes at the end of the method. Mrs Beeton gave instructions for beating the mixture by hand, but you can make the biscuit dough really quickly using an electric mixer – simply mix all the ingredients together. Quantities can easily be halved or quartered, although it is worth making a large batch of biscuits, because they keep well if stored in an airtight tin.

METHOD

Put the butter into a basin and warm it, but do not allow it to oil. With the hand, beat it to a cream. Add the flour by degrees, then the sugar and flavouring. Moisten the mixture with the yolks of the eggs, which should previously be well beaten. When all the ingredients are thoroughly incorporated, drop the mixture from a spoon on to buttered paper, leaving a distance between each cake, as they spread as soon as they begin to get warm. Bake in rather a slow oven for 12 to 18 minutes and do not let the biscuits acquire too much colour.

The oven should be preheated to 325°F (160°C) Gas 3.

NOTES

Flour Use plain flour.

Flavouring and finish For ginger biscuits, sift 1 teaspoon ground ginger with the flour. For lemon biscuits, add ¼ teaspoon lemon essence. For an attractive finish, prick the biscuits in several places with a fork and sprinkle with caster sugar before baking.

Paper Use non-stick baking paper on baking sheets. You will need to make the biscuits in batches according to the size and number of baking sheets you have.

Mrs Beeton writes

" In making the above quantity, half may be flavoured
with ground ginger and the other half with essence of lemon
or currants, to make a variety. With whatever the preparation
is flavoured, so are the biscuits called; and an endless variety
may be made in this manner."

Time ½ to ¾ hour
Sufficient to make 3 or 4
  dozen
Seasonable at any time

INGREDIENTS
½ lb (250 g) butter
1 lb (500 g) flour
½ lb (250 g) caster sugar
flavouring to taste
the yolks of 6 eggs

✎ Savoy Biscuits

Time ½ to ¾ hour
Sufficient for about
  30 biscuits
Seasonable at any time

INGREDIENTS
4 eggs
6 oz (175 g) caster sugar,
  plus extra sprinkling
the grated rind of 1 lemon
6 oz (175 g) flour

Mrs Beeton writes

"Since the establishment
of the large modern
biscuit manufactories,
biscuits have been
produced both cheap and
wholesome, in,
comparatively speaking,
endless variety."

MRS BEETON SAID, 'these biscuits, or ladies'-fingers as they are called, are used for making Charlotte russes, and for a variety of fancy sweet dishes'. Today we are more likely to know them as sponge fingers or boudoir biscuits, which are used in trifles and tiramisù. They are crisp, sweet and light, so are also good for serving with creamy rich desserts and fresh fruit salads.

METHOD
Break the eggs and separate the whites from the yolks, putting them into two different bowls. Beat the yolks well, mix with them the sugar and grated lemon rind and beat these ingredients together until pale and thick. Dredge in the flour gradually. Whisk the whites of the eggs to a solid froth, then fold them into the flour mixture. Draw it along in strips on thick paper to the proper size of the biscuit and bake them in rather a hot oven for 10 to 15 minutes. Watch them carefully as they are soon done, and a few seconds over the proper time will scorch and spoil them. Sprinkle caster sugar over the biscuits when they are old

The oven should be preheated to 375°F (190°C) Gas 5.

NOTES
Beating Use a heavy-duty electric mixer and beat the egg yolks, sugar and lemon rind until the mixture is thick enough to leave a ribbon trail when the beaters are lifted. If you do not have this type of mixer, put the basin of mixture over a pan of gently simmering water and whisk with a hand-held electric mixer or a balloon whisk. Take care to wash and thoroughly dry the beaters or whisk before whisking the egg whites. If there is even a trace of egg yolk or grease on them the whites will not whisk to a froth.
Flour Use plain flour.
Paper Use non-stick baking paper on baking sheets.
Size Mrs Beeton did not give precise measurements for making the biscuits but the 'proper size' she alluded to is about 3 inches (7.5 cm) long. To get a neat finish, pipe the mixture on to the paper using a piping bag with a ½ inch (1 cm) plain nozzle.

Seed Biscuits ⌒

THESE DAYS WE MOST OFTEN associate spicy caraway seeds with Eastern European and German cooking, but in Victorian England they were a popular flavouring ingredient for fruit-based dishes and in many biscuits and cakes – as they had been in Elizabethan days. Seed cake, a plain cake spiced with a liberal amount of caraway seeds, was a famous English cake of the time, but it has lost favour over the years. These caraway-flavoured biscuits are mildly spicy. They are a sweet biscuit, but are also very good served with cheese.

METHOD
Beat the butter to a cream. Stir in the flour, sugar and caraway seeds. When these ingredients are well mixed, add the eggs, which should be well whisked. Roll out the paste and cut out the biscuits with a round cutter. Bake them on greased baking sheets in a moderate oven for 10 to 15 minutes.

The oven should be preheated to 350°F (180°C) Gas 4.

NOTES
Flour Use plain flour.
Round cutter Use a 2¾ inch (7 cm) plain or fluted biscuit cutter.
Baking Sheets Cook the biscuits in batches, depending on the number of baking sheets you have. You can bake two sheets at a time, but they will need to be swapped over halfway.

Mrs Beeton writes

"The tops of the biscuits may be brushed over with a little milk or the white of an egg, and then a little sugar strewn over."

Time ½ hour
Sufficient to make about 40 biscuits
Seasonable at any time

INGREDIENTS
¼ lb (125 g) butter
1 lb (500 g) flour
¼ lb (125 g) caster sugar
2 tablespoons caraway seeds
3 eggs

✍ *Sunderland Gingerbread Nuts*

Time ½ hour

Sufficient for 18 biscuits

Seasonable at any time

INGREDIENTS

1½ teaspoons ground ginger

1½ teaspoons ground
  allspice

1½ teaspoons ground
  coriander

5 oz (150 g) self-raising
  flour

2 oz (60 g) moist soft brown
  sugar

3 oz (90 g) treacle

2 oz (60 g) butter

MRS BEETON SAID THE RECIPE for these biscuits was an excellent one, then elaborated on this by suggesting ways of making them even spicier. Her suggestions make interesting reading, but the biscuits are just perfect as they are, and are plenty hot enough without the addition of cayenne pepper. The quantities given here are less than in the original recipe, which made a huge number of biscuits.

METHOD

Put the spices into a bowl with the flour and sugar and mix these ingredients well together. Warm the treacle and butter together in a saucepan. With a spoon, work them into the flour until a nice smooth paste forms. Drop the mixture from the spoon on to a piece of buttered paper and bake for 15 minutes.

The oven should be preheated to 325°F (160°C) Gas 3.

NOTES

Buttered paper If you use non-stick baking paper there is no need to butter it first. Use 2 baking sheets and space the mounds of mixture well apart on the paper, to allow room for spreading during baking. Swap the sheets over halfway through. The biscuits will still be quite soft at the end of baking, so leave them to cool and harden slightly before transferring them to a wire rack to cool completely.

Mrs Beeton writes

"A little candied lemon-peel mixed with the above is an improvement, and a great authority in culinary matters suggests the addition of a little cayenne pepper in gingerbread. Whether it be advisable to use this latter ingredient or not, we leave our readers to decide."

Scotch Shortbread ❧

THE ORIGINAL RECIPE for this traditional shortbread made a large amount and was rather vague about the size and shape. This version uses the same ingredients and method, but the quantities have been reduced and precise instructions are given for shaping the dough before baking. You can omit the candied peel decoration if you like and sprinkle the shortbread with caster sugar instead. Instructions for this are given in the notes below the method.

METHOD

Beat the butter to a cream, gradually dredge in the flour and add the sugar, caraway seeds and almonds, which should be blanched and cut into small pieces. Work the paste until it is quite smooth and divide it into three pieces. Put each cake on a separate piece of paper, roll the paste out square to the thickness of about 1 inch (2.5 cm) and pinch it on all sides. Prick it well and ornament it with one or two strips of candied orange peel. Bake for 25 to 30 minutes.

The oven should be preheated to 325°F (160°C) Gas 3.

NOTES

Flour Use plain flour.

Almonds Buy ready chopped blanched almond pieces, sometimes called almond nibs or nibbed almonds. Or buy flaked almonds and chop them with a knife.

Paper Line 3 baking sheets with non-stick baking paper and shape one piece of shortbread on each piece of paper. After pricking the dough, mark each piece into 4 triangles with a sharp knife, then decorate it with candied peel, if using, and chill in the refrigerator for about ½ hour before baking. After removing the shortbread from the oven, cut through the knife marks to separate the triangles and sprinkle the shortbread with sugar if you like. Leave the shortbread on the baking sheets until firm, then transfer to wire racks to cool.

Time ¾ to 1 hour
Sufficient to make 12 pieces
Seasonable at any time

INGREDIENTS
½ lb (250 g) butter
1 lb (500 g) flour
2 oz (60 g) caster sugar
1 tablespoon caraway seeds
1 oz (30 g) sweet almonds
a few strips of candied
   orange peel

Mrs Beeton writes

"Where the flavour
of the caraway seeds is
disliked, omit them,
and add rather
a larger proportion
of candied peel."

✥ Victoria Sandwich

Time ½ to ¾ hour

Sufficient for 5 or 6 persons

Seasonable at any time

INGREDIENTS

½ lb (250 g) butter

½ lb (250 g) self-raising
 flour

¼ saltspoon salt

½ lb (250 g) caster sugar

4 eggs

a layer of any kind of jam

THIS QUINTESSENTIAL ENGLISH SPONGE CAKE, made popular in Queen Victoria's reign, used to be called Victoria Sandwiches because it was baked in a Yorkshire pudding tin, then cut into fingers which were sandwiched together with jam. The recipe here has been adapted to its more modern form of two round cakes with a jam filling. The traditional finishing touch is a light sprinkling of caster sugar on the top.

METHOD

Beat the butter to a cream, dredge in the flour, salt and sugar and stir these ingredients well together, then add the eggs, which should be previously thoroughly whisked. When the mixture has been well beaten for about 10 minutes, pour the batter into 2 round cake tins that have been greased. Bake in a moderate oven for 20 minutes. Let the cakes cool for a few minutes, then turn them out of the tins. When cold, spread one of the cakes with a layer of jam, place over it the other cake and press them slightly together.

The oven should be preheated to 350°F (180°C) Gas 4.

NOTES

Weight of ingredients In her original recipe, Mrs Beeton said to weigh the eggs in their shells, then to use the equivalent weight in caster sugar. An egg weighs about 2 oz (60 g), so the approximate weight of the other ingredients is listed here, but it is wise to weigh the eggs and the other ingredients accurately for successful results.

Cake tins To ensure that the cakes can be removed from the tins easily, line the base of each with non-stick baking paper.

All-in-one method If you have a heavy-duty electric mixer you can make this cake very quickly. Put all the ingredients in the bowl and beat for about 5 minutes until light and fluffy. Add 1 to 2 tablespoonfuls warm water to the batter to lighten the texture of the cake (this is a good thing to do whether you are making the cake by hand or machine).

Christmas Cake ↷

MRS BEETON GAVE A CHOICE OF RECIPES for fruit cake, any of which would be suitable for Christmas. This is a traditional English Christmas cake, laden with fruit, nuts, glacé cherries and candied peel, flavoured with ginger and mixed spice and laced with brandy or sherry. If you like a rich, mature cake, make it a month or two ahead of time, wrap it well in greaseproof paper, then overwrap it with foil and store it in a cake tin. Every few weeks, prick the surface of the cake and feed with a few tablespoons of brandy or sherry. This will make the cake moist and dark – and boozily rich.

METHOD

Sift the flour, spice and salt into a basin. Put the butter and sugar in a separate large basin and beat them together until soft and creamy. Add the eggs one at a time, beat well to mix and add some of the flour after the third egg. When all the egg is thoroughly mixed in, beat in the fruit, nuts, ginger and remaining flour. Add the brandy or sherry and beat the mixture for a few minutes until all the ingredients are thoroughly mixed. Spoon the mixture into a prepared cake tin and make a slight hollow in the centre with the back of the spoon. Bake the cake for 45 minutes. Reduce the oven temperature and bake for 1 hour, then reduce the oven temperature again and bake for 45 to 60 minutes. When the cake is done, a skewer inserted in the centre will come out clean. Leave the cake to cool in the tin.

The oven should be preheated to 325°F (160°C) Gas 3, then reduced to 300°F (150°C) Gas 2, followed by 275°F (140°C) Gas 1.

NOTES

Flour Use plain flour.

Moist sugar Use a soft brown sugar, either light or dark.

All-in-one method Simply put all the ingredients in the bowl of a food mixer, turn the machine on and beat for a few minutes until everything is evenly mixed.

Prepared cake tin Use an 8 inch (20 cm) round tin. Line the base and sides with a double thickness of non-stick baking paper or greaseproof paper. To help to prevent the cake from overbrowning, tie brown paper around the outside of the tin to come about 2 inches (5 cm) above the rim.

Time 3 to 3¼ hours
Sufficient for one 8 inch (20 cm) cake
Seasonable at Christmastime

INGREDIENTS

7 oz (200 g) flour
1½ teaspoons ground mixed spice
¼ teaspoon salt
7 oz (200 g) butter
7 oz (200 g) moist sugar
6 eggs
7 oz (200 g) sultanas
7 oz (200 g) currants
7 oz (200 g) raisins
¼ lb (125 g) glacé cherries, cut into quarters
3 oz (90 g) cut mixed peel
2 oz (60 g) walnuts or almonds, chopped
2 oz (60 g) stem ginger from a jar, chopped
4 tablespoons brandy or sherry

Mrs Beeton writes

"To know when a cake is sufficiently baked, plunge a clean knife into the middle of it; draw it quickly out, and if it looks in the least sticky, put the cake back, and close the oven door until the cake is done."

✑ A Nice Useful Cake

Time 1½ hours

Sufficient for one 7 inch (18
  cm) cake

Seasonable at any time

INGREDIENTS

¼ lb (125 g) butter

6 oz (175 g) currants

3 eggs

2 oz (60 g) sweet almonds

1 oz (30 g) candied peel

¼ lb (125 g) sugar

1 lb (500 g) flour

2 teaspoons baking powder

8 fl oz (250ml) milk

DRIED FRUIT, ALMONDS and candied peel make this a most appealing
cake. It is suitable for everyday and special occasions, as its name
suggests. It keeps well in an airtight tin and for this reason it is also
sometimes called 'Cut-and-Come-Again Cake'.

METHOD

Beat the butter to a cream. Wash, pick over and dry the currants.
Whisk the eggs. Blanch and chop the almonds. Cut the peel into neat
slices. When all these are ready, mix the dry ingredients together, then
add the butter, milk and eggs and beat the mixture well for a few
minutes. Put the cake into a buttered mould or tin and bake it in a
moderate oven for rather more than 1¼ hours.

The oven should be preheated to 350°F (180°C) Gas 4.

NOTES

Currants There is no need to wash and dry the currants, but they
should be picked over to remove any stalks and pieces of stone that
might be among them.

Sweet almonds Use blanched almonds and chop them finely, or buy
ready chopped almonds, sometimes called almond nibs or nibbed
almonds.

Flour Use plain flour.

Mould or cake tin Use a 7 inch (18 cm) round tin. Grease the base
and sides and line with non-stick baking paper.

Mrs Beeton writes
───────

"The currants and candied peel may be omitted, and a little lemon
or almond flavouring substituted for them; made in this manner,
the cake will be found very good."

Thick Gingerbread ❧

THIS IS A RICH, DARK spicy gingerbread, the kind which improves with keeping. After baking, leave it to cool in the tin for about 15 minutes, then turn it out on to a wire rack and leave it until completely cold. Wrap it in greaseproof paper, then in foil, and store it in an airtight tin for 2 to 3 days before eating. If it is kept wrapped in this way, it will stay moist and fresh for up to a month.

METHOD

Put the flour into a bowl with the sugar, ginger and allspice and mix these together. Warm the butter with the treacle, add it to the other ingredients and stir well. Make the milk just warm, dissolve the bicarbonate of soda in it, then mix everything into a nice smooth dough with the eggs, which should be previously whisked. Pour the mixture into a buttered tin and bake it for 1 to 1¼ hours or longer, should the gingerbread be very thick. Just before it is done, brush the top over with the yolk of an egg beaten up with a little milk, and put it back in the oven to finish baking.

The oven should be preheated to 325°F (160°C) Gas 3.

NOTES

Flour Use plain flour.
Coarse brown sugar Demerara is the sugar to use in traditional gingerbread.
Buttered tin Use a greased, deep 8 inch (20 cm) square tin, line the base and sides with greaseproof paper, then brush the paper with butter.

Time 1¼ to 1½ hours
Sufficient for one 8 inch
  (20 cm) cake
Seasonable at any time

INGREDIENTS
1 lb (500 g) flour
3 oz (90 g) coarse brown
  sugar
3 tablespoons ground ginger
1 tablespoon ground
  allspice
3 oz (90 g) butter
¾ lb (375 g) treacle
2 fl oz (60 ml) milk
¾ teaspoon bicarbonate of
  soda
2 eggs
the yolk of an egg and a
  little milk to glaze

✂ *Pound Cake*

Time 2¼ to 2½ hours

Sufficient for one nice-sized
cake

Seasonable at any time

INGREDIENTS
½ lb (250 g) butter

½ lb (250 g) self-raising
flour

½ lb (250 g) light soft brown
sugar

½ lb (250 g) currants

2½ oz (75 g) candied peel

½ oz (15 g) sweet almonds

a little ground mace when
liked

4 eggs

THIS TRADITIONAL ENGLISH cake takes its name from the weight of the ingredients used – one pound each of butter, flour, sugar and dried fruit. Some Victorian recipes made one very large cake with this quantity of ingredients, but Mrs Beeton was more sensible and gave instructions for making two cakes. The quantities given here are half of the original, to make just one cake.

METHOD

Work the butter to a cream, dredge in the flour and add the sugar, currants and candied peel, which should be cut into neat slices, and the almonds, which should be blanched and chopped, and the mace if liked. Mix all these well together. Whisk the eggs and let them be thoroughly blended with the dry ingredients. Beat the cake well for 20 minutes and put it into a round tin, lined at the bottom and sides with buttered paper. Bake it from 2 to 2¼ hours, and let the oven be well heated when the cake is first put in. If this is not the case, the currants will all sink to the bottom.

The oven should be preheated to 300°F (150°C) Gas 2.

NOTES

Sweet almonds Buy blanched almonds and chop them with a knife or buy ready chopped almonds, sometimes called nib or nibbed almonds.

Mixing is done by hand in Mrs Beeton's method, but it can be done in an electric mixer in a fraction of the time. Put all the ingredients in the mixer bowl and beat until they are evenly combined.

Cake tin Use a deep 9 inch (23 cm) round tin. Grease the base and sides, line with greaseproof paper, then brush the paper with butter.

Mrs Beeton writes

"To make this preparation light, the yolks and whites of the eggs should be beaten separately, and added separately to the other ingredients. A glass of wine is sometimes added to the mixture; but this is scarcely necessary, as the cake will be found quite rich enough without it."

MOIST, FRUITY AND SPICY with a subtle almond flavour, this eggless cake is excellent – and so quick and easy to make. Mrs Beeton gave no explanation of its name. Some Italian cakes use polenta (ground corn) in fruit cakes in the same way as ground rice is used here. It's possible that Mrs Beeton swapped rice for polenta – but kept the Italian name.

METHOD
Warm the butter to a cream, but without oiling it. Blanch and chop the almonds. Grate the nutmeg. When all these ingredients are prepared, mix them well together with the flour, ground rice, raisins, currants and sugar. Make the milk warm, stir in the bicarbonate of soda and add this to the cake mixture. Mix everything well together. Butter a mould, rather more than half fill it with the dough, and bake the cake in a moderate oven for 1½ to 2 hours, or less time should it be made into 2 cakes.

The oven should be preheated to 325°F (160°C) Gas 3.

NOTES
Sweet almonds Buy ready chopped blanched almonds.
Flour Use plain flour.
Ground rice is finely milled grains of rice that is sold in boxes in the baking section of the supermarket.
Cake tin Mrs Beeton gave no indication of the shape and size of this cake, but it bakes well in a deep 7½ inch (19 cm) round cake tin lined with greased greasepoof paper.

Mrs Beeton writes

"ALMONDS – the almond-tree is a native of warmer climates than Britain, and is indigenous to the northern parts of Africa and Asia; but it is now commonly cultivated in Italy, Spain, and the south of France. It is not usually grown in Britain, and the fruit seldom ripens in this country : it is much admired for the beauty of its blossoms. In the form of its leaves and blossoms it strongly resembles the peach-tree, and is included in the same genus by botanists; but the fruit, instead of presenting a delicious pulp like the peach, shrivels up as it ripens, and becomes only a tough coriaceous covering to the stone enclosing the eatable kernel, which is surrounded by a thin bitter skin."

Time 1½ to 2 hours
Sufficient for one 7½ inch
  (19 cm) cake
Seasonable at any time

INGREDIENTS
¼ lb (125 g) butter
2 oz (60 g) sweet almonds
½ nutmeg
½ lb (250 g) flour
½ lb (250 g) ground rice
½ lb (250 g) raisins, stoned
  and cut into small pieces
¼ lb (125 g) currants
¼ lb (125 g) caster sugar
1 pint (600 ml) milk
1 teaspoon bicarbonate
  of soda

~ Sponge Cake

Time 1½ hours
Sufficient for one 9 inch
  (23 cm) cake
Seasonable at any time

INGREDIENTS
3 eggs
6 oz (175 g) caster sugar
the grated rind of 1 lemon
1 tablespoon brandy
6 oz (175 g) flour

IN HER ORIGINAL RECIPE Mrs Beeton said, 'Put the eggs into one side of the scale, and take the weight of 8 in sugar and the weight of 5 in flour'. Based on this principle, this recipe has the ingredients worked out for you. It is a fatless whisked sponge, a versatile cake that can be served in many different ways. It can be simply sifted with sugar and served plain, split in two or three and filled with whipped cream and jam, or iced. It is also useful as a base for trifles.

METHOD

Separate the yolks from the whites of the eggs. Whisk the yolks, sugar, lemon rind and brandy briefly in a bowl, then set the bowl over a pan of gently simmering water and whisk until the mixture is pale and thick enough to leave a ribbon trail. Remove the bowl from the heat and continue whisking for 3 to 5 minutes. Fold in the flour in batches. Whisk the whites of the eggs to a very stiff froth and fold them in too. Put it into a buttered mould strewn with a little fine sifted sugar and bake the cake for 1 hour. Care must be taken that it is put into the oven immediately, or it will not be light.

The oven should be preheated to 325°F (160°C) Gas 3.

NOTES

Brandy This was in the original recipe, but it can easily be omitted.
Flour Use plain flour.
Whisking Use a balloon whisk or a hand-held electric mixer. If you use a heavy duty electric mixer, there is no need to whisk the mixture over hot water.
Cake tin Elaborate moulds were once popular, but these days a plain, deep 9 inch (23 cm) round cake tin is more often used for a whisked sponge. Brush the base of the tin with butter, but not the sides – the cake needs to stick to the tin slightly as it rises.

Mrs Beeton writes

"The flavouring of this cake may be varied by adding a few drops of essence of almonds instead of the grated lemon-rind."

MRS BEETON SAID, 'These are very nice with a few currants and a little sugar added to the other ingredients; they should be put in after the butter is rubbed in'. These days, tea cakes include sugar and currants as standard ingredients, not optional extras, so you may want to follow her advice. You will need ¼ lb (125 g) currants and 1 oz (30 g) caster sugar. Other additions you might like to include are 2 oz (60 g) chopped candied peel and a pinch or two of ground mixed spice.

METHOD

Crumble the yeast into a cup and mix with it a little of the warm milk so that it shall be as smooth as cream. Set it aside until it froths. Put the flour into a bowl, mix with it the salt and rub in the butter. Stir the yeast into it, then the remaining milk. Knead it well, then cover the bowl and put it in a warm place until well risen, about 1 hour. Form the dough into 8 cakes of equal size. Place them on greased baking sheets, cover and leave in a warm place until well risen – about ½ hour. Bake for 20 minutes.

The oven should be preheated to 425°F (220°C) Gas 7.

NOTES

Yeast Use dried fast-action yeast if you prefer. It is sold in a box containing ¼ oz (6 g) sachets, and you will need 1 sachet for this recipe. The beauty of this type of yeast is that it mixes straight into the flour and only one rising is needed before baking. Follow the instructions on the packet.

Mrs Beeton writes

"These cakes should be buttered, and eaten hot
as soon as baked; but, when stale, they are very nice split
and toasted; or, if dipped in milk, or even water,
and covered with a basin in the oven till hot,
they will be almost equal to new."

Time ½ hour plus rising
Sufficient to make 8 tea cakes
Seasonable at any time

INGREDIENTS
8 fl oz (250 ml) warm milk
1 oz (30 g) fresh yeast
1 lb (500 g) strong plain flour
½ teaspoon salt
¼ lb (125 g) butter

CHAPTER 11

Preserves

Mrs Beeton's recipes for preserves came in a chapter called 'Preserves and Confectionery'. The term 'confectionery' covered a wide range of different sweet foods which were served as the third or dessert course at formal dinners. Among these were fresh and stewed fruits and *compôtes*, and fruits preserved in sugar syrup. Here they are most evocatively described.

'The tazza, or dish with stem, is now the favourite shape for dessert dishes. The fruit can be arranged and shown to better advantage on these tall high dishes than on the short flat ones. All the dishes are now usually placed down the centre of the table. The fruit should always be gathered on the same day it is required for the table, and should be tastefully arranged on these dishes. When fresh fruit cannot be obtained, dried and foreign fruits, *compôtes*, baked pears, stewed Normandy pippins &c., must supply its place, with the addition of preserves, bon-bons, cakes, biscuits &c.'

Many dessert dishes and 'confections' were too difficult to make at home and were best left to the professional confectioner, but it seems that the housekeeper, second in command to the mistress of the house, could be entrusted with some of them.

'The housekeeper, in those establishments where there is no house steward or man cook, undertakes the preparation of the confectionery, attends to the preserving and pickling of fruits and vegetables and, in a general way, to the more difficult branches of the art of cookery.'

The housekeeper was given her orders according to the season:

'In June and July, gooseberries, currants, raspberries, strawberries and other summer fruits should be preserved, and jams and jellies made. In July too, the making of walnut ketchup should be attended to. Mixed pickles may also be now made.'

Now we have refrigerators and freezers, home pickling and preserving is no longer as necessary as it was in Victorian days, but it is still immensely satisfying to make jam or marmalade. Although the fruits you use may not be homegrown, Mrs Beeton's advice on harvesting makes delightful reading.

'Fruits intended for preservation should be gathered in the morning, in dry weather, with the morning sun upon them if possible. They will then have their fullest flavour, and keep in good condition longer than when gathered at any other time. Fruit gathered in wet or foggy weather will soon be mildewed, and be of no service for preserves.'

✑ Apple Jam

Time 1 to 1½ hours
Sufficient for 4 to 5 pots
 of jam
Seasonable in September,
 October or November

INGREDIENTS
3 lb (1.4 kg) apples
3 lb (1.4 kg) preserving
 sugar
the grated rind of 2 lemons
4 tablespoons lemon juice

THIS IS ONE OF THE BEST JAMS to make at home because apples are always in plentiful supply, and they are high in pectin, so the jam sets easily. Mrs Beeton did not specify a type, but she almost certainly would have used Bramley cooking apples. In the autumn you may be lucky enough to get cheap imperfect apples or windfalls, both of which are suitable for making jam.

METHOD
Peel the apples, core and slice them very thin, and be particular that they are all the same sort. Put the peelings and cores in a piece of muslin and tie it into a bag. Put the apples and the muslin bag into a preserving pan, add 1 pint (600 ml) water and let the apples cook gently until quite tender and pulpy – about ½ hour. Remove the pan from the heat, take out the muslin bag and squeeze it hard against the side of the pan with a spoon to remove as much juice from it as possible. Add the sugar to the fruit with the grated lemon rind and juice and stir over a low heat until the sugar has dissolved. Increase the heat, bring to the boil and boil rapidly for about ½ hour, reckoning from the time the jam begins to boil properly. Remove the scum as it rises, and when the jam is done, put it into jam pots. Place waxed discs, wax side down, over the jam, then put on the lids.

NOTES
Testing for a set Before starting to make the jam, put a saucer in the refrigerator to chill. At the end of the recommended cooking time, remove the pan from the heat and spoon a little jam on to the saucer. Leave it undisturbed for a few minutes, then run your finger through the middle. If the jam has reached setting point, it will wrinkle.
Jam pots Before starting to make the jam, wash the jam pots well in very hot soapy water and rinse them thoroughly in very hot water. Drain them, then stand them upright on a baking sheet and dry them in a very low oven preheated to 250–275°F (120–140°C) Gas ½–1 for 15 minutes. They should be warm when they are filled with the hot apple preserve.

Apricot Jam ๏

Fresh apricot jam is as real treat, and yet it can be made very quickly and easily. When you see fresh apricots in the shops in the late summer, buy just enough to make a few pots of jam.

Method

Wash the apricots, cut them in half and remove the stones. Break a few of the stones, blanch the kernels, then put them with the fruit into a preserving pan. Add the lemon juice and 11 fl oz (325 ml) water and bring to the boil. Cover and simmer for 30 to 35 minutes until the apricots are very soft, then remove the pan from the heat and add the sugar. Return the pan to a low heat and stir until the sugar has dissolved, then increase the heat and boil rapidly for about ¼ hour, carefully removing the scum as fast as it rises. When the jam is done, put it into jam pots. Place waxed discs, wax side down, over the jam, then put on the lids.

Notes

Warmed sugar Put the sugar in an ovenproof bowl in a very low oven preheated to 250–300°F (120–150°C) Gas ½–2 for 15 minutes. Warmed sugar dissolves quickly and does not lower the temperature of the fruit when added to it.

Breaking the stones Cover a hammer with a clean cloth and use it to crack the stones. Or use a heavy weight, nutcrackers or a meat mallet. Lift out the kernels.

Blanching Throw the kernels into a pan of boiling water and boil rapidly for 1 minute. Drain.

Testing for a set and preparing jam pots See the instructions opposite.

Mrs Beeton writes

"APRICOTS – The apricot is indigenous to the plains of Armenia, but is now cultivated in almost every climate, temperate or tropical.

There are several varieties. The skin of this fruit has a perfumed flavour, highly esteemed. A good apricot, when perfectly ripe, is an excellent fruit. It has been somewhat condemned for its laxative qualities, but this has possibly arisen from the fruit having been eaten unripe, or in too great excess. Delicate persons should not eat the apricot uncooked, without a liberal allowance of powdered sugar. The apricot makes excellent jam and marmalade, and there are several foreign preparations of it which are considered great luxuries."

Time 1 hour
Sufficient for 4 to 5 pots of jam
Seasonable in August or September

INGREDIENTS
3 lb (1. 4 kg) ripe apricots
3 tablespoons lemon juice
3 lb (1. 4 kg) warmed preserving sugar

Blackcurrant Jam

Time 2 hours
Sufficient for about 4 pots
of jam
Seasonable in July

INGREDIENTS
2 lb (1 kg) blackcurrants
3 lb (1.4 kg) warmed
  preserving sugar

BLACKCURRANTS ARE VERY HIGH IN PECTIN, so they make good jam. They are also very juicy, which gives the jam a soft, runny consistency. Make sure that the skins are very soft before the sugar is added or they will be tough to eat.

METHOD
Let the fruit be very ripe, and gathered on a dry day. Strip it from the stalks and put it into a preserving pan with 1½ pints (900 ml) water. Boil these together for about ¾ hour until the skins are very soft, then remove the pan from the heat and add the sugar. Return the pan to a low heat and stir until the sugar has dissolved, then increase the heat and boil the jam again for ½ hour, reckoning from the time when the jam bubbles equally all over. It may need longer, should it not appear to set nicely when a little is poured on to a cold plate. Keep stirring it to prevent it from burning and carefully remove all the scum. When done, pour it into jam pots. Place waxed discs, wax side down, over the jam, then put on the lids.

NOTES
Warmed sugar See the instructions on page 311.
Testing for a set and preparing jam pots See page 310.

Mrs Beeton writes

"Great attention must be paid to the stirring of this jam,
as it is very liable to burn, on account
of the thickness of the juice."

DAMSONS ARE A BEAUTIFUL COLOUR and they make excellent jam. They have a generous amount of pectin, so the jam sets easily. This recipe can also be used for plums and greengages.

METHOD

Have the fruit gathered in dry weather. Wash it and pick it over, removing the stalks and rejecting any damsons that are at all blemished. Put the damsons into a preserving pan and add 17 fl oz (500 ml) water. Bring to the boil and simmer for 30 to 35 minutes or until the damsons are broken down and pulpy. Remove the pan from the heat and add the sugar. Return the pan to a low heat and stir until the sugar has dissolved, then increase the heat and boil rapidly for 10 to 15 minutes, carefully removing the stones and scum as fast as they rise to the surface. The jam must be well stirred all the time, or it will be liable to burn and stick to the pan, which will cause it to have a very disagreeable flavour. When the jam looks firm and the juice appears to set, it is done. When done, pour it into jam pots. Place waxed discs, wax side down, over the jam, then put on the lids.

NOTES

Warmed sugar See the instructions on page 311.

Stones The flesh of uncooked damsons clings tightly to the stones, which makes removing the stones at the time of preparation fiddly and time-consuming. They quickly come loose during boiling and rise to the surface, making it very easy to skim them off with a slotted spoon.

Testing for a set and preparing jam pots See page 310.

Time 1 hour
Sufficient for 4 to 5 pots of
jam
Seasonable in September or
October

INGREDIENTS
2¾ lb (1.25 kg) damsons
3¼ lb (1.5 kg) warmed
preserving sugar

✑ *Orange Marmalade*

Time 4 hours

Sufficient for 9 lb (4 kg)

Seasonable in January or
February, as Seville
oranges are then in
perfection

INGREDIENTS
2 lb (1 kg) Seville oranges
2 lb (1 kg) warmed
   preserving sugar

Mrs Beeton writes
─────────

"The juice and grated
rind of 2 lemons to every
dozen oranges are a very
great improvement to
this marmalade."

NOTHING MORE THAN Seville oranges, sugar and water, Mrs Beeton's recipe for homemade marmalade 'to resemble Scotch marmalade' is one of the simplest and best. It's up to you whether you make it fine or coarse cut, but take care if you choose to cut the rind into very thick pieces – they must be allowed to get really soft before the sugar is added.

METHOD

Let there be an equal weight of Seville oranges and sugar. Peel the oranges thinly, then cut the peel into strips. Cut the fruit in half and squeeze out the juice. Put the pulp and pips in a piece of muslin and tie it into a bag. Put the shredded peel, orange juice and muslin bag in a preserving pan and add 4 pints (2.4 litres) water. Bring to the boil, cover and simmer for 2 hours or until the peel is completely tender. Remove the muslin bag and squeeze it hard against the side of the pan with a spoon to remove as much juice as possible from it. Add the sugar and heat gently, stirring until the sugar has dissolved, then bring to the boil and boil rapidly for 15 to 20 minutes until set. Remove the pan from the heat, skim off any scum, then leave the marmalade to stand for 15 to 20 minutes. Stir well to distribute the peel through the marmalade, then pour into jam pots and place waxed discs, wax side down, over the marmalade. Leave until the jam is cold before putting on the lids.

NOTES

Warmed sugar See the instructions on page 311.
Testing for a set and preparing jam pots See page 310.

Raspberry Jam ❧

MRS BEETON ADDED redcurrant juice to boost the pectin content of the raspberries and help the jam set. You can make the jam without it, but it will be a little more runny. Loganberries can be used instead of raspberries, if available.

METHOD

Let the fruit for this preserve be gathered in fine weather, and used as soon after it is picked as possible. Take off the stalks, put the raspberries into a preserving pan and let them simmer gently for ¼ hour, keeping them well stirred. Remove the pan from the heat and add the currant juice and sugar. Stir until the sugar has dissolved, then return the pan to the heat and boil again for ½ hour or until the jam is done. Skim the jam well after the last of the sugar is added, or the preserve will not be clear. When done, pour it into jam pots. Place waxed discs, wax side down, over the jam, then put on the lids.

NOTES

Warmed sugar See the instructions on page 311.
Redcurrant juice Strip the currants from the stalks, put them into a saucepan and simmer until the juice is well drawn from the fruit. Strain the currants and measure the juice.
Testing for a set and preparing jam pots See page 310.

Mrs Beeton writes

"The addition of the currant juice is a very great improvement to this preserve, as it gives it a piquant taste, which the flavour of the raspberries seems to require."

Time 1 hour
Sufficient for 4 to 5 pots
of jam
Seasonable in July and
August

INGREDIENTS

3 lb (1.4 kg) raspberries
¾ pint (450 ml) redcurrant
juice
3 lb (1.4 kg) warmed
preserving sugar

THESE QUOTATIONS ARE
FROM 'DOMESTIC
SERVANTS' A CHAPTER
TOWARDS THE END OF
MRS BEETON'S
ORIGINAL BOOK. RULES
AND REGULATIONS
WERE LISTED FOR THE
MANY DIFFERENT
MEMBERS OF STAFF KEPT
IN LARGER HOMES AND
GRAND MANSIONS, BUT
THE ONES HERE
CONCERN ONLY THE
BUTLER AND, TO A
LESSER EXTENT, THE
FOOTMAN. THEY
CONJURE UP A VIVID
'UPSTAIRS
DOWNSTAIRS' PICTURE,
AND HELP TO EXPLAIN
THE HIERARCHY AMONG
THE SERVANTS IN MRS
BEETON'S DAY.

THE NUMBER OF THE MALE DOMESTICS in a family varies according to the wealth and position of the master, from the owner of the ducal mansion with a retinue of attendants, at the head of which is the chamberlain and house-steward, to the occupier of the humbler house, where a single footman, or even the odd man-of-all-work, is the only male retainer. The majority of gentlemen's establishments probably comprise a servant out of livery, or butler, a footman and coachman, or coachman and groom, where the horses exceed two or three.

Duties of the butler

THE DOMESTIC DUTIES of the butler are to bring in the eatables at breakfast, and wait upon the family at that meal, assisted by the footman, and see to the cleanliness of everything at table. On taking away, he removes the tray with the china and plate, for which he is responsible. At luncheon, he arranges the meal, and waits unassisted, the footman being now engaged in other duties. At dinner, he places the silver and plated articles on the table, sees that everything is in its place, and rectifies what is wrong. He carries in the first dish, and announces in the drawing-room that dinner is on the table, and respectfully stands by the door until the company are seated, when he takes place behind his master's chair on the left, to remove the covers, handing them to the other attendants to carry out. After the first course of plates is supplied, his place is at the sideboard to serve wines, but only when called on.

THE FIRST COURSE ENDED, the butter rings the cook's bell, and hands the dishes from the table to the other servants to carry away, receiving from them the second course, which he places on the table, removing the covers as before, as again taking his place at the sideboard.

AT DESSERT, the slips being removed, the butler receives the dessert from the other servants, and arranges it on the table, with plates and glasses, and then takes his place behind his master's chair to hand the wines and ices, while the footman stands behind his mistress for the same purpose, the other attendants leaving the room. Where the old-fashioned practice of having the dessert on the polished table, without any cloth, is still adhered to, the butler should rub off any marks made by the hot dishes before arranging the dessert.

BEFORE DINNER, he has satisfied himself that the lamps, candles, or gas-burners are in perfect order, if not lighted, which will usually be the case. Having served every one with their share of the dessert, put the fires in order (when these are used), and seen the lights are all right, at a signal from his master, he and the footman leave the room.

HE NOW PROCEEDS TO THE DRAWING ROOM, arranges the fireplace, and sees to the lights; he then returns to his pantry, prepared to answer the bell, and attend to the company, while the footman is clearing away and cleaning the plate and glasses.

AT TEA, he again attends. At bedtime he appears with the candles; he locks up the plate, secures doors and windows, and sees that all the fires are safe.

✑ Rhubarb and Orange Jam

Time 2¼ to 2½ hours
Sufficient for about 5 pots
  of jam
Seasonable from February
  to April

INGREDIENTS
6 oranges
1 lemon
2 lb (1 kg) finely-cut rhubarb
2 lb (1 kg) warmed
  preserving sugar

RHUBARB WAS ORIGINALLY USED for making jam in times of hardship when other fruits were scarce, but nowadays it is appreciated in its own right and you will often see pots of homemade rhubarb jam for sale in country markets. Orange and lemon are used both for flavouring and to help make the jam set.

METHOD
Wash and peel the oranges, and remove as much of the white pith as possible. Roughly chop the flesh of the oranges and put it into a preserving pan, discarding the pips. Add the rind of half of the oranges cut into thin strips. Squeeze the juice from the lemon and add it to the pan. Chop the lemon rind, place it in a piece of muslin and tie it into a bag. Peel the rhubarb and cut it into thin pieces. Add the muslin bag, rhubarb and ½ pint (300 ml) water to the oranges and stir everything together over a low heat until the juice runs from the rhubarb. Bring to the boil and boil for 1¼ hours or until the orange peel is tender, removing all the scum as it rises. Remove the muslin bag and squeeze it hard against the side of the pan with a spoon to remove as much juice from it as possible. Add the sugar and heat gently, stirring until the sugar has dissolved, then bring to the boil and boil rapidly for 15 to 20 minutes until the jam is done. Remove the pan from the heat, skim off any scum, then pour into pots. Place waxed discs, wax side down, over the jam. Leave until cold before putting on the lids.

NOTES
Warmed sugar See the instructions on page 311.
Testing for a set and preparing jam pots See page 310.

Strawberry Jam &

STRAWBERRIES ARE LOW IN PECTIN, so they need a little help if they are to make a jam that will set. Mrs Beeton used redcurrant juice, but you can use 4 tablespoons of lemon juice instead.

METHOD

Put the redcurrant juice in a preserving pan, add the sugar and heat gently. Select well-ripened but sound strawberries, pick them from the stalks and when the sugar has dissolved in the redcurrant juice, put in the fruit. Simmer for ½ to ¾ hour, carefully removing the scum as it rises. Stir the jam only enough to prevent it from burning at the bottom of the pan, as the fruit should be preserved as whole as possible. Remove the pan from the heat, skim off any scum, then let it cool for a while before pouring it into pots. Place waxed discs, wax side down, over the jam, then leave until the jam is cold before putting on the lids.

NOTES

Redcurrant juice Strip the currants from the stalks, put them into a saucepan and simmer until the juice is well drawn from the fruit. Strain the currants and measure the juice.

Testing for a set and preparing jam pots See page 310.

Time 1 hour
Sufficient for about 5 pots
  of jam
Seasonable in June and July

INGREDIENTS
1½ pints (900 ml)
  redcurrant juice
3 lb (1.4 kg) preserving
  sugar
3 lb (1.4 kg) strawberries

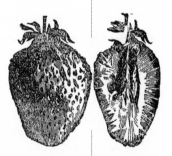

◦ *Lemon Curd*

Time ¼ hour

Sufficient for 1 pot

Seasonable at any time

INGREDIENTS

2 lemons

3 eggs

¼ lb (125 g) butter

½ lb (250 g) granulated
  sugar

MRS BEETON'S RECIPE made twice this amount, but lemon curd does not keep well. It is easy to make, so it is best to make a small quantity when you need it.

METHOD

Carefully grate the lemon rind and strain the juice. Beat the eggs and strain them. Put the butter in the top of a double boiler and heat gently until it has melted. Add the lemon rind and juice, then the eggs and sugar, and keep stirring the mixture over the heat until the sugar has dissolved and the curd begins to thicken. When the consistency is like that of honey, it is done.

NOTES

Lemons When the grated rind is used, as here, it is best to buy unwaxed lemons. If these are not available, scrub the lemons vigorously under cold running water and dry them well before grating the rind.

Storage Keep lemon curd in the refrigerator. It will stay fresh for up to 2 weeks.

Excellent Mincemeat ∽

PACKED WITH JUICY FRUITS and heady with brandy, it is no wonder that Mrs Beeton said this mincemeat was excellent. She suggested making it at the beginning of December and leaving it for a fortnight before use, but in fact it improves with keeping longer and you can safely make it up to 2 months before Christmas. The apples must be baked before being added to the mincemeat; follow the instructions in the notes below.

METHOD

Grate the lemons, squeeze the juice and strain it. Chop the lemon shells, put them in a saucepan and cover them with water. Bring to the boil and simmer them until they are tender enough to chop finely – about 1 hour. Add to this pulp the apples, which should be baked, and their skins and cores removed. Put in the remaining ingredients one by one, and, as they are added, mix everything very thoroughly together. Put the mincemeat into a stone jar with a closely fitting lid and leave to stand in a cold place for 2 days, then pack into pots, cover with waxed paper, wax side down, and then the lids. Leave to mature for about a fortnight before using.

NOTES

Apples Mrs Beeton gave no precise information about how the apples should be baked. The simplest way is to put them in a baking dish and bake them in an oven preheated to 400°F (200°C) Gas 6 for 50 to 60 minutes. Leave to cool, then scoop out all the flesh.

Suet In Mrs Beeton's day, cooks would have shredded their own suet, but we can buy shredded suet in boxes from the baking section of the supermarket.

Teacupful of brandy A Victorian teacup held about 7 fl oz (200 ml).

Time 2 hours plus standing and maturing
Sufficient to make 9 lb (4 kg)
Seasonable in December; it should be made the first or second week

INGREDIENTS

3 large lemons
3 large apples
1 lb (500 g) stoned raisins
1 lb (500 g) currants
1 lb (500 g) shredded suet
2 lb (900 g) soft brown sugar
1 oz (30 g) sliced candied citron
1 oz (30 g) sliced candied orange peel
1 oz (30 g) sliced candied lemon peel
1 teacupful of brandy
2 tablespoons orange marmalade

CHAPTER 12

Beverages

Mrs Beeton began this chapter with an important classification: 'Beverages are innumerable in their variety, but the ordinary beverages drunk in the British Isles may be divided into three classes:

1 Beverages of the simplest kind not fermented.
2 Beverages consisting of water, containing a considerable quantity of carbonic acid.
3 Beverages composed partly of fermented liquors.'

Tea, coffee and chocolate were not included in this classification, although most of Mrs Beeton's 'general observations on beverages' were about tea and coffee, and many different methods were given for making these popular drinks.

She described tea as 'the cup that cheers but not inebriates' and claimed that it had become 'almost a necessary of life'. Tracing its history in Britain back to the middle of the 16th century, she included a charming little quote from *Pepys's Diary*: 'September 25th,1661. I sent for a cup of tea (a China drink), of which I had never drunk before.'

As always, there was plenty of practical advice.

'In the purchase of tea, that should be chosen which possesses an agreeable odour and is as whole as possible, in order that the leaf may be easily examined. The greatest care should be taken that it has not been exposed to the air, which destroys its flavour.'

Mrs Beeton described coffee as a 'delicious beverage for drinking' and made the following interesting observation.

'The demand for it throughout the British Isles is daily increasing, the more especially since so much attention has been given to mechanical contrivances for roasting and grinding the berry and preparing the beverage.'

In the recipe section she not only gave several different ways of making coffee, but she also gave the method for making essence of coffee and instructions for roasting the beans.

Mrs Beeton's original Beverages chapter contained recipes for homemade wines, ginger beer and fruit vinegars. These have not been included in this edition because they are not practical today, but at the end of the chapter you will find a few of her recipes for party drinks, all of which we still enjoy.

_෫ *To Make Hot Chocolate*

Time 5 to 10 minutes
Sufficient for 1 person
Seasonable at any time

INGREDIENTS
¼ pint (150 ml) milk
¼ pint (150 ml) water
½ oz (15 g) chocolate
white sugar to serve

THESE DAYS WE USE drinking chocolate powder to make hot chocolate, but it is interesting to see how it used to be made in Mrs Beeton's time. It certainly tastes much better made with real chocolate rather than powder.

METHOD
Make the milk-and-water hot. Grate the chocolate into it, and stir the mixture constantly and quickly until the chocolate is dissolved. Bring to boiling point, stir well, and serve directly with white sugar.

NOTES
Chocolate The original recipe specified 'cake chocolate'. Use a good-quality block chocolate with at least 70 percent cocoa solids.

Mrs Beeton writes

"Chocolate prepared in a mill is made
by putting in the scraped chocolate, pouring over it
the boiling milk-and-water, and milling it over the fire
until hot and frothy."

"CHOCOLATE AND COCOA – Both these preparations
are made from the seeds or beans of the cacao-tree, which
grows in the West Indies and South America. The Spanish, and the
proper name, is cacao, not cocoa, as it is generally spelt. From this
mistake, the tree from which the beverage is procured has been often
confounded with the palm that produces the edible cocoa-nuts,
which are the produce of the cocoa-tree (*Cocos nucifera*),
whereas the tree from which chocolate is procured
is very different (the *Theobroma cacao*)."

EVEN THOUGH WE NOW HAVE a vast array of different coffee machines to choose from, Mrs Beeton's advice can still be taken – and it makes the most delightful read. Her quantities and method are perfect for making coffee in a jug, percolator or cafetière.

METHOD

To make coffee good, it should never be boiled, but the boiling water merely poured on it, the same as for tea. The coffee should always be purchased in the berry – if possible, freshly roasted – and it should never be ground long before it is wanted for use. There are very many new kinds of coffee-pots, but the method of making the coffee is nearly always the same; namely, pouring the boiling water on the powder, and allowing it to filter through. Coffee should always be served very hot, and, if possible, in the same vessel in which it is made, as pouring it from one pot to another cools, and consequently spoils it.

Mrs Beeton writes

"Many persons may think that the proportion of water we have given for each oz of coffee is rather small; it is so, and the coffee produced from it will be very strong; ⅓ of a cup will be found quite sufficient, which should be filled with nice hot milk, or milk and cream mixed. This is the *café au lait* for which our neighbours over the Channel are so justly celebrated. Should the ordinary method of making coffee be preferred, use double the quantity of water, and, in pouring it into the cups, put in more coffee and less milk."

THE COFFEE PLANT grows to the height of about twelve or fifteen feet, with leaves not unlike those of the common laurel, although more pointed, and not so dry and thick. The blossoms are white, much like those of jasmine, and issue from the angles of the leaf stalks. When the flowers fade, they are succeeded by the coffee bean, or seed, which is enclosed in a berry of a red colour, when ripe resembling a cherry.

Time 5 to 10 minutes
Sufficient for 2 persons
Seasonable at any time

INGREDIENTS
1 oz (30 g) or 2 tablespoons
  ground coffee
⅓ pint (200 ml) water

‹∞ *To Make Tea*

Time 2 minutes to warm the
teapot, 5 to 10 minutes to
draw the strength from
the tea
Sufficient for 1 pot, allowing
1 teaspoonful tea to each
person, and one over
Seasonable at any time

MRS BEETON GAVE SUPERB ADVICE on the making of tea, all of
which still holds good today.

METHOD

There is very little art in making good tea. If the water is boiling and
there is no sparing of the fragrant leaf, the beverage will almost
invariably be good. The old-fashioned plan of allowing a teaspoonful
to each person, and one over, is still practised. Warm the teapot with
boiling water, let it remain for two or three minutes for the vessel to
become thoroughly hot, then pour it away. Put in the tea, pour in
½–¾ pint (300–450ml) boiling water and close the lid. Let it stand
for the tea to draw from 5 to 10 minutes, then fill up the pot with
water. The tea will be quite spoiled unless made with water that is
actually boiling, as the leaves will not open and the flavour will not be
extracted from them. The beverage will consequently be colourless
and tasteless – in fact, nothing but tepid water. Where there is a very
large party to make tea for, it is a good plan to have two teapots
instead of putting a large quantity of tea into one pot; the tea, besides,
will go farther. When the infusion has been once completed, the
addition of fresh tea adds very little to the strength. When more is
required, have the pot emptied of the old leaves, scalded, and fresh tea
made in the usual manner.

Mrs Beeton writes

"TEA – In its general appearance, and the form of its leaf,
it resembles the myrtle. The blossoms are white and fragrant,
not unlike those of the wild rose, but smaller; and they are succeeded
by soft green capsules, containing each from one to three
white seeds. These capsules are crushed for oil,
which is in general use in China."

BEVERAGES

THIS IS A COOL AND REFRESHING summer punch, which looks very pretty if you are lucky enough to have borage leaves and flowers to float on the top. In the original recipe all the ingredients were mixed together and passed round in a special silver 'claret cup' from which each guest sipped in turn – see *Mrs Beeton writes* below.

METHOD

Mix the Maraschino, sugar and nutmeg together in a large jug, then pour in the wine and add the crushed ice, regulating the amount of ice by the state of the weather – if very warm, a larger quantity would be necessary. Lastly, add the soda water and float borage sprigs on the top. Serve immediately.

NOTES

Maraschino is a sweet cherry liqueur. You could also use Kirsch, a pure white spirit made from black cherries, or cherry brandy.

Nutmeg This has a very strong flavour which is not to everyone's liking. Omit it if you are not sure it will appeal.

Bottle sizes Use a standard 72 cl bottle of wine, which contains about 1¼ pints (750 ml) wine, and a large bottle of soda water containing 17 fl oz (500 ml).

Mrs Beeton writes

"Hand the cup round with a clean napkin passed through one of the handles, that the edge of the cup may be wiped after each guest has partaken of the contents thereof."

"CLARETS – Round Bordeaux are produced a number of wines of the first quality which pass under the name simply of *vins de Bordeaux*, or have the designation of the particular district where they are made; as Lafitte, Latour, &c. The clarets brought to the English market are frequently prepared for it by the wine growers by mixing together several Bordeaux wines, or by adding to them a portion of some other wines; but in France the pure wines are carefully preserved distinct."

Time 10 minutes
Sufficient for 4 to 6 persons
Seasonable in summer

INGREDIENTS
1 liqueur glass of
  Maraschino
4 tablespoons caster sugar
¼ teaspoon grated nutmeg
1 bottle of claret
about ½ lb (250 g) crushed
  ice
1 bottle of soda water
sprigs of borage to decorate

⌀ *Champagne Cup*

Time 10 minutes

Sufficient for 6 to 8 persons

**Seasonable for picnics,
    balls, weddings and other
    festive occasions**

INGREDIENTS

1 liqueur glass of brandy
    or Curaçao

2 tablespoons caster sugar

1 lb (500 g) crushed ice

2 bottles of soda water

1 bottle of champagne

sprigs of borage

MRS BEETON MIXED AND SERVED this special occasion drink in a silver cup, and directed her readers to follow the serving instructions she gave in the recipe for Claret Cup (page 327). The instructions here are more practical.

METHOD

Mix the brandy or Curaçao with the sugar in a large jug, then add the crushed ice, soda water and champagne. Top with borage sprigs and serve immediately.

NOTES

Curaçao is an orange-flavoured white spirit, which originally came from the Caribbean island of the same name. Grand Marnier, a Curaçao made from wild oranges in the Cognac area of France, could also be used, so too could Cointreau, which is a white Curaçao made with orange peel in Angers.

Mrs Beeton writes

"Should the above proportion of sugar not be found sufficient to suit some tastes, increase the quantity. When borage is not easily obtainable, substitute for it a few slices of cucumber-rind."

"CHAMPAGNE – This, the most celebrated of French wines, is the produce chiefly of the province of that name, and is generally understood in England to be a brisk, effervescing, or sparkling white wine, of a very fine flavour; but this is only one of the varieties of this class. There is both red and white champagne, and each of these may be either still or brisk. There are the sparkling wines (*mousseux*), and the still wines (*non-mousseux*). The brisk are in general the most highly esteemed, or, at least, are the most popular in this country, on account of their delicate flavour and the agreeable pungency which they derive from the carbonic acid they contain, and to which they owe their briskness."

Lemonade ∽

THERE CAN BE FEW DRINKS more refreshing in hot weather than homemade lemonade. Keep a jug in the refrigerator and serve it in tall tumblers, with ice.

METHOD

Rub some of the sugar lumps on 2 of the lemons until they have imbibed all the oil from them, then put them with the remainder of the sugar into a jug. Add the lemon juice (but no pips) and pour in the boiling water. When the sugar is dissolved, strain the lemonade through a fine sieve or piece of muslin. When cool, it will be ready for use.

Time 10 minutes
Sufficient for 4 to 6 persons
Seasonable in summer

INGREDIENTS
½ lb (250 g) lump sugar
3 large or 4 small lemons
2 pints (1.2 litres) boiling
water

Mrs Beeton writes

"The lemonade will be much improved by having the white of an egg beaten up in it; a little sherry mixed with it, also, makes this beverage much nicer."

"LEMONADE – 'There is a current opinion among women,' says Brillat Savarin, "which every year causes the death of many young women,– that acids, especially vinegar, are preventives of obesity. Beyond all doubt, acids have the effect of destroying obesity; but they also destroy health and freshness. Lemonade is, of all acids, the most harmless; but few stomachs can resist it long. I knew, in 1776, at Dijon, a young lady of great beauty, to whom I was attached by bonds of friendship, great, almost, as those of love. One day, when she had for some time gradually grown pale and thin (previously she had a slight *embonpoint*), she told me in confidence, that, as her young friends had ridiculed her for being fat, she had, to counteract the tendency, been in the habit every day of drinking a large glass of *vinaigre*. She died at eighteen years of age, from the effect of these potions."

⠻ *To Mull Wine*

Time 10 to 15 minutes
Sufficient for 8 to 10 persons
Seasonable in winter

INGREDIENTS
4 cinnamon sticks or blades
    of mace
4 cloves
a pinch or two of grated
    nutmeg
1 pint (600 ml) water
a bottle of red wine
¼ lb (125 g) caster sugar

As you will see from the quotation at the end of this recipe, Mrs Beeton didn't think it was a good idea to give quantities for making mulled wine. They have been included here as a guide, but they can be adjusted according to personal taste.

METHOD
Boil the spices in the water until the flavour is extracted – about 5 minutes. Add the wine and sugar and bring to the boil, then serve.

Mrs Beeton writes

"In making preparations like the above, it is very difficult to give
the exact proportions of ingredients like sugar and spice,
as what quantity might suit one person would be to another quite
distasteful. The spices usually used for mulled wine are cloves, grated
nutmeg and cinnamon or mace. Any kind of wine may be mulled,
but port and claret are those usually selected for the purpose;
and the latter requires a very large proportion of sugar.
The vessel that the wine is boiled in must be delicately clean,
and should be kept exclusively for the purpose."

THIS IS QUITE A POTENT BREW, ideal for a winter party, and you can make it look more festive by floating thin slices of orange and lemon on the top. As to the number of people this quantity would serve, Mrs Beeton made the following observation: 'This information must be taken *cum grano salis* (with a pinch of salt); for the capacities of persons for this kind of beverage are generally supposed to vary considerably'.

METHOD

Rub the sugar over the lemon until it has absorbed all the yellow part of the skin, then put the sugar into a punch bowl. Add the lemon juice (free from pips) and mix these two ingredients well together. Pour over them the boiling water and stir well together. Add the rum, brandy and nutmeg, mix thoroughly and the punch will be ready.

NOTE

Punch bowl Use a punch bowl that will withstand the heat of the boiling water. Pouring the water on to a metal spoon held inside the bowl will be an added safeguard.

Mrs Beeton writes

"It is very important in making good punch that all the ingredients are thoroughly incorporated; and to ensure success, the processes of mixing must be diligently attended to."

"PUNCH is a beverage made of various spirituous liquors or wine, hot water, the acid juice of fruits, and sugar. It is considered to be very intoxicating. Punch, which was almost universally drunk among the middle classes about fifty or sixty years ago, has almost disappeared from our domestic tables, being superseded by wine."

Time 10 to 15 minutes
Sufficient for 4 persons
Seasonable in winter

INGREDIENTS
¼ lb (125 g) lump sugar
1 large lemon
1 pint (600 ml) boiling water
½ pint (300 ml) rum
½ pint (300 ml) brandy
½ teaspoon grated nutmeg

CHAPTER 13

Basic Recipes

This chapter did not appear in Mrs Beeton's original book. The recipes that appear here were originally scattered throughout the first edition and are collected here for convenience. Stocks, for instance, originally came at the very beginning of Soups, the first recipe chapter in the book. Mrs Beeton attached great importance to good stock-making.

'It is on a good stock, or first good broth and sauce, that excellence in cookery depends. If the preparation of this basis of the culinary art is entrusted to negligent or ignorant persons, and the stock is not well skimmed, but indifferent results will be obtained.'

Basic pastry recipes came at the beginning of the Pastry and Puddings chapter. There were fourteen altogether, but only three different pastries are used in the recipes in this edition, so these are the only ones included in this chapter. Mrs Beeton had learnt the art of pastry making when she was a teenager at finishing school in Germany, and she paid particular attention to it. This is what she had to say about puff pastry.

'The baking of pastry requires particular attention. Do not put it into the oven until it is sufficiently hot to raise the paste; for the best-prepared paste, if not properly baked, will be good for nothing. Brushing the paste as often as rolled out, and the pieces of butter placed thereon, with the white of an egg, assists it to rise in leaves or flakes. As this is the great beauty of puff-paste, it is as well to try this method.'

Forcemeats and stuffings were in the same chapter as sauces, pickles and gravies. In the introduction to that chapter, Mrs Beeton gave sound and sensible advice about the preparation of forcemeats, which we would do well to follow today.

'For forcemeats, special attention is necessary. The points which cooks should in this branch of cookery more particularly observe are the thorough chopping of the suet, the complete mincing of the herbs, the careful grating of the breadcrumbs and the perfect mixing of the whole. These are the three principle ingredients of forcemeats, and they can scarcely be cut too small, as nothing like a lump or a fibre should be anywhere perceptible. To conclude, the flavour of no one spice or herb should be permitted to predominate.'

At the end of this chapter there are instructions for making curry powder, boiled rice and sippets, useful recipes that are referred to elsewhere in the book.

∽ Medium Stock

Sufficient for about 4 pints (2.4 litres)

INGREDIENTS

about 4 lb (2 kg) beef and veal bones

½ lb (250 g) lean bacon or ham

1 large onion stuck with 3 cloves

2 or 3 carrots

½ leek

½ head of celery

1 teaspoon salt

½ teaspoon peppercorns

1 large blade of mace

1 small bunch of savoury herbs

THIS IS CALLED A BROWN STOCK because the bones, meat and vegetables are browned at the beginning. Mrs Beeton made it with shin of beef and knuckle of veal and browned the meat and vegetables on top of the stove. Here it is made less extravagantly with beef and veal bones and is browned in the oven, which is more practical. Bacon or ham give the stock a good flavour, but can be omitted. If you include either of these, add salt sparingly.

METHOD

Put the meat bones in a roasting tin and roast them in the oven for ½ hour. Turn the bones over, add the lean bacon or ham and the vegetables and roast for another ½ hour. Transfer the contents of the roasting tin to a stockpot or large saucepan. Pour in 8 pints (4.8 litres) cold water and add the other ingredients. Cover the pan and place over a high heat until the water boils, then simmer very gently for 5 hours. Do not let it boil quickly. Strain the stock through a fine sieve and skim off every particle of grease.

The oven should be preheated to 450°F (230°C) Gas 8.

NOTES

Cutting the meat Ask your butcher to saw through the bones, cutting them roughly into 3 inch (7.5 cm) pieces. Cut the bacon or ham into pieces of roughly the same size.

Savoury herbs Use a bouquet garni of bay leaves, parsley and thyme.

Skimming off the grease The best way to do this is to let the stock go cold after straining, then refrigerate it overnight. The fat will rise to the top and form a solid layer, which can then be lifted off.

Mrs Beeton writes

"This is the basis of many soups, and will be found quite strong enough for ordinary purposes."

WHEN THE MEAT AND BONES are used raw at the beginning of stock making the stock is called a white stock. Here there is a mixture of veal and chicken bones, but it you prefer you can use all chicken. If you have a leftover carcass from roasting a chicken this too can be used, although strictly be speaking the stock cannot then be called a white stock.

METHOD

Cut up the veal and put it with the chicken carcass, trimmings of poultry and the ham into a stockpot or large saucepan, which has been rubbed with the butter. Pour in 4½ pints (2.5 litres) cold water and add the remainder of the ingredients. Cover the pan and place over a high heat until the water boils, then simmer very gently for 5 hours. Do not let it boil quickly. Strain the stock through a fine sieve and skim off every particle of grease.

NOTES

Veal bones Get your butcher to saw these into 3 inch (7.5 cm) pieces.

Skimming off the grease The best way to do this is to let the stock go cold after straining, then refrigerate it overnight. The fat will rise to the top and form a solid layer, which can then be lifted off.

Sufficient for about 2½ pints (1.4 litres)

INGREDIENTS
about 2 lb (1 kg) veal bones, chicken carcass and poultry trimmings
4 slices of lean ham
½ oz (15 g) butter
1 carrot
2 onions
½ head of celery
12 white peppercorns
salt
1 blade of mace

Fish Stock

**Sufficient for about 2 pints
(1.2 litres)**

INGREDIENTS
any kind of fish trimmings
2 onions, sliced
2 carrots, sliced
the rind of ½ lemon
a bunch of sweet herbs
a little salt and pepper

MRS BEETON'S RECIPE listed 2 lb (1 kg) of beef or veal with the fish trimmings, but she did say that the meat could be omitted, so it has not been included in this recipe. She also said: 'When a richer stock is wanted, fry the vegetables and fish before adding the water'. If you would like to do this, melt 1 oz (30 g) butter in the pan, add the fish trimmings and vegetables and fry them until nicely coloured, stirring frequently, for 5 to 10 minutes. Add the other ingredients and proceed with the recipe.

METHOD

Cut up the fish and put it with the other ingredients into a stockpot or large saucepan. Pour in 4 pints (2.4 litres) cold water and bring to the boil, then cover the pan and simmer gently for ½ hour. Skim the liquor carefully and strain it through a fine sieve.

NOTES

Sweet herbs Use a bouquet garni of parsley, thyme, bay leaf and a piece of celery or leek.
Straining To avoid slivers of bone going through the sieve, line it with a piece of muslin or a coffee filter paper.
Storage Mrs Beeton was right to say that fish stock does not keep well (below). If you are not using it immediately, store it in a covered container in the refrigerator and use within 24 hours.

Mrs Beeton writes

"Do not make fish stock long before it is wanted,
as it soon turns sour."

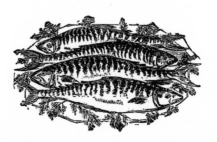

Puff Pastry ೧৶

Mrs Beeton's instructions are not for a true puff pastry, which involves rolling out, folding, turning and resting the dough a total of six times. Hers is a short-cut method, which usually goes by the name of flaky pastry. It is not a difficult pastry to make, but it does need time for the pastry to chill several times, and you must be sure to work in a cool kitchen, keeping the ingredients and your hands and utensils as cool as possible.

METHOD

Carefully weigh the flour and butter, and have the exact amount. Sift the flour with a pinch of salt, see that it is perfectly dry, and proceed in the following manner to make the pastry, using a very clean pastry board and rolling pin. Rub 2 oz (60 g) of the butter into the flour, then add the lemon juice and about ¼ pint (150 ml) cold water, using a knife to mix it with. The water must be added by the spoonful and the amount regulated by the discretion of the cook. If too much water is added and the dough becomes wet, the pastry will be tough when baked. Roll it out until it is a long rectangle with an equal thickness of about ¼ inch (5 mm). Cut 2 oz (60 g) of the butter into small pieces, place these in the middle third of the pastry, sift over it a little flour, then fold the plain flaps of pastry over the butter in the middle. Seal the edges of the pastry by pressing them gently with the rolling pin. Give the pastry parcel a clockwise ¼ turn, then roll it out into a rectangle as before and put another 2 oz (60 g) of butter in the middle. Repeat the rolling and buttering until the pastry has been rolled out 4 times in all and all the butter has been used. Do not omit, every time the pastry is rolled out, to dredge a little flour over that and the rolling pin, to prevent both from sticking. Handle the pastry lightly, and do not press heavily upon it with a rolling pin.

NOTES

Chilling is important, although not mentioned by Mrs Beeton. During chilling the pastry relaxes and the gluten in the flour softens. The pastry should be wrapped in cling film or foil and left in a cold place or chilled in the refrigerator for 20 to 30 minutes when the dough is first made, and after each time it is folded and sealed into a parcel shape.

Consistency of the dough After adding the water, knead the dough very lightly on the pastry board. It should be soft and quite lumpy, but not sticky.

Sufficient for 1 lb (500 g) pastry

INGREDIENTS
½ lb (250 g) flour
½ lb (250 g) cold butter
salt
1 teaspoon lemon juice

∽ Short Crust Pastry

Sufficient for ¾ lb (375 g)
pastry

INGREDIENTS
½ lb (250 g) flour
salt
¼ lb (125 g) butter

THIS IS A VERY GOOD basic recipe using half fat to flour. Short crust is easy to make as long as you work in a in a cool kitchen, keeping the ingredients and your hands and utensils as cool as possible. For crisp, melt-in-the-mouth pastry, work quickly and lightly and handle the dough as little as possible.

METHOD
Sift the flour and a pinch of salt into a bowl. Put the butter into the flour and cut it into small pieces with a round-bladed knife, then rub it lightly into the flour with your fingertips. Mix it to a smooth dough with about 2 to 3 tablespoons cold water, then knead it lightly until it is smooth. Leave it to rest in a cool place for 20 to 30 minutes before rolling it out, and it will be ready for use.

NOTES
Butter Mrs Beeton used all butter, but some cooks use a mixture of half butter and half lard. Other cooks use margarine instead of butter and a hard white vegetable fat instead of lard. Experiment with the different kinds of fat and their permutations to find which pastry you like the best. They are all equally good.

VARIATIONS
Rich short crust Increase the butter to 5–6 oz (150–175 g) or add the yolk of an egg, or add both of these. If you do this, you will need less water, or none at all.
Sweet short crust Add 2 tablespoons caster sugar after working in the butter (see *Mrs Beeton writes* below).

Mrs Beeton writes

"This paste may be converted into an excellent short crust
for sweet tarts, by adding to the flour, after the butter is rubbed in,
2 tablespoonfuls of fine-sifted sugar."

THE QUANTITY OF SUET TO FLOUR specified here makes quite a rich suet pastry, although Mrs Beeton said that as much as ¾ lb (375 g) of suet could be used to every 1 lb (500 g) of flour. On the other hand, she claimed, if as little as ¼ lb (125 g) suet was used this would, 'answer very well for children, or where the crust is wanted very plain'. In her day the suet was bought as a whole piece, which had to be skinned and chopped by hand. Nowadays we can buy it ready shredded in packets from the supermarket.

METHOD
Sift the flour and a pinch of salt into a bowl. Stir in the suet, then work the ingredients to a smooth dough with about 6 fl oz (175 ml) cold water. Knead the dough lightly, roll it out, and it is ready for use.

Mrs Beeton writes

" Some cooks, for rich crusts, pound the suet in a mortar, with a small quantity of butter. It should then be laid on the paste in small pieces, the same as for puff-crust, and will be found exceedingly nice for hot tarts."

INGREDIENTS
½ lb (250 g) flour
salt
¼ lb (125 g) shredded suet

✎ Forcemeat

Sufficient for a turkey, a
 moderate-sized fillet of
 veal, a rolled loin of lamb
 or 2 roast chickens

INGREDIENTS
2 oz (60 g) ham or lean
 bacon
the rind of half a lemon
2 tablespoons finely
 chopped parsley
2 tablespoons finely
 chopped sweet herbs
salt, cayenne pepper and
 pounded mace to taste
6 oz (175 g) bread crumbs
¼ lb (125 g) shredded suet
2 eggs

THIS IS A FRESH HERB STUFFING which has some ham or bacon in it
to add flavour, but you can omit the meat if you prefer. Mrs Beeton's
original quantities for the herbs were rather frugal, so they have been
increased here, but you could add even more. She recommended the
forcemeat be made into balls and fried or baked in the oven, which is
a delicious way to serve it.

METHOD
Very finely chop the ham or bacon and the lemon rind. Mix with the
herbs. Add a seasoning to taste of salt, cayenne and mace, and blend
everything thoroughly together with the bread crumbs and suet.
Now beat and strain the eggs, work these into the other ingredients,
and the forcemeat will be ready to use.

NOTES
Sweet herbs Use herbs that go well with the meat or poultry that is
to be stuffed. For turkey, use thyme; for chicken, use tarragon; for
lamb, use rosemary or mint; for veal, use sage.
Bread crumbs should be fresh.
To make forcemeat balls Roll pieces of forcemeat in wet hands to
make balls about 1 inch (2.5 cm) in diameter. Dust them lightly with
flour, then fry in hot oil until golden brown and crisp on all sides.
Drain on kitchen paper before serving.

Mrs Beeton writes

"No one flavour should predominate greatly, and the forcemeat
should be of sufficient body to cut with a knife, and yet not dry and
heavy. For very delicate forcemeat, it is advisable to pound the
ingredients together before binding with the egg; but for ordinary
cooking, mincing very finely answers the purpose."

Sausagemeat Stuffing ❧

THIS STUFFING IS BASED ON a kind of homemade sausagemeat – lean and fat pork chopped together, then flavoured and seasoned according to taste. Mrs Beeton mentioned that suet could be substituted for the fat pork. If you buy shredded suet, this would save a little time.

METHOD

Chop the meat and fat pork very finely and mix them with the bread crumbs, sage, mace and seasoning, taking care that everything is thoroughly incorporated. Moisten with the egg, then the stuffing is ready for use.

NOTES

Chopping the meat This can be done in a food processor, or even minced in a mincer if you have one.
Bread crumbs These should be fresh.

Mrs Beeton writes

"Equal quantities of this stuffing and forcemeat opposite will be found to answer very well, as the herbs, lemon peel, &c. in the latter, impart a very delicious flavour to the sausagemeat. As preparations, however, like stuffings and forcemeats, are matters to be decided by individual tastes, they must be left, to a great extent, to the discrimination of the cook, who should study her employer's taste in this, as in every other aspect."

Sufficient for a small turkey

INGREDIENTS
6 oz (175 g) lean pork
6 oz (175 g) fat pork
2 oz (60 g) bread crumbs
1 small tablespoon finely
    chopped sage
1 blade of mace, pounded
salt and pepper to taste
1 egg

✎ Sage and Onion Stuffing

Sufficient for 1 goose or a pair of ducks

INGREDIENTS
4 large onions
10 sage leaves
¼ lb (125 g) bread crumbs
1½ oz (40 g) soft butter
salt and pepper to taste
1 egg yolk

SAGE AND ONION is the traditional stuffing for pork, goose and duck. Mrs Beeton gave some sound advice at the end of her recipe about cooking the onions first. If they are parboiled in the way she described they will be easier to digest.

METHOD

Peel the onions, put them into boiling water and let them simmer for 5 minutes or rather longer. Just before they are taken out, put in the sage leaves for a minute or two to take off their rawness. Chop both these very fine, add the bread crumbs, butter and seasoning, and work everything together with the yolk of an egg. The stuffing is then ready for use. It should be rather highly seasoned, and the sage leaves should be very finely chopped.

NOTES

Bread crumbs These should be fresh.

Mrs Beeton writes

"Many cooks do not parboil the onions in the manner just stated, but merely use them raw. The stuffing then, however, is not nearly so mild, and, to many tastes, its strong flavour would be very objectionable. When made for goose, a portion of the liver of the bird, simmered for a few minutes and very finely minced, is frequently added to this stuffing; and where economy is studied, the egg may be dispensed with."

Indian Curry Powder ❧

Mrs Beeton's instructions were based on Dr Kitchener's recipe. Her advice was to 'put all the ingredients in a cool oven, where they should remain one night'. In her day the kitchen range was probably burning all night, whereas today we prefer to use the quickest method – dry-frying on top of the stove.

METHOD

Dry-fry the whole seeds and spices in a non-stick frying pan for a few minutes, tossing them constantly until they give off a strong aroma. Pound them in a mortar with the ground spices, rub them through a sieve and mix them thoroughly together. Keep in an airtight container.

NOTES

Dry-frying means to cook without fat or water. A non-stick pan is ideal because it helps to prevent burning, but it is not essential as long as you keep the spices and seeds on the move. The heat under the pan should be low to moderate.

Sieving makes the powder very fine, but it is not essential. You may prefer to grind the spices in an electric grinder or spice mill.

Quantity It is best to make curry powder when you need it so that the spices taste as fresh as possible. This amount will keep fresh for about 6 months if you store the airtight container in a cool, dry place, but you may prefer to make a smaller quantity than that given by Mrs Beeton.

Mrs Beeton writes

"We have given this recipe for curry-powder, as some persons prefer to make it at home; but that purchased at any respectable shop is generally speaking, far superior, and, taking all things into consideration, very frequently more economical."

Sufficient for about 1 lb (500 g) curry powder

INGREDIENTS
¼ lb (125 g) coriander seeds
2 oz (60 g) cinnamon sticks
1 oz (30 g) brown mustard seeds
½ oz (15 g) allspice berries
2 oz (60 g) fenugreek seeds
¼ lb (125 g) turmeric
1 oz (30 g) ground ginger
½ oz (15 g) cayenne pepper

To Make Sippets

SIPPETS WERE OFTEN USED as a garnish in Victorian times. Today we would call them croûtes, and the smaller version, which are often used to garnish soups, are known as croûtons.

Cut the bread into thin slices and stamp them out in whatever shape you like – rings, crosses, diamonds, etc. Fry them in hot fat. When variety is desired, fry some for a short time until they are a pale golden colour and fry others for longer until they are of a darker hue. Drain them until thoroughly crisp.

NOTES
Hot fat Mrs Beeton suggested boiling lard or clarified dripping, but groundnut or olive oil would be healthier. A combination of half oil and half butter gives the sippets a good colour and flavour.
Croûtons Cut the bread into tiny squares or diamonds with a knife (or use aspic cutters), then fry and drain as for the sippets.
Draining Spread them out on kitchen paper.

VARIATION
If you prefer, you can toast the bread shapes rather than frying them.

To Make Clarified Butter

THIS IS PURE BUTTER which has had its impure milk solids removed. It has a higher smoke point than ordinary butter and is used for frying at high temperatures. When clarified butter is simmered until it has a nutty aroma and taste, it is known as *ghee*.

METHOD
Put the butter into a heavy saucepan over a low heat. When it melts, stir it round once or twice, then let it settle. Pour it gently off into a clean bowl, carefully leaving all sediment behind.

NOTES
Butter Use unsalted butter and clarify ½–1 lb (250–500 g) according to your needs.
Storing Once the clarified butter has cooled, store it in an airtight container in the refrigerator. It will keep fresh for up to 1 month.

IN THE ORIGINAL RECIPE the reader was advised to 'pick over, wash, and soak the rice in plenty of cold water'. Rice often used to have pieces of grit, stones and husks among the grains, so this preparation was essential before it could be cooked. Nowadays, this is only necessary for basmati rice, which should be washed and rinsed until the water is no longer cloudy.

METHOD

Have ready a large saucepan filled with boiling water, add 1 teaspoon salt, then drop in the rice and keep it boiling quickly with the lid uncovered until it is tender but not soft – 12 to 15 minutes. Remove the pan from the heat, drain the water off the rice, then put it in a dish in a warm place to dry. Do not handle it much with a spoon, but shake it about a little with two forks so that it dries evenly. It is now ready to serve, and may be heaped lightly on a dish by itself, or be laid round the dish as a border, with a curry or *fricassée* in the centre.

NOTES

Salt Mrs Beeton cooked the rice in unsalted water, then sprinkled salt over the rice after draining. Rice has more flavour if salted water is used for cooking, as in the method here.

Rice Use long-grain. Basmati is particularly fragrant.

Draining and drying Some cooks drain the rice into a sieve, then pour boiling hot water from the kettle through the grains to help make them separate. To keep the rice hot for a short time before serving, put it into a warm dish, cover loosely with foil and place it in a low oven. If you like, you can put a knob of butter on top of the rice before covering it. Fork the rice through gently just before serving.

Mrs Beeton writes

"Some cooks smooth the rice with the back of a spoon, and then brush over it the yolk of an egg, and set it in the oven to colour; but the rice well boiled, white, dry, and with every grain distinct, is by far the more preferable mode of dressing it. During the process of boiling, the rice should be attentively watched, that it be not overdone, as, if this is the case, it will have a mashed and soft appearance."

Sufficient for 4 persons

INGREDIENTS
salt
¾ lb (375 g) rice

ᏻ Index